BRITAIN'S HISTORIC SHIPS

PAUL BROWN

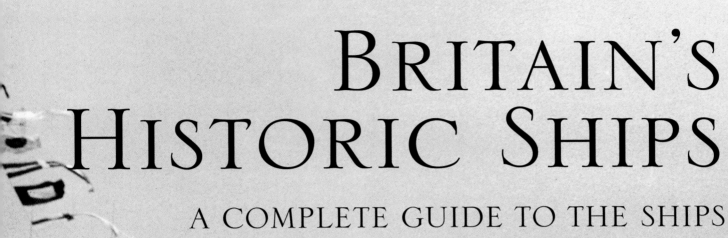

BRITAIN'S HISTORIC SHIPS

A COMPLETE GUIDE TO THE SHIPS
THAT SHAPED THE NATION

CONWAY

PREVIOUS PAGES

The Royal Yacht *Britannia*
at Cowes, 1963.

A Conway Maritime Book

Copyright © Paul Brown 2009

First published in Great Britain in 2009 by
Conway
an imprint of Anova Books Company Ltd
10 Southcombe Street
London W14 0RA
www.anovabooks.com

To receive regular email updates on forthcoming Conway titles, email
conway@anovabooks.com with Conway Update in the subject field.

British Library Cataloguing in Publication Data
A record of this title is available on request from the British Library

ISBN 9781844860937

Distributed in the U.S. and Canada by:
Sterling Publishing Co., Inc.
387 Park Avenue South
New York, NY 10016-8810

Printed and bound by Craft Print International Ltd, Singapore
Colour Reproduction by Dot Gradations Ltd, UK

Contents

Acknowledgements

I would like to thank all those who have provided information and pictures for this book, including: Kim Adamson, Kenneth Anderson, Richard Basey, Phillip Belcher, Jessica Beverly, Leslie Brown, Steve Davis, Peter Dodds, Chris Grenfell, Ben Hedges, Chris Henry, Nick Hewitt, Bryn Hughes, Chris Jones, David Kampfner, Andy King, Philip King, Michael McCaughan, George Malcomson, Nick Marshall, Lisa Massey, Christine Monkhouse, Richard Osborne, David Page, Linda Ross, Philip Simons, Dagmar Smeed, Julia Stephenson, Martin Stevens, Matthew Tanner, Jim Tildesley, Richard Walker and David Walsh.

I am also indebted to the authors of the ship histories listed in the bibliography, which have provided much valuable information on many of the ships featured in this book. They include R. S. Allison (*Caroline*), Ian Buxton (*M33*), Colin Castle and Iain Macdonald (*Glenlee*), Ewan Corlett (*Great Britain*), Richard Johnstone-Bryden (*Britannia*), Andrew Lambert (*Trincomalee*), A. D. Munro (*Wellington*), Ann Savours (*Discovery*), Ken Smith (*Turbinia*), Alan Villiers (*Cutty Sark*), John Wells (*Warrior*) and John Wingate (*Belfast*). The reader is referred to these for further detail.

Finally I would like to thank Alison Moss, John Lee and Nicki Marshall of Conway for their help and encouragement.

Introduction

Britain is an island nation whose history has in no small part been influenced by the maritime activities – both war and commerce – around our shores, and globally, over two millennia. Interest in the rich physical heritage of our maritime past, including historic ships, boats, dockyards, coastal and sea fortifications and maritime museums has increased over the past forty years. These sites now attract large numbers of visitors for leisure and educational activities, while their restoration, preservation and exhibition provides employment, sometimes in a voluntary capacity, for many others.

This book is concerned with what is probably the most fragile part of this heritage – the surviving historic ships that are scattered around the ports and harbours of our coastline. Many of these ships have survived by happenstance, escaping the breaker's yard while languishing in some lowly harbour role. Others had unusually long operational lives that allowed them to survive into a period when the restoration and preservation of historic ships became more common. A few were deliberately retained because, even before the wider emergence of concern for our heritage, their historical importance was recognised by at least a small group of active campaigners.

In the late sixteenth century Francis Drake's ship, the *Golden Hind*, in which he had circumnavigated the globe, was placed on permanent display at Deptford. It remained open to the public until the reign of Charles II in the mid-1600s, and the money paid by visitors was donated to seamen's charities. Perhaps some of it should have been spent on maintaining the ship, for she became rotten and was broken up. This was a rare example of a historic ship being retained for display before the twentieth century. It was only in 1922 that a more successful project was undertaken, when, following representations from the Society for Nautical Research, the Admiralty agreed that HMS *Victory* should be preserved. The funding that was not met by the Admiralty had to be raised by the Society. It was a time of depression and funds were only slowly forthcoming; it was thanks to the generous contribution of the Dundee ship owner Sir James Caird that the initial target was reached and work commenced.

Coincidentally it was also in 1922 that the first move towards preserving the *Cutty Sark* was made. Captain Wilfred Dowman saw the former clipper, then under the Portuguese flag, sheltering from a storm in Falmouth harbour, and resolved to buy her. Soon afterwards he succeeded, and returned the vessel to Britain for use as a cadet training ship at Falmouth and, later, Greenhithe. Eventually she was handed over to the Cutty Sark Preservation Society in 1953. Having led the way, *Victory* and *Cutty Sark* remain the most important preserved ships in the United Kingdom.

The pace of development of the historic ships movement accelerated in the 1970s. The Maritime Trust, founded in 1969, acquired a number of ships including *Discovery*, *Warrior*, *Gannet*, *Kathleen & May*, *Robin*, *Cambria*, *Lydia Eva* and *Portwey*. All have survived and appear in this book. Although they have since passed into the care of other trusts, they are testament to the pioneering work of the Maritime Trust. This nucleus of preserved historic ships has since been expanded through the efforts of many dedicated individuals and groups.

For those who take on the preservation or restoration of a historic vessel the task is daunting. Ships need more maintenance, and their condition deteriorates more rapidly, than most buildings. Simply maintaining a vessel in good condition is a challenge. In many cases the task is much greater, involving a major rebuild or complete restoration. Securing funding for this is difficult, with very little coming from government sources. The Heritage Lottery Fund has come to the rescue of a number of historic ship projects, while lack of funds has put the future of others at severe risk. In 2006 the National Historic Ships Unit was formed, with quite limited government funding, to help address such problems, acting as a focus for advice on all aspects of the preservation of historic vessels, advising the Heritage Lottery Fund on the consideration of applications, and raising awareness of the importance of our historic ships fleet. In order to qualify for inclusion in the register that is maintained by the Unit vessels must be British-built and lying in UK waters, be at least fifty years old, have a minimum length of 40 feet, and be substantially intact. The register of historic ships contains some 1,200 vessels (many of which are quite small). Sixty vessels are in the core collection and are considered to be of national significance, while there are 151 designated vessels of outstanding regional significance. Of these, thirteen of the core collection and twenty-one of the designated vessels were listed in 2007 as being at risk, illustrating the scale of the problems faced. Such is the risk of vessels having to be scrapped that the Unit has produced guidelines for recording and archiving material before a historic ship is broken up. The former Royal Navy motor launch *ML 162* (*Golden Galleon*) was the first vessel to be deconstructed using this advice. One other ship included in the appendix (the tank landing ship *Stalker*) is, at the time of writing, in a breaker's yard at Portsmouth, though efforts to save her are being made. Furthermore, following the liquidation of the Warship Preservation Trust in 2006 its ships (the frigate *Plymouth*, submarine *Onyx*, minesweeper *Bronington* and landing craft *Landfall*) have all faced uncertain futures.

The ships included in this book span five hundred years of maritime evolution. Though the oldest ship, *Mary Rose*, is incomplete, she is remarkable in representing the Tudor navy established by Henry VII and Henry VIII. She was one of the first true warships – purpose built, with an armament of heavy guns firing through ports in her sides. In stark technological contrast, are representatives of the post-war Navy, such as the guided-missile destroyer *Bristol* and the nuclear-powered submarine *Courageous*. Also included are representatives of the postwar merchant navy, such as *Balmoral* and *Shieldhall*. Some of the postwar ships are not yet fifty years old but are nevertheless historic in that they are important examples of types and classes no longer in service.

Within living memory of some people, Britain had the largest navy, the largest merchant fleet, and the biggest shipbuilding industry in the world. Representation of all those ships in our historic ships fleet is very patchy; for example, no large twentieth-century historic merchant ship remains in UK waters, and no capital ship from that century remains. Occasionally though, even now, historic ships are returned to the UK: the Clyde-built three-masted barque *Glenlee* is a glorious and often overlooked example, but efforts to bring the Second World War sloop *Whimbrel* back to Liverpool, where she was based during the Battle of the Atlantic, have foundered. Other important ships already in British waters, such as the clipper *City of Adelaide* (listed here in the appendix), are candidates for major restoration projects if funds can be secured. In these ways the historic fleet will hopefully continue to flourish and grow. Some important British-built ships, such as the liners *Queen Mary* and *Queen Elizabeth 2* are overseas. This book concentrates on the ships that can be seen around the British Isles. Many are open to the public, at locations such as Bristol, Chatham, London, Portsmouth, Gosport, Devonport, Glasgow, Dundee, Edinburgh and Hartepool. As opening times may change from season to season these are not given in the main text but a list of the relevant websites is given at the back of the book so that you can locate the necessary visitor information.

chapter 1: the sailing navy

The ships in this chapter span a period of more than 300 years, thus covering almost all of the main era of the sailing navy, as it is traditionally recognised. From the Tudor *Mary Rose*, one of the first true warships, to the Georgian line-of-battleship *Victory* and frigates *Trincomalee* and *Unicorn*, which show the type at its zenith, we can trace the design evolution of the sailing warship. Also embraced here are the replicas *Matthew*, *Golden Hind* and *Grand Turk*, which give further insights into developments during this era.

Mary Rose

Henry VIII's favourite ship

The remains of this important Tudor warship were raised from the seabed and are on display in a dry dock at Portsmouth Historic Dockyard

On 19 July 1545 a fleet of English ships engaged a French invasion fleet including the flagship *Henry Grace à Dieu* at Spithead. At the newly built Southsea Castle, King Henry VIII watched in horror as the leading English ship, *Mary Rose* – reputedly his favourite ship – sank before his eyes. She was to lie on the seabed for more than 400 years before her remains were raised in 1982. Now surviving partially intact, she is one of the most visited attractions in the Portsmouth Historic Dockyard.

Design

Mary Rose was built between 1510 and 1511, probably in the dry dock that had been completed in 1496 at Portsmouth. Her hull was of carvel construction, a recent innovation; until the end of the fifteenth century English ships had been clinker-built. *Mary Rose* was named after Henry's favourite sister, Mary, and his family emblem, the Tudor rose. Between July 1511 and April 1512 she was fitted out in London, having apparently been towed there from Portsmouth. During the fitting out her masts were stepped and rigged, decks were constructed and she was armed. A successful ship, she was designed to fight at close range by closing with the enemy before firing her guns, then coming alongside to allow the soldiers she was carrying to board and capture the enemy ship through hand-to-hand fighting. Her heaviest guns, mounted low in the stern, were mainly used to bombard shore positions. She was designed to attack the ports of Brittany, which had recently joined in a union with France and posed a new threat to England.

As built, the *Mary Rose* was listed as 500 tons and proved to be a good sailer. She underwent two refits and it is believed that in the second (around 1536) she was rebuilt and may have been uprated to 700 tons; however, changes in her tonnage during her career may have been due to different methods of calculation rather than enlargement of the ship. Her hull was strengthened by the addition of diagonal braces between the orlop (lowest) deck and the hold. The incorporation of gunports in her sides allowed guns to be mounted on the lower decks. The ship was given a powerful broadside battery of heavy cannon that was capable of inflicting serious damage on other ships at a distance. She was equipped to fire her ahead weapons (which were actually mounted on the aftercastle and fired off-centre) before turning to fire first a broadside, then to fire astern, and finally to fire the other broadside; she then made off to reload as other ships took her place. This new emphasis on artillery meant that she was a prototype for the large galleons of the late sixteenth century that defeated the Spanish Armada. Her rebuild helps explain why the only contemporary painting of the *Mary Rose* shows differences from the hull that was lifted at Spithead.

Below the illustration appears handwritten text in a period script (the Anthony Roll):

Gonnepowder — Shotte · of · yron — Shotte · of · Stoey · And · Leade — Bowes Bowestrynge Arrowes · Morys pyck Byllys · Darts for topp

| Serpentyn powder in Barrells | plast for Cannon for ½ Cannon for Culveryn for ½ Culveryn for Sakers | for porte pecys for ffowlers for toppe pecys for Bacys Shotte of leade | Bowes of yough Bonestrynge Lyuer arrowes in ShaVys Morys pykes |

Service History

Mary Rose fought in battles against the French at Brest and Cherbourg during the First French War between 1512 and 1514. In the 1512 action, as Sir Edward Howard's flagship, she led a fleet of eighteen ships which sailed in April and took twelve Breton and French ships, as well as landing soldiers who won several battles and burnt towns and villages for thirty miles around. In August the same fleet returned to the French coast and encountered the French fleet off Brest; *Mary Rose* disabled the French flagship, which then ran aground. Another French ship was boarded by the English Regent but an explosion in the powder magazine of the French ship destroyed both vessels. On the following day the English burnt twenty-seven French ships and captured five others, and landed soldiers who wreaked further havoc ashore. By October 1512 *Mary Rose* was at Southampton before wintering on the Thames, near Eltham. On 19 March 1513 the King visited the fleet at Woolwich after which *Mary Rose* sailed to be part of a race off the Kent coast with other English ships, which she won by sailing on a broad reach after rounding the North Foreland. By early April she was at Plymouth, and sailed on 10 April in an unsuccessful attempt at blockading Brest, during which Admiral Howard was killed in a skirmish with a French galley. His brother, Lord Thomas Howard, was appointed to take command of the fleet on its return to Plymouth, but adverse winds and weather frustrated a second plan to attack Brest and the fleet apparently did not cross the Channel again in 1513.

Later in 1513, however, *Mary Rose* was among the ships sent north to support the English army in its actions against the Scots and landed troops at Newcastle. The Scots were defeated at the Battle of Flodden on 9 September. Between April and June 1514 *Mary Rose* was in active service again as part of plans for an attack on French galleys. By late July she was at

ABOVE The only surviving contemporary illustration of *Mary Rose* appeared in the Anthony Roll, a list of the King's ships published in 1546, a year after the loss of the ship.

PREVIOUS PAGES The replica figurehead of HMS *Unicorn* was unveiled by the Prince of Wales in 1979.

OPPOSITE The hull of
Mary Rose undergoing
preservation, showing the
weather deck, upper deck,
castle deck, sterncastle, and
main deck (all labelled) and,
below the main deck, the
orlop deck.

Blackwall on the Thames, being placed in ordinary (reserve) with only a skeleton crew. She remained in reserve, with only essential maintenance, until June 1520 when she was part of a force that protected Henry VIII on his passage to France to meet the French king, Francis I.

In the Second French War (1522–25) she was again in action. As the flagship of Vice-Admiral Fitzwilliam she left Dover on about 30 May 1522, and at Southampton on 19 June Admiral Thomas Howard, Earl of Surrey, joined *Mary Rose*. The fleet eventually reached Dartmouth on 29 June, and *Mary Rose* then led the fleet to take the French port of Morlaix several days later. Later that year the ship was laid up for the winter at Dartmouth, and then was in ordinary for twenty-three years. During this time she was recorded as laid up at Portsmouth in 1524, and then in October 1526 was at Deptford where a review of her condition revealed that major repairs were needed. These were effected in a specially dug-out dock at Portsmouth in 1527. Further repairs or reconstruction probably took place in 1536, and in 1539 and 1540 *Mary Rose* was recorded as laid up on the Thames.

Capsize at Spithead

Mary Rose met her nemesis in the third war with France, which began in 1543. The French had built up a huge armada of 235 vessels in Le Havre, and in 1545 that fleet sailed with thirty thousand men for England – hoping to capture the Isle of Wight to use as a base to invade the mainland. Henry VIII was aboard the flagship *Henry Grace à Dieu* when the first French ships were sighted rounding Bembridge Point, but he was taken ashore to Southsea. The French were met by eighty English ships which had gathered at Portsmouth, with another sixty on their way from the West Country. Very light winds made engagement between the two fleets difficult. Lord de Lisle, in the English flagship (which was leading the starboard division), ordered his forward ships to try to lure the enemy under the powerful guns of Southsea Castle. *Mary Rose*, which had excellent sailing qualities, was leading the port division and was soon ahead of the others. It was reported that she fired a starboard broadside and then tacked to enable her port broadside to be fired. The change of tack may also have been necessary to help close with the enemy, who was probably to windward of the English fleet. Unfortunately the gunport lids on the port side were not closed and water rushed in as the ship heeled to port following a sudden gust of wind. The admiral, Sir George Carew, whose flag was flown by *Mary Rose*, was reportedly hailed by his nephew, Sir Gawen Carew, who commanded *Matthew Gonson*, asking why *Mary Rose* was handling badly. There had been confusion in raising the sails and the heeling alarmed Sir Gawen who thought that she could capsize. Sir George is said to have replied, 'I have the sort of knaves I cannot rule'. It seems that her crew contained too many senior mariners, including ships' masters, who would not take orders from one another and this contributed to the error.

The exact circumstances of her loss are nevertheless uncertain. She was very heavily loaded, and this together with the top weight of her tall forecastle and aftercastle, may have made her unstable. Once the heeling had begun guns and equipment may have broken loose and fallen to the port side,

further exaggerating the problem, and the men would have struggled to retain their footing as they tried to take remedial action. The ship sank with the reported loss of more than 500 lives, there being only twenty-five sailors and a few personal servants who survived. Unable to engage the English properly, the French turned away and later made landings on the Isle of Wight at Sandown, Shanklin, Bonchurch and Nettlestone, but withdrew in the face of the English forces on the island.

Salvage and Restoration

Following her sinking, expert Venetian salvors attempted to raise the *Mary Rose* between August and December 1545. Although unsuccessful, they did recover sails and parts of the masts and rigging. Some of her guns were subsequently recovered in further salvage operations that lasted until 1549, but for most of the following 300 years the ship lay undisturbed. In 1836 divers discovered the wreck and four guns and some other objects were salved, followed the subsequent year by additional guns and artefacts.

In the 1960s attempts were made to relocate the wreck, and in 1967 sonar detected a discontinuity in the silt that was to prove to be the remains of the *Mary Rose* hull. In 1979 the Mary Rose Trust was formed to raise the wreck and over the following three years divers recovered many timbers and artefacts while the site was excavated and the starboard side of the hull was prepared for lifting. Having lain in the silt of the seabed the structure of this side had been preserved, while exposure to currents and marine organisms had destroyed the

Technical Details

Mary Rose had a keel length of 105ft (32m), a waterline length of about 126ft (38.5m) and an overall length of about 148ft (45m) including the bowsprit. Her beam was 38ft 3in (11.66m) and her draught about 15ft (4.6m). The height of the aftercastle, seen on the preserved section, was 46ft (14m).

She had four masts – the fore and main being square rigged, while the mizzen and bonaventure were lateen rigged (with triangular fore and aft sails which helped the ship sail to windward).

At the time of her loss her armament comprised: 15 heavy, cast-bronze, muzzle-loading guns; 24 heavy, wrought-iron, breech-loading guns; 30 wrought-iron, breech-loading swivel guns; and 30 wrought-iron, breech-loading swivel guns. In addition to the cannon, her crew carried 50 handguns, 250 longbows, 300 pole arms, 480 darts to throw from the fighting tops, and a large number of arrows.

Her crew was listed in 1545 as 200 mariners, 185 soldiers and thirty gunners, although one account suggests there were more than 700 men on board when she sank. This probably included additional soldiers, some of them heavily armoured.

port side. Steel cables were attached to the 280-ton hull structure, which was then lifted onto a specially shaped cradle. The cradle was lifted above the water surface on 11 October 1982 and placed on the deck of a barge ready to be towed into Portsmouth Harbour.

The hull section can now be seen in the historic No. 3 dry dock (built in 1799) which has been covered with an insulated roof. The hull still sits in the cradle used in the lifting operation, and is undergoing restoration. The visitor galleries are separated from the hull by glass screens. The experience of restoring the *Vasa*, a Swedish full-rigged warship that sank on her maiden voyage in 1628, has informed the process on *Mary Rose* (the *Vasa* was raised in 1961 and is now on open display in Stockholm.) Many timbers salvaged from the *Mary Rose* wreck site have been returned to their original positions, and the process of conserving the hull continues. Initially the hull was continuously sprayed with chilled fresh water, to control marine organism growth and maintain humidity. After twelve years polyethylene glycol (PEG) was introduced into the spray system. This wax solution penetrated the timber cells over seven years, replacing the water throughout the timber thickness. Then, in 2003, a different grade of PEG was introduced, to penetrate only the outer walls of the timber. This will eventually be allowed to dry and solidify, providing mechanical support to the fragile cell walls of the timber.

The Mary Rose Museum

Divers at the *Mary Rose* site brought 19,000 objects to the surface, of which 11,000 have been conserved or restored. Mostly undisturbed for four centuries, they provide an unparalleled insight into life as it was on the day that the ship sank, revealing a whole Tudor world in a way that excavation of land sites cannot equal. Discoveries included 172 yew longbows as well as 2,300 arrows, mostly made from poplar and each with an iron head, and twenty-five cannon. The remains of 179 men were found – the majority appeared to be in their twenties with healthy teeth and bones. Symbolically, one unknown mariner was laid to rest in a grave inside Portsmouth Cathedral.

No. 5 Boathouse (1882) in Portsmouth's Historic Dockyard became home to the Mary Rose Museum, and some of the artefacts recovered from the site can be seen there. These include tableware, cutlery, candleholders, cooking pots, musical instruments, a backgammon set, book covers, quill pens and inkpots, together with items of clothing and shoes. As well as cannons and shot, there are swords, arrows and longbows, navigation instruments and many other items of equipment and tooling. A fighting top (possibly intended to be the highest of those on the main mast) was found and has been restored; this and a few additional items of rigging were in storage below deck and escaped salvage by the Venetian divers. A replica section of the main and upper deck has been constructed in the museum and is fitted with original bronze and iron guns which were found protruding through the open gun ports when the ship was excavated. Only one contemporary painting of the *Mary Rose* exists, in the Anthony Roll, a list of King Henry VIII's ships that was completed in 1546. This illustration differs in some respects from the excavated hull. Another illustration, the Cowdray Engraving, shows the scene at Southsea and Spithead as the *Mary Rose* sank. It is an eighteenth-century engraving based on a Tudor wall painting, now lost, that once belonged to Cowdray House in Sussex.

Permanent Exhibition

In 2008 a £21 million grant (as part of a larger £35 million project) was awarded by the Heritage Lottery Fund to complete the conservation of the ship and build a permanent museum to house the hull and the artefacts recovered from the wreck site. As well as the ship, the new museum will house almost 70 per cent of the artefacts, instead of the mere six per cent on display in the old exhibition. Spraying of the hull will continue until 2011 while the museum is built around it: the museum is scheduled to open in 2012. By 2016 the hull will have dried sufficiently for it to be on open display, with very close access from galleries allowing visitors to see both the outside and inside of the conserved hull.

Matthew Replica

A near contemporary of *Mary Rose* was John Cabot's caravel *Matthew*, in which he sailed to Newfoundland in 1497, becoming the first European of his day to land in North America. To celebrate the 500th anniversary of this voyage a replica of the *Matthew* was built between 1994 and 1996 at Bristol (from where John Cabot had sailed, and where the original ship was built on Redcliffe Wharf, less than a quarter of a mile from where the replica was built). In 1997 the new *Matthew* retraced Cabot's voyage and sailed to Newfoundland. She is now on display and open to the public on the SS *Great Britain* site at Bristol.

Colin Mudie designed the replica, but with no plans, no contemporary pictures and very few historical references he had to synthesise a design based on what was known about ship design and construction in the late fifteenth century. It was known that the original *Matthew* had a displacement of about 50 tons, a crew of eighteen or nineteen, and she sailed from Bristol to Newfoundland in thirty-four days and returned in just fifteen days (equating to an average speed of about 5 knots). Mudie based the underwater lines on *Mary Rose* whose hull, he claimed, was one of the most beautiful he had ever seen, with very smooth laminar flow and good 'lift' (for sailing to windward), giving a hull that could be sailed efficiently in all conditions. The hull was carvel-planked in larch on sawn, doubled oak frames. The stempost and sternpost were also of English oak, and the keel of opepe, while the decking and masts were of Douglas fir. The *Matthew* replica has a waterline length of 62 feet (18.9 metres), a beam of 19 feet (5.8 metres) and three masts, two of which are square-rigged, like *Mary Rose,* while the mizzen mast is lateen rig, like the two after masts on *Mary Rose*; she also has fore- and after castles so, although smaller than *Mary Rose,* the *Matthew* replica does give an impression of what *Mary Rose* was like.

RIGHT *Matthew* at the 2001 Festival of the Sea, Portsmouth.

Golden Hinde Replica

Carracks such as *Mary Rose* were superseded by Elizabethan galleons. These had a larger length-to-breadth ratio and the forecastle was moved back so that it no longer projected over the bow, thereby raising the bows and making control of the ship's head easier. In December 1577 Francis Drake led an expedition to South America in the privateer galleon *Pelican,* which Drake renamed *Golden Hinde* in honour of his patron, Sir Christopher Hatton.

Drake raided ports and captured Spanish ships off the west coast of South America , accumulating large amounts of gold, silver and other treasure. He sailed on to the west coast of North America, possibly present-day California, claiming it for England as Nova Albion. He then sailed westwards across the Pacific to the East Indies and thence to the Cape of Good Hope. In September 1580 he arrived at Plymouth, having completed the first circumnavigation by an Englishman, and was later knighted by the Queen aboard his ship at Deptford.

The replica *Golden Hinde* now displayed in St Mary Overie Dock on London's South Bank, was built at Appledore in 1973 and has also circumnavigated the globe. She has a length of 120 feet (36.5 metres) overall, 102 feet (31 metres) on the waterline, and a breadth of 22 feet (6.7 metres), and is 'armed' with twenty-two guns. She is open to the public at certain times and also offers special educational events. Another *Golden Hind* replica open to the public has been permanently berthed in Brixham harbour since 1963.

ABOVE Stern view of the *Golden Hinde* replica in the St Mary Overie dock.

RIGHT Detail of the topsides on *Golden Hinde*.

Victory

Nelson's flagship at Trafalgar

The most famous of all British warships; this First Rate Ship of the Line is now preserved and open to the public in a dry dock at Portsmouth Historic Dockyard

The Navy's last Ship of the Line

HMS *Victory* is a remarkable symbol of the Royal Navy's success in the age of fighting sailing ships. The oldest commissioned warship in the world, she is the only surviving three-decked ship of the line and has been restored to magnificent condition. No visitor to Portsmouth should miss a tour around her. Open every day except Christmas Day, she is visited by more than 350,000 people a year. In the summer months a guided tour begins every five minutes.

That she has survived to this day is probably attributable to three things. First, her massive oak construction; she lay for six years under construction in a dry dock and her timbers were thus fully seasoned by the time she entered the water. Secondly, she had a long operational career. *Victory* represented the zenith of ship-of-the-line design, and although forty years old when she fought at Trafalgar she was still a powerful and competitive force. When she retired from active service she was nearly fifty years old. (Even so, her design was used as the basis of two new Second Rates – *London* of 1810 and *Princess Charlotte* of 1825.) Thirdly, having been Nelson's flagship at Trafalgar, probably the Navy's proudest victory, she was retained in commission in harbour roles at Portsmouth long after her contemporaries were scrapped. *Victory* is now the flagship of the Second Sea Lord and Commander-in-Chief Naval Home Command and can be seen flying the White Ensign in No. 2 dry dock where she has lain since 1922.

Design and Build

Construction of *Victory* was authorised by parliament on 18 December 1758 as part of the 1759 Navy Estimates. She was designed by Sir Thomas Slade, Surveyor of the Navy, 1755–71, who based her lines on *Royal George*, a First Rate launched at Woolwich Dockyard in 1756. *Victory*'s construction was supervised by John Lock, master shipwright at Chatham Dockyard until his death in 1762, and completed by his successor Edward Allin. Lord St Vincent was later to describe *Victory* as 'by far the handiest [ship] I ever set my foot on, sailing remarkably fast and being of easy draft of water.'

She was laid down in a dry dock at Chatham Dockyard on 23 July 1759, but not floated-out (launched) until 7 May 1765. (The old single dock at Chatham in which she was built dated from 1623 and was replaced in 1858 by the present No. 2 dock.)

Her hull was constructed from approximately 6000 trees, 90 per cent of which were oak, the remainder being elm (for the keel) and fir, pine and spruce (for the masts and yards). This equates to 100 acres (40 hectares) of woodland. A total of 26 miles (42 kilometres) of cordage was to be used to rig the ship when she commissioned. In the rigging there were 768 elm or

ABOVE The decorated stern of HMS *Victory*.

ash blocks (pulleys) and a further 628 were used on the gun carriages.

Victory's Guns

Victory was a First Rate, the largest of only four such ships in the fleet at the time of her completion. First Rates had 100 guns or more, and were usually employed as senior flagships. Third Rates – the most numerous ships-of-the-line – had between sixty-four and eighty guns. *Victory* was completed with 100 guns of four different types, the heaviest being 42-pounders (referring to weight of the iron roundshot). The guns were all muzzle-loading and were arranged over three decks, with the heaviest on the lower deck and the lightest on the upper deck to help preserve a low centre of gravity. By the time of Trafalgar the number of guns was 104, but the original 42-pounders had been replaced by 32-pounders in 1778, on the orders of Admiral Keppel, because they were cumbersome (requiring a larger crew) and had a slow firing rate. After Keppel left the ship they were reinstated, but were taken out again in 1803. Although twelve Napoleonic-era iron guns remain on the ship today they are unlikely to be those used at Trafalgar because the originals were replaced in the 1806–08 refit.

Each 32-pounder required a crew of thirteen and the emphasis was on rapid firing rather than accuracy. It had a maximum range of 2,366 metres (2,600 yards), though in action ships often engaged at close quarters. A well-trained crew might fire their gun every two minutes. The broadside fired by *Victory* weighed 1,148 pounds (522 kilograms), and most of her guns could be fired treble shotted – giving 3,240 pounds (1,473 kilograms) total weight in a broadside. Broadsides would be directed at either the rigging (favoured by the French, to disable the ship), or hull (favoured by the British who wished to overcome the ship at short range prior to boarding and taking the enemy ship as a prize). At close range the powder charge would be reduced to prevent the ball passing right through the hull of the enemy vessel. Bar shot and chain shot were also used to cut through rigging and spars. At Trafalgar two heavier guns, 68-pounder carronades, were carried on the forecastle. These were low-velocity close-range weapons. The first shot fired by *Victory* at Trafalgar was from the port-side carronade, which hit the stern of the French flagship *Bucentaure*.

Victory's Early Service History

Following the end of the Seven Years War in 1763 Britain was at peace with France, so on her completion in 1765 *Victory* undertook sea trials but was then placed in ordinary at Chatham. In 1778, after France had entered the American War of Independence, *Victory* was taken into the dockyard for five or six weeks to be fitted out for sea. She was commissioned on 12 March 1778 under Sir John Lindsay and sailed from Chatham on 13 April. In May she joined the Channel Fleet under Rear Admiral John Campbell and Captain Jonathan Faulkner, as the flagship of Admiral Augustus Keppel, and thereafter was nearly always an admiral's flagship. In July 1778 she led the fleet in the indecisive battle off Cape Ushant, which was followed by three weeks under repair in the dockyard at Plymouth. In April 1780 she entered Portsmouth dockyard for a refit, during which her hull was sheathed in copper sheeting below the waterline to combat the teredo worm that bored into wooden ships' hulls. In 1781, as Admiral Kempenfelt's flagship, she led a squadron which intercepted a French fleet off Ushant in the Bay of Biscay. Fourteen French ships of the line were escorting a large convoy of military transports bound for the West Indies. Kempenfelt caught the convoy to windward of its escorts and was able to capture fifteen transports while the remainder of the fleet scattered. In April 1782, under the flag of Lord Howe, *Victory* took part in action off Cape Spartel and in the Relief of Gibraltar, when Howe successfully evaded the Franco-Spanish fleet and delivered into Gibraltar the thirty merchantmen he was escorting. In November 1782 she paid off for a refit at Portsmouth before entering ordinary there. In October 1787 *Victory* was made ready for service, due to a brief crisis with the Netherlands, but returned to reserve two months later. In May 1790 she was commissioned under Captain John Knight as Lord Hood's flagship in the Channel Fleet, but paid off in January 1791 to recommission as the flagship of Commodore Hyde Parker.

After a refit in 1792, *Victory* again became the flagship of Lord Hood in June 1793, at the start of the French Revolutionary War. Hood, who was now Commander-in-Chief of the Mediterranean Fleet, captured Toulon briefly and destroyed nine French ships of the line. The fleet then captured, but was unable to hold, the island of Corsica. Horatio Nelson, then a young captain commanding *Agamemnon,* lost the sight of his right eye in this action. In December 1794 *Victory* returned to Portsmouth (where the ailing Hood, now aged nearly seventy struck his flag) and entered the dockyard for repairs and updating. On 23 May 1795 she sailed for the Mediterranean as the flagship of Rear Admiral Sir John Man, and was in action with the French off Hyeres. *Victory* suffered fairly extensive damage to spars and rigging during the battle and these were repaired at Gibraltar. In December, when her captain was Robert Calder, Admiral Sir John Jervis transferred his flag to *Victory* and in 1796 she was part of a blockade of Toulon.

On 14 February 1797, still under Jervis, *Victory* and fourteen other ships of the line engaged a Spanish fleet of twenty-seven ships of the line off Cape St Vincent. Jervis secured a notable victory, in which Nelson, commanding Captain, played an audacious part – capturing two Spanish ships and earning himself a knighthood and promotion to Rear Admiral. *Victory* came home to pay off at Chatham in November 1797 and became a hospital ship for prisoners of war on the Medway. This could have spelt the end of her active service. There was a shortage of First Rates, however, and in 1800 she underwent a major refit and recommissioned in 1803 for further service in the Mediterranean. The fragile peace brought about by the Treaty of Amiens in March 1802 was now ending. *Victory* was undocked at Chatham in April 1803 and arrived at Portsmouth on 14 May. War was declared with France on 18 May, and Nelson boarded his new flagship on that day. *Victory* under Captain Samuel Sutton sailed from Portsmouth two days later, with Lord Nelson flying his flag as the newly appointed Commander-in-Chief of the Mediterranean Fleet. On 28 May she retook the Fifth Rate *Ambuscade*, which had been captured by the French in 1798. Once on station Sutton was relieved by Captain Thomas Hardy.

While Nelson's main fleet was at Sardinia he blockaded Toulon, from where the French fleet eventually escaped in May 1805. Napoleon had amassed an army and landing barges in the vicinity of Boulogne as part of his plan to invade Britain. Admiral Villeneuve was required in the Channel to support the invasion but would first cross the Atlantic as a diversionary tactic intended to disguise his true intentions.

Technical Details

Displacement:	3,500 tons (3,556 tonnes)
Length:	226ft 6in (60.9m) overall (including bowsprit), 186ft (56.6m) on lower gun deck
Beam:	51ft 10in (15.7m)
Hull thickness at waterline:	3ft (0.91m)
Masts:	(with exception of bowsprit, heights are taken from waterline
Mizzen mast:	152ft (46.3m);
Main yard:	102ft (31.0m).
Sails:	Ship-rigged, 37 sails with total area 58,590sq ft (5,443 sq m)
Speed:	Maximum approx 10 knots; Normal fair weather 8 knots
Crew:	821, including Vice Admiral Lord Nelson, at the Battle of Trafalgar
Storage of provisions:	920 tons (940 tonnes)

Chased by Nelson to the West Indies and back, the French were then bottled up in Cadiz. Nelson briefly returned to Portsmouth in *Victory* in August 1805. He sailed from there for the last time on 15 September, for Cadiz, from where he pursued the French and Spanish to the engagement off Cape Trafalgar.

The Battle of Trafalgar

Admiral Villeneuve, commanding the combined Franco-Spanish fleet in Cadiz, was criticised by Napoleon for failing to engage the British decisively, and a replacement commander-in-chief was assigned to the fleet. Before that replacement could arrive in Cadiz, however, Villeneuve sailed, on 19 October 1805, with thirty-three ships of the line bound for Italy carrying troops to reinforce Napoleon's army there. Their departure was observed by the schooner *Pickle* and reported to Lord Nelson, who was cruising between the capes of St Mary's and Trafalgar. Early the next morning Villeneuve's fleet was sighted by Nelson's frigates and pursued by the British fleet as it made for the Straits of Gibraltar. At 6.10 on the morning of 21 October Nelson signalled from the *Victory* to his fleet to form the Order of Sailing in Two Columns. One column of twelve ships was led by *Victory,* while to leeward another column of fifteen ships was led by Admiral Collingwood in *Royal Sovereign.* Nelson planned that his two columns would allow him to cut the enemy line at two points, separating it into three sections. The two British lines would attack the middle and rear sections respectively. By the time the vanguard had turned round and entered the battle the British would be ready to deal with them. At 6.22 am Nelson signalled 'Prepare for Battle'. Villeneuve wore his ships round so that they headed roughly north-north-west and the British steered towards the north-east to cut off a retreat to Cadiz. Ahead and to leeward of them lay the French and Spanish ships, arranged in two lines which converged to present a crescent like formation.

In light winds, the first engagement was between *Fourgueux* and *Royal Sovereign,* at about 11.30 am. At 11.48 am Nelson made his famous signal 'England Expects That Every Man Will Do His Duty'. Within minutes *Victory* was under fire from all quarters, suffering heavy losses. While *Royal Sovereign* fought the Spanish flagship *Santa Ana, Victory* steered towards the giant *Santissima Trinidad,* but then identified *Bucentaure* as Villeneuve's flagship and fired her first shots at point blank range. The French ship was effectively disabled, and *Victory* then broke through the enemy line, moving alongside *Redoutable,* which had been close to *Bucentaure.* The upper decks of the two ships became a maelstrom of shot and carnage. Nelson, in full uniform on the quarterdeck of *Victory,* was targeted at 1.15 pm by a musketeer in the mizzen-top of *Redoutable,* 49 feet above him. A musket ball entered his left breast and he fell, mortally wounded. *Temeraire* came to *Victory*'s assistance and *Redoutable* was forced to strike her colours, with more than 300 dead.

A French lieutenant later recalled how superior the English gunnery had been:

> 'The audacity with which Admiral Nelson had attacked us, and which had so completely succeeded, arose from the complete scorn which, not without reason, he professed for the effects of our gunfire. At that time our principle was to

aim at the masts and, in order to produce any real damage, we wasted masses of projectiles which, if they had been aimed at the hulls, would have felled a proportion of the crews. Thus our losses were always incomparably higher than those of the English, who fired horizontally and hit our wooden sides, letting fly splinters which were more murderous than the cannon ball itself. We were still using the linstock match to fire our guns, which dispatched the ball with an excruciating delay, so that if the ship was rolling, as it was on October 21, complete broadsides flew over the enemy's mastheads without causing the slightest damage. The English had flintlocks, rather than our crude linstocks.'

ABOVE 'The Fall of Nelson' by Denis Dighton, circa 1825, depicts the moment Nelson is mortally wounded on the upper deck of *Victory* during the Battle of Trafalgar.

The battle continued until about 4.30 pm. Nelson's strategy of splitting the enemy into three parts had succeeded: Villeneuve had surrendered, seventeen enemy ships were captured as prizes and one sank. Four of the surviving ships were taken two days later, with the remainder retreating to Cadiz. *Santa Ana* was recovered by the Spaniards from her small prize crew, and other prizes foundered or were wrecked in the gales that followed the battle. As a result only four prizes were brought home by the British. All of the British ships survived, though many were dismasted or heavily damaged. Nelson died a hero's death, breathing his last at 4.30 pm. He was one of fifty-seven to die on *Victory,* more than on any other British ship. In all 449 men died in the British fleet, but losses on the Franco-Spanish fleet were much higher – it is estimated that about 4,400 perished and thousands were taken prisoner. The captured Villeneuve was repatriated the following year, but committed suicide – 'a gallant man but without talent' remarked Napoleon. Britain's naval supremacy was once again assured, and the threat of invasion by the French was averted.

W L Wyllie

H.M.S. VICTORY & B1 SUBMARINE. PORTSMOUTH.

ABOVE HMS *Victory* afloat at Portsmouth before the First World War (with the submarine *B1* alongside) showing the later beakhead design.

PREVIOUS PAGES

The restoration of *Victory* at Portsmouth, painted by W. L. Wyllie in 1925.

Victory fired nearly 30 tons of shot at Trafalgar but was heavily damaged and dismasted. On 24 October she was taken in tow by *Polyphemus* but the tow soon parted in the gale and she had to weather the storm on her own. When the gale had subsided she was taken in tow by *Neptune* and arrived at Gibraltar on 28 October. Under jury rig, and with Nelson's body still aboard, she left there on 3 November and anchored in St Helens Roads, off the Isle of Wight, on 4 December.

Victory After Trafalgar

After urgent repairs at Portsmouth *Victory* sailed to the Thames, arriving at Sheerness on 22 December. There Nelson's remains were transferred to a yacht for passage to Greenwich, to lie in state in the Painted Hall at Greenwich Hospital. Men from *Victory* joined both the river procession to Westminster (the Royal barge carrying Nelson's coffin being rowed by sixteen of them) and the funeral procession from the Admiralty to St Paul's Cathedral. According to Lady Elizabeth Hardy, 'The show altogether was magnificent, but the common people, when the crew of the *Victory* passed, said, "We had rather see them than the whole show!"'

Able Seaman John Brown, aged 25, a pressed man from Wakefield, wrote home:

'While we expect to be drafted aboard the new Ocean *as Lord Collingwood is going to have her (him that was Second in Command in Action) there has been great disputes between admirals and captains wanting this Ships company but government will let nobody but Lord Collingwood have them as he was Commander in chief when lord Nelson Fell. There is three hundred of us Pickt out to go to Lord Nelson Funral we are to wear blue Jackets white Trowsers and a black scarf around our arms and hats besides gold medal for the battle of Trafalgar Valued £7 1s. around our necks. That I shall care of until I take it home and Shew it to you.'*

Victory paid off at Chatham in January 1806 for a major refit and repairs and then entered reserve on the Medway. She recommissioned in January 1808 under Captain John Searle, and her last seagoing service was in the Baltic, as flagship of Rear Admiral de Saumarez, and off the coasts of Spain. She was involved in a number of skirmishes with the Danes in the Baltic, and transported troops to and from the Iberian Peninsula in support of Wellington. From March 1808 she was commanded by Captain Philip Dumaresque and was involved in the evacuation of Corunna in 1809.

During her operational career *Victory* was awarded six battle honours: Ushant 1778, Ushant 1781, Toulon 1793, St Vincent 1797, Trafalgar 1805 and Baltic 1808.

ABOVE Carronade on the forecastle of *Victory*.

She paid off into reserve at Portsmouth in November 1812, and from 1813 to 1816 underwent major repairs and reconstruction there. Her ornate beakhead bow was replaced with a more practical round one, her bulwarks were built up square, and her sides were painted with black and white horizontal stripes. After a further spell in ordinary at Portsmouth (until 1823) she was guardship there between June 1823 and January 1824. *Victory* then became the flagship at Portsmouth of, successively, the Port Admiral in 1825, the Admiral Superintendent of the Dockyard in 1837, and the Commander-in-Chief, Home Fleet, in 1847. In 1869 she paid off and was used for accommodation and storage as a tender to the new flagship, *Duke of Wellington*. In 1887 her lower masts, which had rotted, were replaced by lighter hollow iron masts removed from the armoured frigate *Shah*, and thus date from that ship's construction in 1870. In 1899 the custom began of flying Nelson's 'England Expects' signal from her masts on Trafalgar Day (21 October).

Restoration

On 23 October 1903 the battleship *Neptune*, which was passing through the harbour mouth at Portsmouth under tow bound for the ship breakers, in strong winds, broke loose from her tugs and was swept back by the flood tide into the harbour where she collided with *Victory*. She so badly damaged her on the port quarter that *Victory* began to sink and had to be dry-docked for repairs. Together with the general deterioration over time of the fabric of the ship, this incident raised questions about her future but nothing was resolved before the First World War and *Victory* remained afloat in Portsmouth Harbour. In 1921 a report on the ship's condition was prepared by the Society for Nautical Research and passed to the Admiralty. It indicated that unless something was done the days of the ship were numbered. The Admiralty agreed to make a permanent dry dock available and the Society launched a public appeal to fund the ship's restoration. In December 1921 *Victory* was moved into No.1 Basin to prepare her for docking, and in the following month was moved to her present dry dock to commence restoration. A steel cradle was fabricated to support her hull. On 8 April 1925 she was refloated for the last time to adjust the cradle so that her waterline was level with the top of the dock, allowing her lines to be seen to the best advantage.

On 17 July 1928 King George V visited Portsmouth to open the ship to the public. During the Second World War she was closed to visitors and stripped of her upper masts and rigging. She was used for a time as an accommodation ship for junior ranks from the Royal Naval Barracks, and for gunners of the Portsmouth anti-aircraft defences. In 1941 she narrowly escaped destruction in a night-time raid when a 500lb high-explosive bomb fell into the dry dock and burst under her port bow, blowing a hole 8 feet by 15 feet in the ship's side. Since the war continuous restoration and maintenance has been necessary. The Death Watch beetle, a notorious pest of structural oak woodwork, had been discovered in 1932, and between 1954 and 1956 a programme of fumigation was carried out, but the problem re-emerged in the 1970s so an annual treatment using insecticide emulsion and smoke was introduced. On enclosed timbers the replacement of decayed oak by teak and iroko has also helped reduce the beetle problem. Many of the remaining wooden spars, which were difficult to repair, were replaced with mild steel in the seventies though Douglas fir continues to be used for some.

Meals on the Lower Deck

The men were allowed three-quarters of an hour for breakfast and one and a half hours for dinner, which was taken at noon or shortly after. Drums were beaten at mealtimes. In the evenings the ship's band played music, when the men danced and the boys skylarked.

Breakfast: Cold oatmeal porridge ('burgoo'), and a hot drink called 'Scotch coffee' made from charred crushed biscuit which was boiled with water and sweetened with a little sugar.
Dinner: Salted beef or pork stew with dried peas and oatmeal.
Supper: Biscuits with butter or cheese.

When available fresh meat and vegetables were served. Livestock was embarked at the start of a voyage, for example twelve cattle or thirty sheep. Temporary pens were erected on the upper deck to house them, and there was also a manger on the lower gun deck. Poultry – chickens, geese and ducks – were kept in coops on the forecastle, quarter deck or in the ships' boats. At ports of call more livestock, fruit and vegetables would be purchased and fresh water obtained.

Lime juice was issued to help prevent scurvy. Each man was provided with a daily allowance of half a pint of rum or brandy, diluted with two pints of water, or eight pints of beer, or two pints of wine. For much of the time on a long voyage little fresh water was available.

The Layout of *Victory*

In 2004 the hold and the grand magazine were opened to the public for the first time. The hold is a large area below the orlop that held shingle ballast and the ship's stores – enough for six months, with barrels containing salt beef, pork, fish and water, sacks containing dry stores such as biscuits, oats, peas and pulses, and casks of butter and cheese. At the after end of the hold the beer, wine and spirits were stored under the guard of a marine sentry. The grand magazine is a large compartment comprising three rooms forward in the hold that contained the main gunpowder store. Visitors can also tour the orlop, lower, middle, and upper gun decks and the upper deck.

The orlop deck contains the sail room, anchor cable stowages, storerooms for the gunner, boatswain and carpenter, and magazines for the 12- and 24-pounders. It also provided accommodation for the surgeon, purser, ship's steward, captain's servant, boatswain, carpenter and midshipmen. The oak deck planking on the lower deck is original. This deck served as the main living quarters for the seamen – 480 men slept in hammocks slung from the beams. At meal times some 560 men, divided into messes of four to eight men, sat at about ninety tables fitted between the guns. At the after end of the lower deck is the officers' wardroom.

Food for the entire ship's company was cooked on a Brodie stove in the galley on the middle deck. This versatile stove was invented by Alexander Brodie, a Scotsman, in 1781. It was fuelled by coal or wood and contained two coppers for boiling food, with capacities of 250 and 150 gallons respectively, a grate for grilling, two ovens for baking 80 pounds of bread, seven external 'hanging stoves' for cooking separate meals for officers, and a distiller to convert sea water into a small quantity of fresh water. The marines also lived on

this deck. The capstans on this deck and the lower deck were used for heavy tasks such as hoisting sails and anchors. Up to 200 men could be employed, with ten men pushing with their chests against each capstan bar.

ABOVE The lower gun deck of *Victory*, with 32-pounders.

Forward on the upper gun deck is the sick berth, which is separated from the rest of the deck by a removable wood and canvas bulkhead which allowed the space to become part of the gun deck during battles, while the sick berth was moved to the orlop deck (where Nelson died). At the after end of the upper gun deck is the great cabin, where the admiral lived, with a dining cabin, a day cabin and a replica of Nelson's cot. On the upper deck astern of the main mast is the quarterdeck, where a plaque marks the spot on which Nelson fell. Astern of this is the captain's cabin, the quarters of Captain Hardy at the time of Trafalgar. This was one of three stern galleries that are seen clearly on the ship's decorated stern (the others being the admiral's cabin and the wardroom).

In 2005 *Victory*'s fore topsail went on display again (in No. 10 Storehouse in Portsmouth Historic Dockyard) after the latest of several conservation programmes. Initially made in the Sail Loft at Chatham in 1803, it is the only surviving sail from the Battle of Trafalgar. Measuring 80 feet at its base, 54 feet at the head, and 54 feet deep, the sail has an area of 3,618 square feet. The sail cloth was woven in Dundee and is pockmarked by some ninety shot holes and further apertures, some of which may have been caused by nineteenth-century souvenir hunters.

Today *Victory*'s crew still comprises officers and ratings of the Royal Navy. She has been commanded by approximately eighty different admirals in her lifetime, and still wears the admiral's flag at her masthead. Her captain is a lieutenant-commander who is responsible for the ship's daily running. She has been restored to her Trafalgar appearance: the black and yellow hull colours of 1800 were adapted by Nelson who ordered the gunport lids to be painted black, producing the distinctive chequer pattern that became standard in the Royal Navy thereafter.

Trincomalee and Unicorn

19th-century sailing frigates

Wooden Fifth Rate frigates from the last era of the sailing navy; both are afloat and open to the public, at Hartlepool and Dundee respectively

Frigates in Nelson's days were fast, manoeuvrable ships, with between twenty-eight and forty-four guns concentrated on the main deck. They were rated as either Fifth Rates, which had thirty-two or more guns, or Sixth Rates which had fewer than thirty-two. Frigates were ubiquitous commands of post-captains, and their roles included scouting for the battlefleet, or operating independently in trade defence, such as convoy protection, actions against the enemy's commerce and privateers and raiding coastal positions. Sometimes they gave more direct support to the battlefleet by repeating admirals' signals, acting as a decoy to draw fire away from beleaguered ships of the line or towing damaged ships out of the line. Of the British frigates from the late sailing-navy era, two survive – the sister ships *Unicorn* and *Trincomalee*.

Design

The archetypal frigate design was first proposed by Lord Torrington in 1689, during the reign of William and Mary, to protect trade from the new French threat. These frigates were two-deckers but were unarmed on the lower deck (at waterline level). This gave better living conditions than on a line-of-battle ship and was more suitable for the long cruises often undertaken by frigates. Extra guns were soon added to the lower deck, however, and the type proposed by Torrington did not really take off until 1748. French frigates often had the best hull forms and were faster, while their British counterparts were more robustly built and seaworthy. Often the Admiralty copied French designs, at least to experiment. After the outbreak of war with the French in 1793 there was a need for more frigates. In 1796 the 38-gun *Leda* was ordered with a hull form identical to the French *Hebe*, which had been captured in 1782. Although rated as a 38-gun ship she usually carried forty-six. *Leda* was a success, and a further eight were ordered between 1802 and 1808 and another four in 1812. One of the *Leda* class, *Shannon*, was engaged in a very successful single-ship action against USS *Chesapeake* in 1813. This contributed to a decision to order an additional three by 1815. A modified version followed, to a design by Sir Robert Seppings, with a round stern and a short timber and diagonally braced structure. This group totalled twenty-three ships (including *Unicorn*), making the *Leda*s the largest class of sailing frigates ever built.

Building *Trincomalee*

Two of the 1812 ships – *Amphitrite* and *Trincomalee* – were built of teak from the Malabar forests, at the East India Company's Bombay Dockyard under the direction of Jamsetjee Bomanjee, the great Parsi master shipbuilder. Teak is generally superior to oak as a shipbuilding material, being both stronger and more durable, and this has contributed to the longevity of *Trincomalee*. Teak also seasoned much more quickly than oak, allowing rapid building of ships that could be used in the hot and humid climates of the Indian Ocean and China Seas. It also helped alleviate the shortage of oak for British shipbuilding during the Napoleonic wars.

The name *Trincomalee* was chosen to honour the action in 1782 between the British and French off the port of that name in Ceylon (now Trincomali in Sri Lanka). It was generally the case that the Royal Navy's ships built in Bombay had names with connections to the Indian subcontinent. Her keel was laid down on 25 April 1816, and *Trincomalee* was floated out on 12 October 1817. At a total cost of £30,323, she was accepted by the Navy on 30 May 1818 at Trincomalee.

The Passage Home

By 1818 Britain was at peace and it was first suggested that *Trincomalee* be laid up in reserve there. Instead, she commissioned in mid-October with the crew of HMS *Challenger*, and for the passage home had a temporary rig and an armament of four 12-pounder guns. She left Trincomalee on 27 October for the voyage to England, accompanied by HMS *Towey*, a Sixth Rate. The two ships called at Port Louis in Mauritius from 26 November to 9 December to take on stores, allow shore leave and entertain visiting dignitaries. *Trincomalee* arrived at Simon's Bay, near the Cape of Good Hope, on 27 December 1818. She then moved to Table Bay on 9 January 1819 to load bullocks and other supplies for St Helena, where a squadron was still stationed to ensure that Napoleon did not escape. Thence, with calls at Ascension Island and Fayal in the Azores, she headed north. At every stop in her passage invalids had embarked, twenty of whom did not survive the voyage.

In Ordinary (Reserve)

Trincomalee arrived at Spithead on 29 March 1819. After entering Portsmouth Harbour she was stripped of her jury masts and bowsprit and paid off at sunset on 27 April 1819. Her upper deck was roofed over for protection, and she was placed in ordinary at a mooring in Portsmouth Harbour. Ten years later she was moved into the dockyard for her bottom to be

BELOW *Trincomalee* and her sister-ship *Amphitrite* beat out of San Francisco on 23 September 1854, heading for Hawaii.

Her Majesty's Ships "Amphitrite" & "Trincomalee" Beating out of San Francisco in Sep.r 23.d 1854.

re-coppered, but then returned to her mooring. During twenty-six years in reserve she had become obsolete as a frigate but her hull was still in good condition. In 1845 she was reduced from forty-two guns to a twenty-six-gun corvette, as was *Amphitrite*, for service on the more remote stations. *Trincomalee* was in dockyard hands from March to November 1845 for this conversion. Her square stern was made elliptical to give a much improved arc of fire from her after guns, and the gunports were altered to accommodate heavier guns.

The after magazine was converted to a shell room and the masts moved. Technological advances such as iron freshwater tanks, anchor chains and compressors were also fitted.

The First Commission – the West Indies

On 23 July 1847 *Trincomalee* commissioned for active service for the first time, on the North America and West Indies Station, with a crew of 240 men. She joined *Amphitrite* at Spithead before both ships sailed together for Lisbon, entering the Tagus on 2 October, and joining the Western Squadron. On 7 October the ships went to sea for gunnery practice and sailing trials with the squadron. Eight days later both left the squadron, *Amphitrite* for the west coast of Africa, and *Trincomalee* for Bermuda – where she arrived on 6 November. She was employed in the West Indies, and from February to April 1848 was off Venezuela protecting British interests during a period of local instability. A refit at Antigua then followed, before *Trincomalee* returned to cruising around the West Indies. From August to September part of her crew were involved in repairing hurricane damage to the dockyard at English Harbour, Antigua. In April 1849 she sailed north to the Newfoundland fishing grounds, calling at Halifax in mid-May, for fishery protection duties, necessary because of French fishery activity, until the end of September.

On her return to the Caribbean *Trincomalee* was sent to Cuba, both for anti-slavery patrols and to provide a British presence to support the security of Spanish Cuba, which was vulnerable to American attempts to annex the country. On 30 and 31 January 1850 the ship landed a party for firing drill with field gun and muskets and to cut local timber for boat knees without permission from the Spanish authorities. This caused a diplomatic incident, with the Spaniards complaining that *Trincomalee* had infringed their territorial rights, leading to an official complaint against her captain, Richard Warren, from the Foreign Office. Between patrols, the ship returned to Port Royal, Jamaica, for stores and maintenance. In June 1850 she prepared at Port Royal for her voyage home, loading condemned stores and a group of invalids. *Trincomalee* sailed on 26 June, and anchored at Spithead on 5 August to discharge the invalids, before beating back down the Channel and entering Plymouth Sound on 9 August. She was paid off on 16 August to spend nearly two years in ordinary.

The Second Commission – the Pacific

Trincomalee was recommissioned at Devonport on 24 June 1852 for service on the Pacific station, with a crew of 157 – including twenty supernumerary boys who had been drafted to other ships in the squadron. She sailed out of Plymouth Sound on 21 August and called at St Vincent in the Cape Verde Islands for provisions and water. She then visited Rio de Janeiro, and Port Stanley in the Falklands. At the latter *Trincomalee* was run into by the Liverpool merchantman *Helena* and the damage took four days to repair. After rounding Cape Horn, *Trincomalee* entered the Pacific on 21 November, and arrived at Valparaiso, the headquarters of the Pacific Squadron, on 12 December. She was soon to meet up with her sister ship *Amphitrite*, which had been on the station for nearly three years, and in April 1853 exercised with her and HMS *Portland*, the squadron's flagship. *Trincomalee*'s first voyage on the extensive Pacific station took her to Esquimalt, in what is now British Columbia, New Archangel (then a Russian port, now Sitka in Alaska), and the Queen Charlotte Islands, where part of the sound was charted and named Trincomalee Channel. She was next in San Francisco Bay with *Amphitrite* in November, and then returned to Valparaiso.

Her second Pacific voyage began in June 1854, when *Trincomalee* sailed for the Sandwich Islands (now Hawaii). This was the first stop on a journey north to support the Arctic mission of HMSs *Enterprise* and *Investigator*, which had passed through the Bering Straits in search of the explorer Sir John Franklin. Meanwhile, unbeknown to *Trincomalee*'s captain, war had broken out with Russia against England and France. *Trincomalee* sailed to Port Clarence at the entrance to the Bering Straits, where provisions for the Arctic ships were unloaded. She then returned to the Sandwich Islands, where her presence was required to deter American attempts to annex the territory.

After returning to Valparaiso, *Trincomalee* sailed with HMS *Monarch,* the new flagship, for the Siberian coast, where at Petropavlovsk an Anglo-French squadron had sustained heavy

The Diary of Eliza Blunt

Eliza Blunt married the boatswain John Blunt at Alverstoke in July 1816 when she was expecting their third child. They may have married because John, then serving in HMS *Victory*, had just been appointed boatswain of the dockyard at Trincomalee. The family took passage in HMS *Minden* which arrived at Trincomalee in March 1817. Their son John was born at sea off the Cape of Good Hope. Unfortunately his father did not survive long in Ceylon, dying in July 1818 of 'the fever'. After he died Eliza and her two youngest children (Charlotte and John) were given passage home by the Admiralty in Trincomalee, while her eldest son, William, remained in Ceylon for some years. By March 1819 the ship was in the Atlantic, north of Ascension Island, and in her diary Eliza wrote:

9 March: 'Blowing a gale of wind, not able to carry sail, tremendous sea, everything flying in all directions, cannot either sit or stand. Children crying, fell down and broke my wash-hand basin. Dinner brought in, soup all spilt, obliged to sit on the deck and pick a bit. All of us had two or three more tumbles. Tea brought in – the cabin floor soon washed with it, teapot upset and rolled into the lee scuppers. Glad to go to bed, servant tipsy, cot clews [fixing for the cot] broke – Charlotte fell out of bed. Pots and plates falling off of the shelves on our heads. God help us poor creatures, no one to console us. Poor Poll [Eliza's parrot] shared the same fate, fell down three times, cage broke into pieces, obliged to get out of my cot and put her in a safe place – bruised my arm and leg tumbling over things.'

10 March: 'Arose at eight o'clock after a sleepless night, wind abated, sea very high with sudden squalls. Ship rolling very much, not able to stand. A sea came in forward and put the fire out, washed the baker's rolls away. Full of disasters and trouble. Servant tipsy again.'

12 March: 'A good breeze this morning, ship going very fast. Had a sheep killed, stock getting very short. Wind increasing, obliged to leave off writing, ink bottle being upset twice, both the children fell down and Betsy and myself flying from one side of the cabin to the other. Cannot either sit or stand. Servant too drunk to put our cots down.'

13 March: '… had a visit from Captain Bridges, obliged to entreat with him not to flog Edwards [the servant] as he has promised me faithfully not to get tipsy any more. Another duck died …. Captain Bridges sent for me into the cabin this evening to take wine.'

On 18 March the ship arrived at Fayal in the Azores and the weather improved:

19 March: 'Thank God we are blessed again with a beautiful day. Sun shines clear and bright – boats alongside with oranges, eggs and potatoes.'

losses and the Commander-in-Chief of the Pacific station, Rear Admiral Sir David Price, had committed suicide. On their arrival in June 1855, *Monarch* and *Trincomalee* found that the Russian ships had eluded them and they rejoined the fleet at Esquimalt. *Trincomalee* was next at San Francisco, blockading American ships that might supply Russia, and then sailed for Honolulu and finally Valparaiso.

Her fourth voyage began in April 1856 and ranged from the Pitcairns, Tahiti and the Sandwich Islands to Esquimalt. Here there occurred what now seems a rather ugly incident. A large landing party of men from *Monarch* and *Trincomalee* was assembled to arrest a native American chief who had apparently shot and wounded a settler whom he suspected of seducing a woman the chief was to marry. The chief was tried and executed. By April 1857 *Trincomalee* was back at Valparaiso preparing for the voyage home. She sailed on 2 May, and after rounding Cape Horn called at Rio de Janeiro. On 29 August she entered Plymouth Sound to take on stores, and arrived at Sheerness on 3 September 1857 to pay off. She was moved to Chatham the following day and entered ordinary again. Between 1852 and 1857 on her Pacific commission she had sailed 110,000 miles and spent 944 days at sea and 882 in harbour. Her life as a seagoing warship was now at an end, with steam power gradually replacing sail.

Drill Ship

In 1860 *Trincomalee* was modified as a drill ship for the Royal Naval Reserve and was commissioned at Chatham on 16 December. The following month she was towed to Sunderland to join HMS *Castor*, to train naval volunteers aged fifteen or sixteen who had signed up to serve for ten years once they reached the age of eighteen. At this time *Trincomalee* was fitted with ten 32-pounder muzzle-loading guns and six 8-inch shell-firing muzzle loaders. During her time as a drill ship her gunports were moved or modified several times to suit different types of training armament. In 1862 she was moved to the Union Dock in West Hartlepool for further service as a drill ship. In 1870 she was refitted with new guns, a re-caulked deck and a roof to protect her from the weather. She remained at West Hartlepool until February 1877 when she was towed to Southampton Water, again for service as a drill ship. In 1881 she received a new upper deck, galley house and other additions; in October 1895 she was replaced by HMS *Medea* and was reduced to reserve with permission granted to use her as a depot ship.

Sale and Service as *Foudroyant*

In May 1897 *Trincomalee* was sold to Read's Shipbreakers of Portsmouth Camber, and dismantling began. However, she had a last-minute reprieve. She was bought by Geoffrey Cobb, the owner of coal mines and a philanthropist, for use as a static training ship, preparing pauper boys for service in the Royal and merchant navies. Cobb had just lost the former Second Rate HMS *Foudroyant*, Nelson's flagship between 1799 and 1800, which had been wrecked at Blackpool. *Trincomalee* was at East Cowes for five years, during which time she was repaired. She moved to Falmouth in 1902 and was refitted and repainted and renamed *Foudroyant,* before commencing her training duties in September 1903. In June 1904 she moved to Milford Haven, returning to Falmouth in September 1905. There she was joined in 1912 by the former HMS *Implacable* to expand the capacity of Cobb's training establishment. In 1927 *Foudroyant* moved back to Milford, but following Cobb's death in 1931 both she and *Implacable* were

Technical Details – *Trincomalee*	
Displacement:	1447 tons
Length:	Hull – 170ft, (51.81m); overall – 270ft (82.30m)
Beam:	40ft (12.19m)
Draught	20ft (6.10m)
Height of mainmast:	165ft (50.2m)
Sail area:	18,320sq ft (1,702sq m)
Designed armament:	Upper deck – 28 x 18-pounder guns; Forecastle – 2 x 9-pounder guns and 2 x 32-pounder carronades; Quarterdeck – 2 x 9-pounder long guns (by 1815 probably replaced by 2 additional 32-pounder carronades), 12 x 32-pounder carronades, 1 x 12-pounder boat carronade
Corvette armament:	Quarterdeck – 2 x 56-pounder guns, 6 x 32-pounder guns; Main Deck – 6 x 8-inch shell guns, 12 x 32-pounder guns
Complement:	286 as designed, 240 as corvette

towed to Portsmouth to continue training under the auspices of the Implacable Committee. Harold Wyllie, son of the artist W L Wyllie, revised the role of the ships to that of providing short residential adventure training holidays for boys and girls. Between 1932 and 1939 some 10,000 young people were to take holidays on the ships, though whether many regarded drill and seamanship training as a holiday is debatable.

During the Second World War the ships were used by the Navy, initially for storage, and during this time they suffered a bomb hit which damaged *Foudroyant*. On 3 July 1943 they were commissioned as a new naval establishment, HMS *Foudroyant*, providing signaling and seamanship training for new naval ratings. They were returned to the Implacable Committee on 8 May 1947. *Implacable* was deemed beyond repair and was scuttled at sea. The renamed Foudroyant Committee returned the remaining ship to her youth training role, supported by numerous different sponsorship and fundraising schemes. However, in the 1980s the number of trainees dwindled and the training ceased in January 1987.

ABOVE *Unicorn* in the Victoria Dock at Dundee.

Preservation

In July 1987 *Foudroyant* was moved on a heavy-lift barge to West Hartlepool for complete restoration to her original condition, though at the time of her move no funds were available for this and her final destination was uncertain. In the event the best offer of initial support came from Teesside Development Corporation, with £1 million, provided that the ship was restored and located in Hartlepool. Restoration began in 1990, re-employing many who had worked on *Warrior*. The Foudroyant Trust was renamed the HMS Trincomalee Trust and *Foudroyant* reverted to her original name in 1992. The restoration was to take eleven years, and initially the ship was alongside, but in August 1996 she entered the restored dry dock in the Historic Quay area. In May 2000, with work almost finished, *Trincomalee* was re-floated in the dock; restoration was finally completed in April 2001. She is the oldest ship afloat in Britain and retains more than sixty per cent of her original hull timbers. Visitors have access to most of the ship, including the five main deck levels; the upper deck (quarterdeck, waist and forecastle), gun deck, mess deck, orlop and hold.

HMS *Unicorn* – In Ordinary

Unicorn has been at Dundee for more than 130 years. For most of this time she was a drill ship for the Royal Naval Reserve (RNR) or Royal Naval Volunteer Reserve (RNVR), but this role ended in 1968 and the ship is now in urgent need of renovation. One of the final group of *Leda*-class frigates, *Unicorn* was laid down on No. 4 Slip at Chatham Dockyard in February 1822 and launched on 30 March 1824, but was never completed for sea. As this was during a prolonged period of settled peace her weather deck was roofed over immediately and she was laid up in ordinary at Chatham. Her tonnage was 1,084 and her dimensions 151.5 x 40.5 feet.

Her hull construction is of particular interest, being the only surviving example of Seppings' diagonal bracing system, in which wrought-iron straps are fixed to the inside of the hull below the gundeck to strengthen it. The hull also shows the very early use of wrought-iron knees (joining the deck beams to the side frames) which were stronger and lighter than oak knees. The round stern (in contrast to *Trincomalee*'s weaker square stern with larger windows) was an improvement to the original *Leda*-class design and could accommodate 9-pounder stern chasers.

In 1857 *Unicorn* was lent to the War Department for use as a powder hulk at Woolwich, until 1862. She then returned to ordinary, this time at Sheerness. In October 1871 she was offered to the Medway Sanitary Authorities for use as a cholera hospital ship to lie in Stangate Creek. This offer was, however, declined and she was converted to a drill ship for the Royal Naval Reserve at Dundee; the HM Paddle Sloop *Salamander* towed her to her new home in November 1873.

Drill Ship at Dundee

Unicorn was commissioned in her new role on 1 January 1874, and was armed with ten muzzle-loading guns comprising one 9-inch, one 6-inch, four 64-pounders, and four 32 -pounders. In 1906 she was taken over by the newly formed RNVR, and when the Reserves were combined after the Second World War she came under the new, unified RNR. During both World Wars she played an important part as the Area Headquarters of the Senior Naval Officer, Dundee. During the Second World War Wrens were accommodated aboard the ship during their wireless telegraphy training at centres in Dundee. In August 1939 the Polish submarines *Orzel* and *Wilk* made dramatic escape voyages from the Baltic, and Dundee became their base with their crews temporarily attached to *Unicorn*. Three Norwegian submarines and a squadron of Norwegian minesweepers were also based at Dundee. The ship was also a designated reception point for enemy prisoners captured by naval forces in the area, including the crew of *U2326* in May 1945.

Just before the Second World War, when the First Lord of the Admiralty was asked to select a name for a new aircraft carrier he chose *Unicorn*, so the old frigate was renamed *Unicorn II* in February 1939. This created confusion with mail and drafting, so on 20 November 1941 she was renamed *Cressy*. On 14 July 1959 she regained her original name, following the scrapping of the aircraft carrier.

For almost a century, since her arrival in Dundee, *Unicorn* had been berthed at the Earl Grey Dock, but in 1961 the Admiralty was informed that this dock was to be filled in to make way for the new Tay Road Bridge, and it was decided that the ship should be scrapped. A former captain of *Unicorn,* Captain J. C. L. Anderson, succeeded in having this decision reversed and on 13 November 1962 *Unicorn* was moved down river to the Camperdown Dock. In the following year she moved to a new berth in the Victoria Dock, where she can still be seen. In 1967 work commenced on a new shore headquarters for the Tay Division RNR, which was given the name HMS *Camperdown,* and again *Unicorn*'s future hung in the balance.

Preservation

Captain Rennie Stewart, her last RNVR captain, initiated a move to ensure her permanent preservation, and the outcome was the formation, in 1968, of the Unicorn Preservation Society. On 26 September 1968 Prince Philip accepted HMS *Unicorn* from the Navy on behalf of the newly formed society. Limited restoration began in 1972: two signal masts and various offices and training facilities were removed, and officers' cabins and two wooden replica 24-pounder guns were added. An extensive area of the port side above the waterline was replanked, and the ship was opened to the public in 1976. Later the Carron Co. of Falkirk donated two 32-pounder carronades, which can be seen on the upper deck, and fibreglass replica 18-pounder guns (on oak carriages) were added; there are now eight reproduction guns on the gun deck. In 1979 Prince Charles unveiled a new figurehead, and in 1981 the bowsprit was added. Visitors to the ship can tour the covered upper deck, the gundeck, including the captain's cabin and galley, the mess (lower) deck – which also includes officers' and warrant officers' cabins, the orlop deck and the hold. Displays on the upper deck cover themes such as the Tay Division RNR, the role of the ship during World War Two, and previous ships named *Unicorn*.

Although opened to the public from 1976 onwards, there has been no major restoration, and the roofing over her weather deck is believed to be the original structure from 1824 – thus making *Unicorn* a unique example of a historic ship in ordinary. This roofing had helped preserve the ship and, unusually for a vessel of her age, her fabric is ninety-five per cent original, but the deteriorating condition of *Unicorn,* and the lack of funding to address the problem, led to her being placed on the Vessels At Risk list of the National Historic Ships Committee (now Unit) in the early twenty-first century. In December 2005 work began on installing the first section of a new weather covering forward, using an innovative textile construction supported by trusses. It is hoped to raise sufficient funds for the ship to be preserved under a canopy, still with her original wooden 'roof' in place, as part of the new Dundee Central Waterfront Development: this would give her a permanent berth in a better position (within close proximity to *Discovery*) that would attract larger numbers of visitors.

Grand Turk, Replica Sixth Rate

The Sixth Rate was the smallest frigate rating, with between twenty and twenty-eight guns. *Grand Turk* was built in Marmaris, Turkey, in 1997, for Michael Turk as a replica of the 20-gun HMS *Blandford,* which had been built at Deptford in 1741. *Blandford* was seized by the French in August 1755 in retaliation for the seizure by the British of French ships in Canada in time of peace, but was later released. The last Sixth Rate to be built was *Niobe* of 1849.

The *Great Turk* was built for the ITV production of the Hornblower series and has appeared in other films and television series'; she has also been used for corporate and private charter work. Latterly she has been based at Whitby, and is owned by Phoenix Turk Ltd. She is 152 feet (46.3 metres) long, has a beam of 34 feet (10.4 metres) and a draught of 10 feet (3.1 metres). The foremast and mainmast are square-rigged, and the mizzen mast is square-rigged on top with a fore-and-aft spanker below, while the bowsprit carries a flying jib and an outer jib. In total there are twelve working sails, augmented by two 450 hp diesel engines.

BELOW *Grand Turk* passing between the frigate *Lancaster* (left) and RFA *Wave Ruler* (right) at the rehearsal for the Trafalgar 200 Review in June 2005.

chapter 2: merchant sail

The merchant sailing ships surviving from the mid- to late nineteenth century show the type in its final stages of development. They include the clipper *Cutty Sark,* built for speed with premium cargoes, and the steel–hulled barque *Glenlee,* designed for the slower, more economical transport of bulk cargoes during the last days of merchant sail, and incorporating newer materials yielded by the Industrial Revolution.

Cutty Sark

Beautiful tea clipper

A fast and graceful clipper ship, which brought tea from China and wool from Australia, now in a dry dock at Greenwich; undergoing a major conservation programme, after which she will again be open to the public

Evolution of the Clipper

Merchant sailing ship design was naturally greatly influenced by the trades in which the vessels served. The economic need to maximise the load that could be carried was usually one of the most important considerations, but in some trades speed was paramount. The clipper evolved in response to this requirement for speed and became one of the most beautiful sailing ships ever seen. The origins of the clipper lie in the American War of Independence when fast, schooner-rigged privateers were built to harass British ships. The Baltimore clippers, as they became known, were also suited to illicit trades such as slavery and, later, drug running in the China opium trade. Their design developed to incorporate fine lines with high, steeply raked hollow bows, a generous sheer to a low stern and raked masts.

It was in the China tea trade that the form reached its pinnacle of success, though the participating American and British tea clippers differed. The *Rainbow* of 1845 was to lead the way as the first of the great Yankee clippers that helped elevate America to the status of Great Britain as a maritime nation. The clipper was ideally suited to the tea trade, with races to bring back the first tea of the new season (which attracted a high price) stimulating the need for fast ships with only modest cargo-carrying capacity. But the tonnage law of Great Britain favoured slow, deep-hulled ships to minimise taxation, while the navigation laws restricted competition, and the fast tea clippers remained largely an American phenomenon for five years. After the repeal of the navigation laws the American clipper *Oriental* landed tea in the West India Docks in December 1850, ninety-seven days after leaving Hong Kong – faster than any contemporary British ship.

This galvanised British ship owners into action, leading to a series of orders for tea clippers. Alexander Hall of Aberdeen won the first building contract for the new, larger and faster clippers – *Stornoway* for Jardine, Matheson & Co., of Hong Kong, and *Chrysolite* for Taylor and Potter of Liverpool, both of which completed fast maiden voyages in 1851. The following year they raced one another home from Whampoa, remaining in visual contact for the first forty-five days. *Chrysolite* was first home, taking 104 days to reach

Technical Details

Gross Tonnage:	963
Length:	280ft (85.34m) overall; 212ft 6in (64.77m) between perpendiculars
Beam:	36ft (10.97m)
Draught	22ft 6in (6.86m)
Height of masts:	Mainmast – 146ft (44.50m); foremast – 130ft (39.62m); mizzen – 109ft (33.22m)
Mainyard length:	78ft (23.77m); bowsprit: 40ft (12.19m)
Sail Area:	32,000sq ft (2,973sq m)
Speed:	Up to 17½ knots
Complement:	28

ABOVE 'The *Cutty Sark*' in the 1880s Wool Trade, by Geoff Hunt RSMA.

PREVIOUS PAGES *Cutty Sark* on display at Greenwich.

Liverpool. The demand for her tea was so great that the *Liverpool Mercury* recorded: '*Chrysolite* was docked on Saturday morning at 9 am, and before night a considerable portion of the cargo was landed, weighed, duty paid, and about 100 chests of tea were on their way to distant parts of the Kingdom, while a quantity of it was in the hands of retailers in the town, so no doubt it was actually on the tea tables of some of the people of Liverpool the same night – an instance of dispatch unparalleled in this or any other port of the Kingdom.'

Building the *Cutty Sark*

In the 1850s and '60s many more British tea clippers entered service, and by 1869 – when *Cutty Sark* was built – the type was at its zenith. She was built as a challenger to the newly completed *Thermopylae*, which in 1869 made it home from Foochow in ninety-one days. Scott and Linton, of Dumbarton, received the order for *Cutty Sark* from Captain John Willis, a Scottish sailing ship owner whose business was based in London. He was known as 'Old White Hat' because he always wore an immaculate white top hat. Willis took the name *Cutty Sark* from a Robert Burns story in which a witch named Nannie wore a short petticoat known as a cutty sark. The new ship's figurehead showed Nannie grabbing the tail of a horse ridden by the fleeing Tam O'Shanter, a farmer who escaped from the witch's clutches on his now tailless horse. Willis lavished carving and gold leaf decoration (known by the sailors as gingerbread work) on the ship: the ship's name and 'Port of London' raised in letters of gold were encircled by wreaths of laurel on her stern, while the gilded inscription 'Where there's a Willis a way', a

ABOVE *Cutty Sark* entering the Millwall Dock on 28 February 1951, on her way to a dry dock to be surveyed in order to establish whether she could be preserved permanently.

pun on the owner's name, was on the taffrail, and on the topsides were two gilded rubbing strakes. Also, a golden shirt or cutty sark was fitted over the pin on the main truck after the clipper's 1885 fast voyage home from Australia, when she beat *Thermopylae*'s time by seven days.

Designed by the young Hercules Linton, one of the partners in Scott and Linton, *Cutty Sark* was launched on 22 November 1869. Her lines were based in part on Willis's favourite ship *Tweed*, which had been built in Bombay as a frigate for the East India Marine, using lines from a French frigate of renowned speed. *Cutty Sark*'s demanding specification coupled with the highly competitive contract price bankrupted her builders, who had never built a ship of this size before; the company failed before she was completed. So the ship was towed to Greenock for William Denny and Brothers to complete work on her masts and rigging. By this time the Suez Canal had just opened and steam-assisted ships were entering service. For these reasons *Cutty Sark* was almost obsolete on completion. Willis, however, could not bring himself to recognise that the trade in which he had been brought up as both ship master and owner was being transformed, and the new ship's service in the tea trade was to be short lived.

In the Tea Trade

After being brought round to London in January 1870 to load general cargo, *Cutty Sark*'s first voyage began on 16 February when she sailed for Shanghai via the Cape of Good Hope. Her captain, George Moodie, had stood by the ship during her building so knew her well. Nevertheless the outward voyage was plagued by minor accidents and problems with the rigging, which still required tuning to get the best out of the ship. She took 104 days on that outward passage, which was hardly a record, but less important than the speed of the return passage. After discharging her cargo in Shanghai *Cutty Sark* loaded tea for London, and completed the return voyage in 110 days, five days longer than *Thermopylae* – though as she departed a month later and from a different port (Foochow) the two voyages were not directly comparable. This was the first of eight passages she made from China to England with tea, one each year from 1870 to 1877. In 1871 the run home from Shanghai was again not in direct competition with her rival, though *Cutty Sark* did race with *Ariel* and beat her by one week. However, while *Ariel* was regarded as a crack ship she had a new master who possibly did not get the best out of her.

Racing with *Thermopylae*

In 1872 the two protagonists finally came into direct competition for the first and only time. *Cutty Sark* and *Thermopylae* left Shanghai on the same tide, but soon entered heavy fog, which delayed them for three days. They then raced in close company all down the China Sea, with the lead alternating between the two ships, before *Cutty Sark* was crippled by a heavy gale in the Indian Ocean in which she lost her rudder, at a time when she was 400 miles ahead of her rival. *Thermopylae* stormed on to win the race while her rival's crew made and fitted a new makeshift rudder at sea during six days when the ship was hove to. She sailed on, only to suffer further damage to the rudder in a succession of fierce gales, which necessitated unshipping it for repairs before refitting it. The ship's carpenter, Henry Henderson, was a hero of the drama and was to be rewarded by the grateful owner with a testimonial and £50, perhaps not surprising for, as was Willis's custom, the ship and her cargo were uninsured.

Moodie's seamanship in handling these problems was widely applauded by the shipping community, many of whom regarded him as the moral victor, though not by Robert Willis, brother of the owner. He had taken passage in the ship and when the rudder was lost he argued fiercely with Captain Moodie, cursing and raving and demanding that the ship should make for the nearest port. Moodie swore at him and told him to go to hell, and for the rest of the passage Willis remained a sullen critic of the captain. Once home Moodie resigned his command in protest, and went into steam.

ABOVE Stripped of her superstructure and upper masts, *Cutty Sark* is towed towards Greenwich on 10 December 1954.

New Masters

Command passed to Captain F. W. Moore, previously John Willis's marine superintendent, who did not drive the ship as hard as Moodie. Moore's natural inclination was not to risk the fabric of the ship. *Cutty Sark* left London on 26 November 1872, sailing to New South Wales for coal, which she took to Shanghai. There she loaded tea alongside *Thermopylae*, and sailed on 7 July 1873 (two days before her rival), but did not make a fast passage – 117 days compared with *Thermopylae*'s 101.

Captain Moore came ashore, to be replaced by Captain W. E. Tiptaft, another competent master who again did not sail the ship to her limits. Departing in December 1873, *Cutty Sark* took a general cargo to Sydney where coal was loaded for Shanghai. With growing competition from steamships, clippers were finding it increasingly difficult to find cargoes, and Tiptaft found no tea available in Shanghai. (Such cargoes as might have been available by this time were often offered at uneconomic rates for the clippers.) The ship's agents, Jardine, Matheson, finally secured a cargo of tea at Hankow, which was a 600-mile tow up the great Yangtze river. The passage to London, where she arrived on 21 October 1875, took an unimpressive 118 days. *Cutty Sark* left London a month later and made it out to Sydney in seventy-three days, a record passage in which speeds of 17 knots were recorded. In six consecutive days in the Roaring Forties she logged 2,163 miles. Again she took on coal for Shanghai before loading tea at Hankow, and once more had a slow passage home, of 122 days.

The Final Tea Cargo

In 1877 *Cutty Sark* loaded her last China tea cargo at Hankow, clearing Woosung on 6 June and reaching London 127 days later. Sheltering from a violent gale off the Downs at the start of her next outward passage in November, her anchors parted and, out of control, she drove through two ships causing considerable damage and was nearly wrecked on the Goodwins. Pulled clear by two tugs, which were awarded salvage, she was taken back to the Thames for repairs. She finally made Sydney and took coal to Shanghai. There was no tea to be had either there or at Hankow, and Captain Tiptaft died while she was at Shanghai. He was replaced by his mate, Captain J. S. Wallace, who was a real driver of ships, the first such man in command. Wallace took her to Sydney for coal and returned to Shanghai in a fruitless attempt to get tea; on both of these passages *Cutty Sark* made good times. The ship returned to Australia and loaded her first wool cargo for New York – rounding Cape Horn for the first time.

Ocean Tramping

Rather than a racing clipper carrying valuable cargoes she was now reduced to tramping – seeking whatever cargo she could find at ports around the world, trying to compete with far larger ships, both steam and sail. Willis reduced *Cutty Sark*'s sail plan so that he could economise on crew numbers: the lower masts were shortened, her yards reduced in proportion, and her skysails and stunsails were removed.

In May 1880 she loaded coal at Penarth for the United States Navy's China Squadron; it was a charter that Willis would bitterly regret for the voyage was both a tragedy and financial failure. Against maritime tradition the ship sailed on a Friday, which was regarded by superstitious sailors with horror, and the doom-mongers among the crew forecast dire consequences. At first the passage went well: despite the early setback of a south-west gale the ship quickly reached the south-east trades of the Indian Ocean. At this time the American mate Sidney Smith, a 'bucko' or bully, was provoked by a lazy foremast hand named Francis who failed to respond to an order when the yards were being squared during a course alteration. In a rage the mate grabbed a capstan bar and hit Francis with it, killing him. The crew rebelled, near to mutiny, and the mate locked himself in his cabin. When the ship reached Java, Wallace foolishly allowed Smith to leave the ship to join an American ship rather than face trial, and the crew openly mutinied. Wallace had to sail the ship without them, using apprentices and petty officers. On 5 September *Cutty Sark* became becalmed in the Java Sea for three days and, with the crew still in a state of great unrest, Wallace did not leave the decks. By the morning of the fourth day, the strain became too much for him: at four o'clock in the morning he jumped over the side and was taken by sharks. The second mate had to take charge and was ordered by Willis to proceed to Yokahama to deliver the cargo, but proved unequal to the task. The exasperated owner had to recruit a Dutch pilot to take her to Singapore where the troublesome crew members were discharged and a new captain, William Bruce, was drafted in from another of Willis's ships, *Hallowe'en*, then at Hong Kong, on which he was mate.

Cutty Sark resumed her tramping but Bruce, although a good navigator, was in many ways an incompetent captain – often drunk to mask his lack of confidence and ruling the ship through tyranny and petty bullying. In the spring of 1882 the ship was bound for New York from Cuba but, being under-provisioned, her crew became half-starved and Bruce had to cadge provisions from passing ships. Bruce was removed from the ship in New York and Captain F. W. Moore, who had commanded her in 1872–3, was transferred from *Blackadder*. In the winter of 1882–3 *Cutty Sark*'s cargoes in the Indian Ocean included redwood, palm sugar, dye nuts and deer horns. The treacle-like palm sugar, known as jaggery, leaked into the bilges and had to be pumped out daily. She returned to London in June 1883, and Captain Moore remained in command of *Cutty Sark* for two further successful years, taking general cargo to Australia and returning to England via Cape Horn with wool. Fast times were made, such as the return passage from Newcastle, New South Wales, of eighty-three days in 1884, beating any other ship that year by at least twenty-five days.

Preparing for a Tea Race from Foochow

The crack ships were always the first to load and began to assemble about the end of April; until the tea came down they were all engaged in painting, varnishing and smartening themselves up in such ways as sheathing over their channels, preparing for the fray. Then what a sight they made when all was spick and span, with their glistening black hulls, snow-white decks, golden gingerbread work and carving at bow and stern, newly varnished teak deck fittings, glittering brass, and burnished copper!

Each ship of course had her distinctive mast and bulwark colours. Some went so far as to paint elaborate landscapes or posies of flowers on their bulwark panels. But none of them could excel the Aberdeen White Star clippers, such as *Thermopylae* and *Jerusalem*, when it came to looks. Their green sides, white figureheads, white blocks, white lower masts, bowsprit and yardarms, gold stripe, and gold scroll work were the admiration of sailors wherever they went.

When all the ships had been polished up, and lay with their yards crossed and sails bent, all ready for the arrival of the tea, a day was set aside for a grand regatta, in which all the boats of the fleet took part. This was always a great occasion, a holiday for the crews, with liberal prizes for the best cutters, gigs and sailing yawls; and naturally the rivalry between the ships was intense.

The tea came down the river in sampans to the Pagoda Anchorage where it was loaded with all the hustle of coaling a man-of-war against time. The tea (in tea chests) was beautifully stowed, tier by tier, by Chinamen using big mallets. Arthur H. Clark in his *Clipper Ship Era* (1920) provides an account of the scene:

'Cargo junks and lorchas were being warped alongside at all hours of the day and night; double gangs of good-natured, chattering coolies were on board each ship ready to handle and stow the matted chests of tea as they came alongside; comfortable sampans, worked by merry, bare-footed Chinese women, sailed or rowed in haste between the ships and the shore; slender six-oared gigs, with crews of stalwart Chinamen in white duck uniforms, darted about the harbour; while dignified master mariners, dressed in white linen or straw coloured pongee silk, with pipe-clayed shoes and broad pith hats, impatiently handled the yoke lines. On shore the tyepans with their clerks hurried about in sedan chairs, carried on the shoulders of perspiring coolies, with quick firm step to the rhythm of their mild but energetic 'Woo ho-woo ho-woo ho!"

(Adapted from Basil Lubbock, *The China Clippers*, Brown, Son and Ferguson, 1914)

Fast Voyages Under Captain Woodget

Cutty Sark's years as a wool clipper were to be her most successful and continued until 1895. Richard Woodget commanded her from 1885 to 1895 and proved to be her most outstanding master. Hailing from Burnham Norton, Norfolk, he was a fine seaman and a driver of the ship, getting the best out of her in all conditions. On his first voyage in 1885, he made Sydney in seventy-seven days and returned in seventy-three, the latter time beating the *Thermopylae*'s by seven days (*Thermopylae* had left Sydney two days later than *Cutty Sark* and arrived off the Downs nine days after her). This firmly established *Cutty Sark* as the fastest of the Australia wool clippers, able to take late cargoes from up country at high rates and still make the January wool sales in England. By this time Willis had reduced the crew by a third and was employing boys, some of them as young as twelve or thirteen years of age, to make up half of the crew, so Woodget's achievements were all the more remarkable. He would sail further south than any other captain in order to get the best of the Roaring Forties trade winds, bringing the ship in close proximity to icebergs.

For ten years *Cutty Sark* made the fastest passage home with wool. Nevertheless the economics of the operation were parlous: *Cutty Sark* would often have to wait months for her wool cargo in Australia and could only manage one round voyage a year. During the idle time in Sydney the crew would often make music, gathered by the main hatch, singing to the accompaniment of simple instruments such as an old whistle or a jew's harp. There would be picnic parties using the ship's boats at weekends, and evening concerts organised by the Australians. The food on board was perhaps not that appetising – one fifteen-year-old apprentice, Clarence Ray, mentioned eating salt tram horse.

The ship's performance under Woodget inspired Willis to make one last attempt at the China tea record in 1886. He sent the ship to Shanghai but no cargo could be found and *Cutty Sark* had to make for Sydney and take on wool again. In 1889 she was involved in a chance

contest with the P & O steamship *Britannia*: on the night of 25 July she sighted the liner, which was making between 14½ and 16 knots. *Cutty Sark* overhauled her at a speed of 17 knots. But the old clipper's heyday was over, for she was competing against both much larger wool clippers and steamers, and in 1895 Willis bowed to the inevitable, selling *Cutty Sark* for £2,100 to J. Ferreira & Co. of Lisbon, Portugal, who renamed her *Ferreira*.

Portuguese Service

Under the Portuguese flag the new *Ferreira* returned to tramping, often to parts of that country's empire – Mozambique, Angola, and the Cape Verde Islands – as well as Rio, New Orleans and even occasionally the United Kingdom, at Liverpool, Cardiff and London. For more than twenty years she continued to be ship rigged, but in May 1916 was dismasted in heavy weather and was re-rigged as a barquentine (her main and mizzen masts being converted to fore and aft rig). In 1922 *Ferreira* was seen by Captain Wilfred Dowman, an old sailing ship master, at Falmouth, having put in there to repair gale damage; he recognised her as the old *Cutty Sark* and resolved to buy her. Although the ship returned to Lisbon, where she was sold to another Portuguese owner and renamed *Maria di Amparo*, Dowman soon managed to purchase her.

ABOVE The bows of *Cutty Sark* in her dry dock at Greenwich.

Training Ship

In 1923 Dowman had the ship towed to Falmouth where she reverted to the 'red duster' and her original name. He re-rigged *Cutty Sark* as a ship to approximate to her original appearance, and she remained in the harbour as a cadet training ship, preparing boys for naval careers, and as a museum ship.

Dowman hoped to return her to sailing condition, but died in 1936 before achieving his aim. His widow presented the ship to the Thames Nautical Training College at Greenhithe, where she was moored close to the college's other training ship, *Worcester*, again to provide training for boys who wanted to pursue a seafaring career. By 1949 she was no longer needed by the college and was offered to the National Maritime Museum which, lacking the resources to take on the ship, approached London County Council (LCC) where the idea was immediately welcomed. An independent committee was set up to further the aim, and *Cutty Sark* was moved to a mooring off Greenwich for the 1951 Festival of Britain. The Cutty Sark Preservation Society was formed under the patronage of Prince Philip, and the old clipper was formally handed over to the Society as a free gift from the Thames Nautical Training College on 28 May 1953.

Restoration and Conservation

Restoration work began on the ship while she was in the East India Docks and a new dry dock was built at Greenwich on land donated by LCC. On 10 December 1954 *Cutty Sark* entered her new home, as described by *The Times*' naval correspondent: 'At Greenwich the crowds were thickening, and beyond the college could be seen the neat white concrete dock where the ship is to lie. Heaving lines were passed to the shore, hawsers were passed to the clipper's passage crew and, for the last time, the rhythmic orders, "Heave … Heave … Heave" were heard on board the *Cutty Sark*. On the muddy dockside young sub-lieutenants and WRNS officers from the college cheered, and the sight of masts moving among the chimneys of Greenwich brought crowds running down the side-streets to the dock, which is now to become so striking a landmark on the river bank.' Finally, on 25 June 1957, with restoration complete, the ship was opened to the public by the Queen accompanied by Prince Philip. Since then *Cutty Sark* has been visited by more than 15 million people.

Major Conservation Project

By 1998 it was becoming evident that a major conservation project would be needed to counter corrosion of *Cutty Sark*'s wrought-iron frames and copper-zinc alloy fastenings, and deterioration of the teak and rock-elm planking. The project was expanded to include replacement of the main deck, keel and the copper-zinc sheathing below the waterline, and raising the ship by 3 metres in the dry dock – to allow visitor access underneath the hull. The ship will be supported in a steel cradle with both internal and external members, to relieve the physical stresses that threaten to destroy her shape.

A glass canopy will be erected at waterline level to give weather protection to the hull and give space in the dry berth for visitors to see the graceful lines of the hull, the figurehead collection and memorials to the merchant marine. Other interpretation areas are being created: in the entrance area, the significance of the ship and its trades is explained; the lower hold details the construction of the ship , the science of the conservation, loading with tea cargoes and the human stories through live interpretation; the tween deck shows the voyages and trades of the *Cutty Sark*, tea tasting, and the people and cultures the ship encountered; the main deck explores rigging and ship handling; and the aft deckhouse will interpret sailors' living conditions.

Work on the £25 million conservation scheme began in November 2006: more than half of the ship's structure, including the masts, gear, deckhouses and saloon, and 400 teak planks, was removed to give access to her frames and decking, and a temporary wooden roof was installed to provide cover for those working on the vessel. The work involved treating and conserving the original fabric (about 90 per cent of the hull is original) – consolidating the planks (542 in all) and treating the iron for the effects of corrosion.

Early in the morning of 21 May 2007 disaster struck; local residents described being awakened by an explosion at about 4.45 am. A huge blaze engulfed the ship, causing significant damage, setting back her conservation by at least a year and adding £10 million to the cost. Fears that the additional funding would not be found were allayed in January 2008 when the Heritage Lottery Fund awarded a further £10 million to the project. The Cutty Sark Trust has said that less than two per cent of the original fabric of the ship was lost in the fire, though there has been some distortion to the diagonal ties under the decks. The Trust aims to complete the project by 2010.

BELOW The Nannie figurehead on the *Cutty Sark*.

Glenlee

Barque that traded worldwide in competition with steamships

Clyde-built sailing barque from the late nineteenth-century merchant navy; later served for many years in the Spanish navy; now restored and open to the public afloat in Glasgow

The Last British Deepwater Sailing Ships

In some trades the merchant sailing ship was to survive long after the introduction of compound-engine steamships. British-built and -flagged square-rigged ships and barques continued to be built in large numbers during the shipping boom of the 1880s and early 1890s, and it was not until about 1897 that market conditions turned against them, by which time there were more than 250 such vessels. The introduction of steel production by new processes meant that the wrought iron and wood used in ship construction could be replaced by steel for hulls, spars and wire rigging, greatly increasing the size and cargo capacity of British merchant sailing ships. With efficient sail plans to minimise crew numbers, hulls with full ends and long square sections to maximise the load of bulk cargoes, and no need for coal or fresh water for boilers, they could still be an economic proposition in bulk cargo deepwater voyages. They took coal from the United Kingdom, returning with cargoes such as timber from the forests of North West America, canned salmon from British Columbia, guano, nitrates and copper ore from Chile, grain from San Francisco and jute from Calcutta. The ship also provided what was sometimes called 'the cheapest warehouse in the world', with low-cost storage for cargoes that often changed hands a number of times during a long passage.

A New Ship for the Glen Shipping Company

One such ship was the *Glenlee*, built at Port Glasgow by Anderson Rodger & Co. for A. Sterling & Co. (colloquially known as the Glen Shipping Company, as all their ship names were prefixed with 'Glen'). Like the other ships owned by the company, *Glenlee* had been built to her builder's account. Archibald Sterling, in whose name she was registered, was the brother-in-law of Anderson Rodger, who was the majority shareholder in each of the company's ten ships, while Sterling (who was the ship manager) had only 1/64th share in each. All ten ships were built by Anderson Rodger between 1893 and 1897, and his diversification into ship ownership and management was probably stimulated by a trough in orders for Scottish shipbuilders in 1893.

Build

Glenlee was laid down at Rodger's Bay Yard, and the ship was ready for launching into Port Glasgow's Inner Harbour on 3 December 1896, when she was moved by tugs to the Bay Yard's fitting-out berth. The masts and yards were already in place, so fitting out was a quick affair, taking only ten days. A three-masted barque, she was one of the first deepwater sailing ships to carry a 'bald headed' or 'jubilee' rig (so called because it had first appeared in 1887, the year of Queen Victoria's Golden Jubilee), with no royals on the fore and main masts. The fore and main masts each carried five sails, with two sails on the mizzen mast. There were three jibs and a staysail forward of the foremast, and three staysails were slung between the masts.

Trials were carried out on the Lower Firth, and on 13 December the ship continued to Liverpool to load her first cargo, for Portland Oregon. She handled well and achieved a mean speed of 8 knots in blustery conditions but, as her passage times demonstrate, she was not a fast ship.

Under Sterling Colours

Glenlee's first master was Charles Morrison who had been born on the Inner Hebridean island of Islay in 1853; *Glenlee* was his second command. The men he signed on at Liverpool included seven Scots, three English, two Germans, two Norwegians, a Swede, an Austrian, a Finn, a Russian, a Dane and a Japanese, demonstrating the cosmopolitan nature of sailing-ship crews at that time. On 21 January 1897 the ship sailed with a general (mixed) cargo, headed south to clear the Old Head of Kinsale on the southern coast of Ireland, and continued the long voyage south via Cape Horn and up the western coasts of South and Central America; she finally arrived off the mouth of the Columbia River on 28 June, berthing briefly at Astoria, 159 days out from Liverpool, before being taken in tow up the river to Portland to discharge her cargo. After nearly three months in Astoria and Portland, during which time nine crewmembers deserted, *Glenlee* left Astoria on 26 September with a cargo of wheat for Queenstown, Ireland, via Cape Horn. Arriving off Queenstown the ship was given orders for Gravesend, Kent, where she arrived on 21 February 1898 after a passage of 148 days. She then proceeded upriver to the Eastern Dock, Wapping, to discharge her cargo. This round voyage of 306 days was the only one made under the Sterling colours; one month later she moved to the Surrey Commercial Docks and was surveyed prior to being put up for sale.

BELOW *Glenlee* served in the Spanish navy as the training ship *Galatea*, seen here entering Portsmouth Harbour in July 1935.

Renamed *Islamount*

Her new owner was Robert Ferguson of Dundee and she sailed for Philadelphia on 14 April 1898 with a general cargo under the command of William Fraser of Fife. *Glenlee* arrived there on 3 June, after a passage of fifty days. Eleven men deserted before she sailed for Nagasaki on 13 July, the high desertion rates probably due to the Klondike gold rush. The passage to Nagasaki took 168 days, reaching the port on 29 December. There followed a passage of twenty-eight days to Portland, Oregon (here another ten men jumped ship), and then 147 days to Queenstown for orders that took her to Cardiff to discharge her cargo of grain. She docked at Cardiff on 25 August 1899, twenty-eight months after leaving the United Kingdom. On 9 September she was renamed *Islamount* to conform with other ships in Ferguson's fleet, whose names were all suffixed 'mount'.

A further five voyages were to be completed under the Ferguson flag, taking her to Australia each time, as well as Vancouver via Cape Horn, Chile, Peru, Rotterdam and Germany, loaded variously with coal, wheat, nitrates and wood along with mixed cargoes. At Vancouver, where she arrived on 16 June 1903, nineteen of her crew deserted.

Islamount's final voyage under Ferguson's ownership began in London on 2 November 1904, taking general cargo to Wallaroo, Australia, via Cape Horn, a passage of ninety-six days. Here a number of crew deserted and the remainder refused to sail, claiming that the ship was short-handed. The Liverpudlian captain, William Bevan, produced the ship's articles to demonstrate that the minimum crew was eighteen, when in fact twenty-four were aboard. The crew were still adamant and Bevan was forced to sign on ten men, but once clear of the port they were returned in one of the ship's boats and the cost of hiring them was charged to the crew's wages. *Islamount* returned via the Cape of Good Hope with wheat and made Falmouth in 135 days to unload. From there she was sent in ballast to Liverpool where she docked on 23 August 1905.

Thirteen Years with a New Owner

She was sold to Robert Thomas & Co., of Liverpool, completing seven voyages under their house flag, including three circumnavigations, between 1905 and 1918. Command passed to Richard Owens, a Welshman from Nevin. The first of these voyages commenced at Liverpool on 23 October 1905, for Fremantle and thence with coal from Newcastle, New South Wales, to Caleto Colosa, Chile, for nitrates which were destined for Dunkirk, where the ship arrived on 27 March 1907.

The next voyage took coal from Barry to Caleta Colosa, but off the River Plate the crew mutinied because they believed that the cargo had overheated and might spontaneously combust. *Islamount* was towed into Montevideo where a survey showed these fears to be unjustified – the cargo was only slightly above the normal temperature and the surveyors recommended shifting about 150 tons in order to ventilate it. Five crew members were found guilty by a Naval Court of neglect of duty and disobedience of lawful commands, and were imprisoned for twelve weeks. The ship then spent five months in Chile discharging and waiting for a cargo of nitrates with which she arrived at Antwerp on 28 September 1908. Another long passage ensued, with coal from Barry to Callao, Peru, in 124 days, returning with nitrates to Rotterdam, which she reached on 2 November 1909.

Islamount's next voyage, which began at Gravesend on 26 January 1910, took her away from home waters for nearly two years. Delivering her general cargo to Adelaide, she proceeded to Melbourne for repairs after running aground, then secured a cargo of grain for Chile, returning to Australia

Technical Details

Gross Tonnage:	1,613
Length:	310ft 6in (94.7m)
Beam:	37ft 6in (11.4m)
Draught:	24ft 6in (7.4m)
Sail Area:	25,200sq ft (2,341sq m)
Sails:	19 sails comprising four headsails, double topsails, double topgallants, main and mizzen staysails, spanker and gaff
Height of mainmast:	159ft (48.2m); bowsprit: 44ft (13.6m)
Complement:	28 (with accommodation for 32)

ABOVE Bow view of *Glenlee* at Yorkhill Quay.

with nitrates. After another Pacific crossing she finally returned to Gravesend with a cargo of guano on 12 December 1911.

The subsequent passage was also eventful. Taking general cargo from London to East London, east Africa, the ship encountered a hurricane off the Cape of Good Hope and sustained damage to deck fittings, lifeboats and sails. After fifteen days in East London she moved north to Delagoa Bay in Portuguese East Africa. Her voyage continued to Newcastle, New South Wales, and Callao, Peru, after which she took guano from the Don Martin Islands to Antwerp where she arrived on 17 November 1913.

Another epic voyage began on 14 February 1914 when *Islamount* cleared Antwerp bound for Buenos Aires. She continued on to Newcastle, New South Wales, and loaded coal for Talcahuano. By this time Britain was at war with Germany and, unbeknown to *Islamount*'s Captain Evans, the German East Coast Pacific Squadron was at large off South America. The action in which the British cruisers *Good Hope* and *Monmouth* were sunk took place only fourteen miles south of Talcahuano on 1 November 1914, but the German ships had moved south by the time *Islamount* entered the area in late November. *Islamount* took nitrates from Tocapilla to Port Natal (now Durban), from where she sailed on 8 June 1915 for Rangoon. Her return passage to Queenstown took a staggering 199 days, and concluded in the perilous Western Approaches where U-boats were highly active. *Islamount* reached Liverpool safely on 10 April 1916.

Her final voyage under the Red Ensign was, at three years and five months duration, the longest, and she never returned to the British Isles. She left Liverpool on 18 May 1916 and was finally paid off at Cette, France, where she arrived on 20 October 1919. In between she went to New York, Melbourne, Bordeaux, Hampton Roads, Sydney, Table Bay, Samarang (in Java) and Port Natal. Early in 1918 her owners relinquished their shipping interests and she was acquired by the British Shipping Controller.

Under the Italian Flag

On 17 December 1919 *Islamount* was sold at Cette to Societa di Navigazione Stella di Italiana of Genoa. Renamed *Clarastella*, she was modernised with two auxiliary diesel engines, electric lighting and a tween deck at La Spezia in the winter of 1920/21. However her time under the Italian flag was short, perhaps because of the shipping recession at this time, which sounded the death knell for many of the surviving sailing ships – whose lives had in many cases been extended by the shortage of shipping tonnage during the First World War. On 14 January 1922 *Clarastella* was sold to the Spanish navy for use as a sail training ship.

Spanish Navy Training Ship

She was renamed *Galatea* and converted at Trieste for her new role, in which she was to serve for thirty-seven years. While her rig remained little changed, the internal spaces were reconfigured to accommodate the large crew, which at full strength included seventeen officers, thirty petty officers and 260 ratings and cadets (in contrast to the crew of twenty-eight during her trading days). The poop deck was extended to take four lifeboats, a large midship house was built for galley space and a flying bridge was erected forward of the mizzen mast. Two Ansaldo diesels of 220 bhp each were installed, to give a top speed of about 8½ knots. On her delivery passage to Cartagena *Galatea* met heavy storms and was reported lost. A search was instituted – but she made Cartagena on 20 December 1922.

She was based at La Grana naval base, Ferrol, in north-west Spain and was initially used for officer training, undertaking cruises of about three months' duration. In 1927 she became an NCO training ship. On New Year's Day 1954 she lost seven sails in a hurricane off New York, and twenty cadets suffered broken limbs. Her last time at sea was in 1959, and in February 1962 she was decommissioned. A further ten years were spent as a static-rigging training ship, and the ship then languished in lay up at Ferrol and Seville. There were abortive attempts to preserve her but the vessel was vandalised and sank at her moorings. *Galatea* was later refloated and put up for sale by auction in 1992. She was sold to Hamish Hardie on behalf of the Clyde Maritime Trust on 30 June of that year.

Restoration

On 1 June 1993 *Galatea* left Seville in tow of the tug *Wallesey* and reached the Clyde on 9 June. At a ceremony at Yorkhill Quay, Glasgow, on 6 July 1993, she was renamed *Glenlee*. A major restoration project was implemented to return her to her 1896 appearance, though the lower tween decks and the main engines (which had been replaced in 1950 by twin Polar Atlas diesels) would remain in place. First, huge amounts of concrete, pig-iron and scrap metal ballasting had to be laboriously removed from the hull, the Spaniards having added 1,200 tonnes of ballast when she was converted for sail training. Also, much of the extra accommodation and equipment installed at this time had to be stripped out before restoration could commence. Grants from the European Union Regional Fund and the National Heritage

Lottery Fund, together with contributions from Glasgow City Council and the Glasgow Development Agency, were secured to finance the ship's full restoration. The steel masts and yards were returned separately from Spain where they had been in storage, though – having been fabricated in the 1950s – they were not the originals.

On 16 July 1998 all three lower masts were erected and by spring of the following year she was fully rigged. In July 1999 the transformation was completed when *Glenlee* was dry docked and her hull painted in her original colours – red boot-topping, blue-grey hull, white band with black ports and black upper topsides. For four days she was a major attraction at the Tall Ships gathering at Greenock, and was visited by more than ten thousand people, before returning to Yorkhill Quay. Here she is open to the public seven days a week throughout the year.

As restored, the main deck is made from opepe, an African hardwood, although originally it was of Baltic pine. In the forecastle are the hospital, lamp room and the heads, and above it hangs the ship's brass bell. A reproduction figurehead is mounted on the bow, the original having been retained by the Spanish navy. The main deckhouse accommodated the crew, and would often have been flooded by waves that rolled across the deck. The galley and poop cabin (the latter accommodating the captain, two mates and the steward), the charthouse and the wheel are also on the maindeck.

The tween deck accommodated the sail locker forward, and was otherwise for cargo. The lower decks were constructed by the Spanish navy for cadet accommodation. The cargo hold contained fresh-water tanks, cargo and ballast.

Life aboard *Glenlee*

The master's (captain's) and mates' accommodation was located below the poop deck and comprised an elegantly furnished saloon with mahogany panelling, a white ceiling and a decorative skylight from which hung a paraffin lamp. Leather settees surrounded a mahogany table and there was a snug copper fireplace with a mirror above the mantelpiece. A barometer and clock was fixed to the bulkhead. The saloon provided access to the officers' cabins and was also used to entertain visitors such as ship owners, agents and other masters.

The rest of the crew were quartered in the main deckhouse, a bare, featureless place with wooden bunks and bunkboards to prevent the occupant falling out. Mattresses, nicknamed 'donkeys' breakfasts' by the crew, were made of coarse linen and stuffed with straw, affording the sleeper little comfort. In the corner stood a small stove called a bogey. A solid wooden mess-table occupied most of the remaining space so that each man was compelled to sit on his sea chest or a bench. A solitary lamp suspended from the bulkhead provided the only source of light during the hours of darkness. Adjoining this were two double-berthed cabins used by the 'idlers' (the senior day men – the bosun, carpenter, sailmaker and cook). Further aft was the galley. All accommodation was subject to the vagaries of climate: the crew were cold and frostbitten in winter, and sweltering in summer. After months at sea the fetid smell of lamp-smoke, tobacco and stale sweat pervaded.

Personal hygiene was something that even the most fastidious found hard to maintain. Washing was done on deck with salt water, each man using part of his fresh water ration for shaving, drinking and washing clothes. Lavatories were provided on either side of the forecastle.

Shipboard routine consisted of a number of laborious and repetitive tasks, among which were taking the helm and steering by the compass or by the set of the sails, painting or chipping rust from the hull, sanding the teak rails, polishing brasswork, working the capstan, splicing wire and rope, making repairs to the standing and running rigging, and swabbing or 'holystoning' the deck. However, working with the sails and rigging was without question the most hazardous task. Other than the idlers, the men were divided into the port and starboard watches, each consisting of six or more men and boys who would be required for hoisting and hauling. Over a 48-hour cycle each watch served five full watches of four hours each and two dog watches of two hours each, totalling 24 hours on deck – but more in bad weather when both the port and starboard watches might be required on deck together. The crew had to grab sleep when they could – the system of watches starved a seaman of sleep for months on end.

(Adapted from Colin Castle and Iain MacDonald, *Glenlee, The Life and Times of a Clyde-built Cape Horner*, 2005)

chapter 3:
coastal sail

Small merchant sailing ships were built in large
numbers for the coastal and short sea trades around
Britain. Included here are survivors of some of the
most important types: the schooners *Result* and
Kathleen & May, the ketch *Garlandstone* and the Thames
sailing barges. All are of designs that had evolved to
their final form in the late nineteenth century, though
they continued to be built in the early decades of the
twentieth century, and gained auxiliary engines to
extend their working lives.

Kathleen & May

One of the last sailing coasters

This topsail schooner carried coal to Ireland and is now restored to seagoing condition; she can normally be seen at Bideford but is not usually open to the public

The last few sailing coasters, usually schooner or ketch rigged, traded until the middle of the twentieth century and were based out of the north Devon ports of Bideford, Appledore and Barnstaple. In the early 1900s hundreds of these vessels traded, commonly to West Country, south coast, cross-Channel, Irish and Welsh ports carrying cargoes such as coal, china clay, cement, cattle food, bricks, scrap iron and pit props. Their lives were extended after the First World War by the introduction of auxiliary engines, which greatly reduced their passage times.

The schooner rig developed in colonial America and became popular for coastal sailing ships in Britain from about the middle of the nineteenth century, replacing the square-rigged brig. The schooner's fore and aft rig (with either two or three masts) required a smaller crew and could sail closer to the wind.

They were often owned and sailed by seafaring families, but some were built and operated on the share system with sixty-four shares covering the costs and sharing the profits.

The last trading schooner in the British Isles was *Kathleen & May*. She had been launched as *Lizzie May* by Ferguson and Baird at Connah's Quay, near Chester, in April 1900 for Captain John Coppack, a leading shipowner in the town, who named her after his two daughters (one of whom, Elizabeth Ellen Coppack, launched the ship). The Coppack family was of Norwegian descent and had settled in Wales in the early seventeenth century. The schooner was planked with 2.5–3-inch thick pitch pine, which had been seasoned for ten to twelve years, laid on heavy doubled frames of oak and fastened with trennels and galvanised iron bolts. Her design was that of a traditional three-masted schooner, rigged fore and aft with four staysails, foresail, mainsail and mizzen, with topsails on the main and mizzen masts, but carrying two square-rigged topsails on her foremast. She was launched fully rigged, so was quickly fitted out to embark in May 1900 on her maiden voyage from Connah's Quay to Rochester with 226 tons of firebricks. Over the next eight years she traded wherever cargoes could be found, ranging from Oban to London, the Channel Islands and Ireland, completing 139 passages (twenty of which were light) and carrying, on average, 249 tons per month. In a typical year she sailed about 4,500 miles.

In September 1908 *Lizzie May* was sold at Rochester to M. J. Fleming of Youghal, County Cork, and renamed *Kathleen*

Technical Details

Gross Tonnage:	136
Length:	98ft 4in (30m)
Beam:	23ft 2½in (7.1m)
Depth of hold:	10ft (3.1m)
Propulsion (auxiliary):	Now fitted with Detroit diesel, 400 bhp, twin screws
Sail Area:	4,550sq ft (423sq m)
Mast height:	74ft fore; 78ft main; 73ft mizzen
Bowsprit length:	43ft 6in
Gross cargo tonnage:	250 tons
Complement:	6

& May after the owner's two daughters. She loaded cement at London for the Bristol Channel but en route ran aground on the Goodwins. Fortunately she was floated off and taken to Dover, where her cargo was discharged and temporary repairs effected. Eventually she reached Appledore for full repairs, having required towing for the final part of the passage. When these repairs were complete in late January 1909, she entered her owner's coal trade between the Welsh ports of the Bristol Channel and Youghal, in which she was employed almost continuously until 1931, except for periods during the 1920s when she was laid up for lack of cargoes. Her average cargo during this period was 170 tons per month, and she completed 372 passages (of which 107 were light). In April 1931 she took her last cargo to Youghal under Fleming's ownership and was sold to Captain Tommy Jewell and his father William, of Appledore. They removed her topsail yards, reduced the height of the topmasts, and added an 80 bhp Beardmore auxiliary engine (which was replaced in 1943 by a more powerful Deutz engine).

Under the Jewells' ownership *Kathleen & May* remained in the Welsh coal trade to Youghal, with occasional cargoes to other ports – for example, taking china clay from Cornwall to the Mersey. Her work continued during the Second World War, when she regularly crossed the Irish Sea armed with a Lewis gun and a rifle. In February 1943 she delivered china clay from

PREVIOUS PAGES
Thames sailing barges, including *Mirosa* and *Thistle*, racing in light airs.

BELOW *Kathleen & May* under sail in the Bristol Channel.

Fremington, on the River Taw, to Crosshaven, County Cork, for the Calligarine Pottery, a trade in which she later became esablished. After collision damage at Swansea in July 1947 she was refitted at Appledore – her short topmasts were removed and a new 36-foot bowsprit was fitted. Under Tommy Jewell she was well maintained – *Kathleen & May* was noted for her smartness and only the soundest in gear and sails was allowed – no doubt contributing to her longevity. A new Crossley diesel was installed in 1952 and around this time she was also fitted with a Lister powered winch, a radio telephone and two radio receivers. Appledore roller-reefing gear was used on all three masts, allowing the sail to be reefed by a ratchet lever that engaged cogs on the boom, thus winding the sail around it (this gear has been retained on the restored vessel). In the 1950s she ranged from the Mersey to Par, and across the Irish Sea as far as the south-west coast of Ireland. In 1959 she carried 7,829 tons, an average of 652 tons per month, more than double her load during the years under sail alone. In September 1960 Captain Tommy Jewell retired and *Kathleen & May* was laid up and sold early the following year.

A succession of owners came and went during the 1960s when she was used for cruising, but in 1967 she was again laid up. In 1971 the schooner was bought by the Maritime Trust and was on display and open to the public at Plymouth until 1978. She was then towed to London to join the Trust's historic ships collection at St Katharine's Dock, before moving in 1985 to St Mary Overy Dock, Southwark. Although the Maritime Trust spent significant amounts of money on her in the early years of its ownership, her condition later deteriorated because of lack of funds, and the trust sold her in 1996 to T. Neilsen & Co. of Gloucester, who were rebuilding the ketch *Garlandstone*. There the forlorn looking *Kathleen & May* attracted the attention of Steve Clarke, a Bideford businessman who noticed the port of registry (Bideford) on her stern. Clarke acquired the vessel and lavished money on an extensive renovation at Bideford, so that she could be displayed there as a tourist attraction, as well as returning her to sailing condition, with new topmasts. Some eighty-five per cent of the planking, sixty per cent of the frames, and all but two of the oak deck beams were replaced, and new decking was laid using balau, an Indonesian hardwood. *Kathleen & May* was relaunched in 2001 and a new set of sails was bent. She has sailed across the Irish Sea and the Bristol Channel several times visiting festivals and her old home port of Youghal, and across the Bay of Biscay to Bilbao. In 2008 the schooner was put up for sale at Bideford. In July 2008 she attended the Brest Maritime Festival and returned with a cargo of 12,000 bottles of wine, which was taken to Dublin as part of a promotion.

BELOW: *Kathleen & May* moored at the East-the-Water quayside on the River Torridge at Bideford, Devon.

Result

Schooner that served in the First World War

Steel sailing coaster, which survives on display ashore as a museum exhibit at Cultra, Northern Ireland

Result was a contemporary of *Kathleen & May* that continued trading until 1967, and differed from her in being built of steel rather than wood. She was launched in January 1893 for Thomas Ashburner & Co., and was registered at Barrow. In fact Ashburner lived at Connah's Quay (where *Kathleen & May*'s first owner also resided) and it was from there that his fleet mainly operated.

Result's lines were more graceful and yacht-like than many schooners because she was conceived by Richard Ashburner, a yacht designer, and Paul Rodgers of Carrickfergus, a well-regarded yacht builder. (Due to financial difficulties suffered by Rodgers, *Result* was completed by Robert Kent of Ayr.) With a counter stern, and clipper bows with a generous sheer, she was rigged as a three-masted topsail schooner with double square topsails on her foremast. At first a flying topgallant was also set on her foremast, but this was soon removed. Her good looks were complemented by her speed, for she was one of the fastest of the later schooners. *Result*'s trading from Connah's Quay took her to Ireland, the Isle of Man and Furness. In 1908 she was sold to Captain Henry Clarke of Braunton, North Devon, where she was the largest of the port's coastal sailing vessels. In 1914 she was fitted with a 45 bhp auxiliary engine and her square topsails and yards were removed.

In November 1916 she was requisitioned by the Admiralty and by January 1917 had been converted at Lowestoft to a decoy ship, numbered *Q23*. The Q-ships carried a concealed armament with which they hoped to sink any U-boat that attacked believing them to be a merchant ship; this tactic was successfully used by some. *Result* was armed with two 12-pounder guns, fore and aft of the mainmast, a 6-pounder gun forward and two fixed 14-inch torpedo tubes aft, and the navy reinstated her square topsails. She encountered her first U-boat at the southern end of the Dogger Bank on 15 March 1917 and was engaged by *UC45* at a range of about 2,000 yards. As the submarine closed on her the schooner opened fire and scored two hits on the conning tower, causing *UC45* to dive and retreat. *Result* suffered damage, mainly to her sails

ABOVE: *Result* on display at Cultra, May 2008.

Technical Details

Gross Tonnage:	122
Length:	102ft (31.1m)
Beam:	21ft 8½in (6.6m)
Draught:	7ft 6in (2.3m)
Complement:	5

and rigging – the foresail alone retained thirteen holes. Another U-boat was engaged later the same night. *Result* fired a torpedo which missed, and gunfire was exchanged, apparently without either ship being hit, before the submarine dived and made off. On 5 April, near the North Hinder Lightship, a third submarine was encountered; *Result* was hit amidships by a 4.1-inch shell, setting the magazine on fire and injuring two of the ammunition party. When she returned fire the submarine dived and the Q-ship dropped a depth charge which led to the U-boat's retreat.

In August 1917 *Result* was returned to her owners who once more removed the square topsails, though they were later reinstated in one of many alterations to her rig over the years. In 1921 she carried slate from Porthmadog to the continent, and later in the 1920s was working the short sea trade along the south coast. By this time her ownership was shared between Captains Clarke and Welch and in the late 1930s the latter acquired full ownership. During the Second World War *Result* carried coal in the Bristol Channel trade from south Wales ports. In 1946 she was refitted, her topmasts were removed and a 120 bhp engine was installed. On one passage, under the command of Captain Welch's son, she sailed from Cardiff to Falmouth

ABOVE *Result* under sail in about 1951, when chartered for filming.

with her midships awash after being overloaded with a cargo of fertiliser. In a fresh breeze she was soon in trouble and ran for the safety of Barry harbour, but grounded as she was entering and split her stern post. The engine compartment flooded, stopping the machinery, and with the schooner's stern submerged the mate had to be lashed to the wheel to avoid being swept overboard. Captain Welch headed for Ilfracombe to ground the ship on a sandy beach, by which time only the bows remained completely above water and it was impossible to reduce sails. The ship was temporarily repaired there and successfully refloated on the next tide.

At some point the mainmast was removed and *Result* continued as an auxiliary ketch, trading in the Bristol Channel, along the south coast, and to the Channel Islands and French Channel ports until 1967. With cargoes in short supply Welch decided to convert the hold into passenger accommodation for charter work, but he died before this could be completed. After three years in the care of the Exeter Maritime Museum, Mrs Welch sold *Result* to the Ulster Folk and Transport Museum in 1970. In 1979 she was craned out of the water at Belfast Lough and taken on a road transporter to be put on display, without masts and on dry land, at the museum at Cultra, County Down, where she remains.

Garlandstone

West Country trading ketch

*Sailing coaster built on the River Tamar for trade with Ireland; now preserved
and open to the public afloat on the Tamar in Devon*

Trading ketches, somewhat smaller than the coasting schooners, survived longest in the West Country where they could serve the many small harbours, coves and open beaches, carrying bulk cargoes such as coal, stone, grain, flour, salt, bricks and tiles. A small crew of two men and a boy could easily handle them, and they often loaded and unloaded the vessel themselves using a spare gaff as a derrick.

One of the last ketches to be built was *Garlandstone*, a product of a small yard owned by James Goss on the River Tamar in the parish of Bere Ferrers near Calstock. Her construction began in late 1904; she was built as a speculative venture and progress on her was delayed by other work; she was finally completed in late 1908. *Garlandstone* was first registered in January 1909 at Milford Haven by her first master, Captain J. D. Russan, of Dale, Pembrokeshire, who had bought her outright. He named her after a large conical rock close to the isle of Skomer, off the Pembrokeshire coast. As built she had a cabin aft where the crew ate together and the master and mate were berthed, the two seamen having berths in the forecastle. By 1912 the after cabin had been replaced by an engine space containing a two-cylinder paraffin engine, and a bulkhead moved to enlarge the accommodation forward. In 1919 Captain Andrew Murdoch became her master and co-owner, and in the following year acquired full ownership. He operated *Garlandstone* in the Irish trade to and from the Bristol Channel until 1943. In 1941, after discharging a cargo in the small southern Irish port of Courtmacsherry his Irish crew refused to sail back to England with him and Murdoch, then an elderly man, had to sail the ketch single-handed to Portishead, with forty-eight hours at the wheel. There he laid her up before selling her and she continued in the Irish trade under two further owners.

For some of the time under Captain Murdoch's ownership *Garlandstone*'s mate was Edward Eglinton who, in his book *The Last of the Sailing Coasters*, wrote of her:

'I found the Garlandstone lying loaded in the Lydney Canal. Having never seen her before I was happy to find such a pretty little vessel with a beautifully rounded counter stern: a sharp and jaunty bow, even her sides showed a gentle curve throughout, and the narrow planking of her deck followed that beautiful curve. She had a wheelhouse with a half-curved back; a roomy galley and a curved back toilet, like a sentry box forward of the fore rigging … A big tall man on her deck wearing a stiff collar and a bowler hat, introduced himself to me. He was Andrew Murdoch, her master and owner. Captain Murdoch wore a bowler hat (and shore-going clothes) at sea and

Technical Details

Gross Tonnage:	76
Length:	76ft (23.2m)
Beam:	20ft 2½in (6.2m)
Draught:	9ft (2.7m)
Propulsion (1912):	Two-cylinder paraffin engine, 40 hp
Speed:	8 knots
Cargo capacity:	approx. 100 tonss
Complement:	4

ashore, and the only other kind of headgear I ever saw him wear was a sou'wester …'

'The Garlandstone sailed on, we had now lost all sight of the Irish coast and we were now feeling the full power of the following seas that no part of Ireland had hindered in their drift from the broad Atlantic. To me, familiar with only the narrows of the Bristol Channel, those mighty volumes of water, galloping up astern and overtaking our little ship, was a magnificent and awe-inspiring performance. As her stern lifted high and broke through over the crests of those majestic travellers there was a hiss and a roar, the surface foaming white over the deep blue of the water, the vessel seemed to fly stern first into the troughs while she was actually racing ahead at nearly ten knots. In the troughs the Garlandstone looked dwarfy and puny but we had nothing to fear, not a drop of water – solid water – came aboard.'

In August 1943 *Garlandstone* was purchased by Alfred Parkhouse of Braunton and fitted with a more modern engine; after the war her foremast was shortened and the sail area reduced. She mainly operated in the Bristol Channel area for three years until being sold to a US citizen.

Her new owner probably intended to convert her into a yacht but this never happened and she lay at Barmouth for many years. She was rescued by Mr R. A. Kiffin and Mr Colin Lansdown and towed to Porthmadog for restoration, to become the centrepiece of the privately owned Garlandstone Museum, which was later absorbed into the Gwynedd Maritime Museum – at one time *Garlandstone* had carried slate from Porthmadog. The ketch was eventually purchased by the National Museum of Wales. In 1987 she was leased to the Morwellham Quay Industrial Museum on the River Tamar, Devon, and became their property in 2000. Full restoration took place in the 1990s during which the after cabin was reconstructed.

BELOW *Garlandstone* berthed on the Tamar in 2008.

Thames Sailing Barges

Sailing barges of the Thames and East Coast

More than sixty of these tan-sailed workhorses of the Thames estuary survive, and many are regularly on the water; see them at Maldon, Faversham, Pin Mill, and elsewhere

The characteristic design of the Thames sailing barge evolved to its final form in the late nineteenth century. The spritsail rig with mainsail and foresail had superseded square sails in the previous century and, in the early 1800s as barges became larger, the small mizzen sail had been introduced. By the 1830s the topsail had been added, except on the so called stumpie barges, which usually worked under Thames bridges by lowering their main masts. The hull design gradually changed from the shape still seen on dumb lighters to a straight stem and broad transom, with a chine running for much of the length amidships. Although most barges were built of wood, some were of iron and, later, steel; they also had leeboards that could be lowered when working to windward. Flat bottomed with a shallow draught they could serve the small up-river quays and creeks of the east and south-east coasts, while the largest could trade as far as Exeter and Hull and to the near continent.

ABOVE A Thames barge on the River Thames near Tower Bridge and City Hall.

Craft built for the short seas of the Thames estuary and the east coast were generally more shapely than those built for use on the Thames and Medway rivers. The men who crewed sailing barges were known as sailormen, and it was common to have a crew of only two, sometimes a man and a boy, although crews of up to six operated the largest. The barges' design thus was both versatile and economical, and their numbers grew so that by 1860 there were around 5,000. As they grew in size fewer were required and by 1900 their numbers had fallen to approximately 2,000. Their cargoes were very varied: stone, bricks, sand, cement and timber for the burgeoning capital's building trade; hay and straw for its horses; flour and malting barley; sugar, chemicals, rubbish, gunpowder, manure and a host of other goods.

The last sailing barges were built in the early 1930s and by this time some had been fitted with auxiliary engines. Inevitably their numbers dwindled as lorries, tugs and lighters, and small motor coasters took their trade. By the 1950s many of the survivors had dispensed with

Thames Sailing Barges Listed in the Core and Designated Lists of the National Historic Ships Register				
Name	**Year**	**Builder**	**Gross tonnage**	**Location**
Cabby	1928	London and Rochester Trading Co., Rochester	76	Maylandsea, Essex
Cambria	1906	William Everard, Greenhithe	109	Sheerness, Kent
Centaur	1895	John & Herbert Cann, Bathside, Harwich	61	Maldon, Essex
Edith May	1906	John Howard, Maldon	64	Lower Halstow, Kent
Gladys	1901	John & Herbert Cann, Bathside, Harwich	68	London
Greta	1891	Stone, Brightlingsea	46	Faversham, Kent
Ironsides	1900	Clarke & Stanfield, Grays	78	Faversham, Kent
Lady Daphne	1923	Short Brothers, Rochester	85	St Katherine's Dock, London
May	1891	John & Herbert Cann, Bathside, Harwich	70	Ipswich
Mirosa	1892	John Howard, Maldon	49	Faversham, Kent
Reminder	1929	F. W. Horlock, Mistley	108	Maldon, Essex
Seagull II	1901	Gill & Sons, Rochester	25	Chatham
Thalatta	1906	W. B. McLearon, Harwich	92	St Osyth, Essex
Xylonite	1926	F. W. Horlock, Mistley	51	Maldon, Essex

BELOW: *Mirosa* in trade. She is seen heavily laden in about 1937 when her skipper was 'Billy' Bunter.

sails altogether and become fully motorised, but a few sailed on – still in trade, in some cases without even an auxiliary engine, until the 1960s. Since then there has been a renaissance of the Thames sailing barge as the survivors have been restored and re-rigged for use on holiday charters, for corporate hospitality or as private yachts. Altogether about sixty-eight survive, though not all are in sailing condition.

Mirosa was built as a stackie for Charles Gutteridge of Vauxhall and carried hay, straw and timber between London and the rivers on the Essex, Kent and Suffolk coasts. The stackies were developed by Howard of Maldon as flat beamy barges that could load stacks of hay or straw up to half the height of the mainmast. With the mainsail brailed up to accommodate this, they had a long sprit and flat topsail head to compensate. Originally named *Ready*, and renamed in 1947, *Mirosa* was the last barge to trade entirely under sail, which she did until 1955. She became a timber lighter until 1964, and in the following year her rig was restored. She has a full suit of flax sails and manilla running rigging. To this day she has never had an engine fitted, and has raced extensively since 1965, probably winning more races than any other barge.

The diminutive *Seagull II* was built to carry ordnance and stores at Pembroke Dockyard. *Greta* also carried ammunition in the Second World War, taking it from Upnor on the Medway to warships in the Thames Estuary. She also took part in the Dunkirk evacuation in 1940. As her name suggests, *Ironsides* is built of iron. Several barges have corporate owners – such as *Gladys* (Allied Mills) which has the smiling Sunblest logo on her topsail, and *May* (Tate and Lyle).

Centaur is owned by the Thames Sailing Barge Trust (who also own *Pudge*, of 1922, which at the time of writing

is undergoing a major rebuild). *Centaur* traded until 1955 when she became a timber lighter. A typical Essex coasting barge, she has been restored to her original attractive appearance, with a graceful sheer to her bows and an elegant transom. Her rig is typical of a true trading barge, unlike many sailing barges which have been re-rigged with large gear for racing.

Cambria was a coastal trader with Everard's, the Greenhithe firm that both built and owned sailing barges. She ranged between the Humber and Cornwall, and cross-channel to the near continent, with cargoes such as coal, coke, pitch, oil cake and wheat. In 1927, the first year since the First World War that the Thames sailing barge races took place, *Cambria* won the coasting class in both the Thames and Medway matches, and in the following year she again won on the Medway. In 1966 her ownership passed to Bob Roberts, a grammar school boy from Poole who had run away to sea in a barquentine at the age of fourteen, and had been *Cambria*'s skipper since 1954. Roberts kept *Cambria* working as the last trading auxiliary sailing barge until 1970, after which she was acquired by the Maritime Trust for display at St Katherine's Dock, London. *Cambria* is now owned by the Cambria Trust and a grant of nearly £1 million from the Heritage Lottery Fund has facilitated a full restoration programme, which began in 2007 at Faversham.

Edith May sailed in trade until the Second World War, when she was converted to a motor barge, and worked as such until 1961. Later she was re-rigged and became one of the most successful racing barges of the post-trade era. Recently she has been completely rebuilt at Lower Halstow, Kent, where sailing barges used to load bricks from the local brickworks.

Other barges active under sail include *Adieu*, *Alice*, *Ardwina*, *Beric*, *Betula*, *Cygnet*, *Decima*, *Edme*, *Ethel Ada*, *Henry*, *Hydrogen*, *Kitty*, *Lady Jean*, *Marjorie*, *Montreal*, *Nellie*, *Phoenician*, *Repertor*, *Thistle*, *Victor*, and *Wyvenhoe*.

Sailing Barge Races

Organised barge races were introduced in 1863 and helped improve both the status of sailormen and the design of barges. The idea came from William Dodd who made his fortune from refuse disposal (he became known as the Golden Dustman) and owned a fleet of sailing barges. In his book *Down Tops'l* (Harrap, 1971), Hervey Benham describes the intense competition in the races which meant that sail was not reduced until the last possible moment:

'Certainly the barge races were a spectacle unequalled even by the J-class yachts. To have participated must have been a tremendous ordeal. Jim Stone [a Mistley skipper] reckons 1929 was the hardest race he ever was in. *Reminder* [a champion barge on the Thames and Medway] was ready to capsize at any moment going up the Lower Hope. She began a sickening, unnatural, lurching roll, and he told a hand to stand by the tops'l halyard. Over she began to go, and only the order "Down tops'l!" saved her. Her crew, in addition to handling four thousand square feet of canvas, were trimming her by shifting thirty-five fathoms of anchor-chain about the deck, and when they finished they fell down on the hatches where they stood and lay there exhausted till some one said "Come on. Let's get ashore out of this."'

The races had died out by the 1930s but have been revived in recent years, including on the Medway.

chapter 4: the transition from sail to steam

Technological change accelerated in the Victorian age, with ships adopting steam power and iron or steel hulls. At first, sails were retained to supplement paddle or screw propulsion because steam engines were relatively inefficient and coaling stations were not always available where required. The ships in this chapter illustrate this transitional period before steam completely replaced sail, from which the survivors include both warships such as *Warrior* and *Gannet*, and merchant ships such as *Great Britain* and *Discovery*.

Great Britain

Brunel's revolutionary steamship

*The first screw-driven ocean liner, designed by Brunel as the world's largest ship;
open to the public in the dry dock in which she was built, at Bristol*

Brunel's Atlantic Liners

The visionary engineer Isambard Kingdom Brunel was responsible for some of the groundbreaking developments in ship design in the early Victorian era. Though trained as a civil engineer to produce bridges, docks and railways, he was able to see the potential offered for ships by emerging technologies, and combine them in the design of a radical new transatlantic liner. As consulting engineer for the Great Western Railway he dreamed of offering a through service from Paddington to New York via Bristol, and in 1837 launched a 1,320-ton wooden paddle steamer, *Great Western*, to take on the fast American sailing packets that then dominated the transatlantic passenger trade. She was the largest steamship in existence and was able to cross the Atlantic in fifteen days. As competition from other paddle steamers emerged, notably from the Liverpool ship owner Samuel Cunard, Brunel conceived the idea for a much larger wooden paddle steamer, to be named *City of New York*. Through a series of revisions to her design she was to become the largest ship in the world, more than 100 feet longer than her rivals, and would be iron-hulled. Her name was changed to *Mammoth*, and she would be built in the Great Western Dock at Bristol, which had been constructed for the building of the *Great Western*.

Design Evolution

Fabrication of the keel officially began on 19 July 1839, the anniversary of the launch of the *Great Western*, though the actual laying of the keel in the dry dock did not take place until December. In May 1840 the experimental propeller-driven *Archimedes* visited Bristol and excited the interest of the Great Western Steamship Company's Building Committee, which recommended that the construction of the new ship's engines should be halted together with any part of the hull that would be affected by a change in engines and propulsion. The Company chartered the *Archimedes* for some months and Brunel, who supported the review, was asked to investigate the possible adoption of the screw propeller. In December 1840 Brunel presented his report to the directors who recommended that screw propulsion be adopted for the *Great Britain*, as the new ship was now named.

Technical Details

Net registered tonnage:	1,016
Gross tonnage:	3,443
Displacement:	3,675 tons (loaded)
Length:	322ft (98.15m)
Beam:	50ft 6in (15.39m)
Draught:	16ft (4.88m); 18ft (5.49m) fully loaded
Propulsion:	Four-cylinder 'Triangle' steam reciprocating engine, single screw, 1,800 ihp
Speed:	12½ knots (under steam)
Bunker capacity:	1,100 tons coal
Sail area:	16,000sq ft
Passengers:	252 (with berths)
Cargo capacity:	1,200 tons
Complement:	130

To suit the new propulsion the engines had to be redesigned, and the Triangle engine, patented by Isambard's father Marc, was selected and adapted to drive a screw. In addition, the ship was to step six masts on which sails would be bent.

All of the masts were fore-and-aft rigged (with standing gaff sails which brailed into the mast), except No. 2 which was square rigged, and she had a single funnel. The gaff-rigged masts had topmasts for gaff topsails, but these were rarely set and the topmasts were housed to reduce windage when on passage. The rig was unorthodox, making full use of ironwork in place of wood, and of iron wire rope in place of the traditional hemp, and its design minimised the necessity for work aloft so that it could be handled by a very small deck watch.

The Grand Launching

Construction proceeded apace from the spring of 1841, and in 1843 the date of launch was chosen – again 19 July. Prince Albert travelled from London by train for the ceremony. After breakfasting at Bristol Temple Meads station he rode in procession through the crowd-lined streets of the flag-bedecked city and reached the Great Western Dock at noon. Here he toured the ship and then, while the dock was being flooded, attended a sumptuous banquet in the company of a host of VIPs, including Sir Marc and Lady Brunel, Isambard's ageing parents. After the banquet, at the invitation of Prince Albert, the naming ceremony was performed by Mrs Miles, the wife of one of the directors of the Great Western Steamship Company. The *Bristol Journal* reported on the scene:

> 'The vessel was decorated with the colours of all nations and as far as the eye could reach in every direction nothing was to be seen but flags, banners and emblems and masses of human beings. All around arose the masts of ships dressed out in chequered and flaunting colours. Boats and barges were crowded and the various adjacent wharves and quays were lined with anxious spectators … From the water's edge upwards rose tier upon tier of spectators … Brandon Hill (which provided a natural amphitheatre) was covered with not less than 30,000 persons.'

PREVIOUS PAGES A view of the upper deck of *Warrior*.

BELOW The launch of the steamship *Great Britain* at Bristol on 19 July 1843, by Joseph Walter.

As the ship was edged out of the dock under tow of a small screw steamer, the *Avon*, Mrs Miles released the champagne bottle towards the bows. However the towing line broke and the bottle missed the ship by about ten feet. As the ship veered towards the royal pavilion under a new line Prince Albert seized another bottle of champagne and threw it at the ship – this time the bottle hit, showering glass and wine onto the heads of workers below who were pushing her side off from the dock.

Sea Trials

There were delays to the fitting out and it was not until 12 December 1844 that the *Great Britain* proceeded down the Avon under her own power for the first time for a sea trial. On 8 January 1845 sea trials continued, and on 14 January the six-masted vessel was formally registered, being described on the certificate as 'schooner rigged with standing bowsprit, square stern and carvel built with false galleries and a Royal Arms figurehead'. On a trial run to Ilfracombe and back on 20 January the *Great Britain* averaged a speed of more than 11 knots, the maximum achieved being 12½ knots. Both her engines and the six-bladed propeller were judged to be most successful, a remarkable achievement for such an innovative design.

On Public Display

The ship's first commander was Lt James Hosken, a half-pay naval officer who had commanded the *Great Western* on sixty-four transatlantic voyages (he was later to become a vice admiral). Late on 23 January 1845 the *Great Britain* left Bristol for London and in the small hours of the following day was struck by a strong north-westerly gale off Lundy, and suffered some damage to fittings on her upper hull and forecastle deck. Another gale was encountered off the Nore but the ship arrived safely at Blackwall in the afternoon of 26 January. She remained on the Thames for five months during which time she was visited by many thousands of people (who paid a small admission charge), the directors being apparently keen to attract the maximum publicity to the ship, despite the high cost of delaying her entry into service. On 23 April Queen Victoria and Prince Albert were joined by the Board of Admiralty when they embarked on a royal tender at Greenwich Palace to visit the *Great Britain*, which was dressed overall for the occasion.

The decision had been taken to base the ship at Liverpool rather than Bristol and it was for the former port that the ship finally left on 12 June on her maiden voyage. With eighty passengers on board she sailed past Cowes and called at Plymouth, where fourteen thousand people visited her. While there her passengers were disembarked into hotels and a day trip

RIGHT *Great Britain* aground in the Falkland Islands, where she had served as a storage hulk.

around Eddystone Lighthouse was undertaken with six hundred people aboard. *Great Britain* called at Dublin on 3 July before making Liverpool on the following day where, as *The Times* reported, 'Numerous steamers, crowded with expectant passengers, put to sea to meet her. The pier-heads were crowded, and a warm welcome was given to this noble and wonderful ship.' Again she was opened to the public, attracting 2,500 visitors each day.

Entering Atlantic Service

On 26 July 1845 *Great Britain* sailed from Liverpool on her first transatlantic voyage to New York, waved off by thousands of cheering spectators who lined the banks of the Mersey, or followed her down the river in ferries and launches. This enthusiasm was not quite matched by paying passengers, of whom there were only forty-five – perhaps because of apprehension about the new form of propulsion. The ship was also carrying 360 measurement-tons of cargo. The weather was poor: there were westerly gales for much of the crossing and thick fog on the American side. Even so, the time of fourteen days twenty-one hours, covering a distance of 3,304 nautical miles at an average speed of 9.4 knots, was considered a success. Compared to paddle steamers there was very little vibration, though the ship was susceptible to rolling. As she steamed up the Hudson with colours streaming from each of her six masts, *Great Britain* was greeted by an immense crowd. Once again she was thrown open to the public, attracting around 21,000 visitors.

While in New York a significant number of her crew deserted and the quality of their replacements meant that the ship was less ably manned when the return voyage began on 30 August. Fifty-three passengers had been embarked, together with a cargo of 1,200 bales of cotton. Again the voyage was largely successful, although difficulties in maintaining steam pressure (probably due to the excessive rolling affecting her stokers) meant that *Great Britain* placed considerable reliance on her sails. The main topmast snapped about half way down due to there being insufficient seamen to take in the topsail in a sudden squall of wind, and one seaman had his arm smashed when trying to remove the debris. This necessitated an amputation by the ship's surgeon and the passengers collected £25 for the seaman as compensation. The passage was made in thirteen-and-a-half days at an average speed of about 9 knots, despite largely unfavourable easterly winds. The first round voyage had vindicated the new method of propulsion but had shown that further development was necessary to get the best out of the ship.

The Second Atlantic Voyage

The second westwards transatlantic crossing began on 27 September 1845, with 104 passengers, and was more eventful, and slower, than the first. Strong adverse winds were encountered for the first ten days of the passage; in a heavy squall on 2 October the foremast was carried away and some hours were spent fishing the sails and spars out of the water. Early on 5 October, while it was still dark, a heavy sea was shipped which, because the skylights were inadequately fastened, came through into the forward cabin in large quantities, causing great alarm among the passengers. Navigational errors then put the ship among the Nantucket shoals where she touched ground and badly damaged the propeller. The ship had little coal left and was extricated from the shoals with great difficulty. The captain had to send a boat to the shore to determine where the ship was, and consulted with a fisherman about the best course to follow. The ship had to put into Holme's Hole in the island of Martha's Vineyard to take on more coal. *Great Britain* finally docked in New York on 15 October after a passage of eighteen days, which one passenger described as 'tedious and not without danger'. Another reported that among the rules for passengers it stipulated that boots must be cleaned by 8 o'clock, and gentlemen must not play cards on Sunday.

After dry docking for repairs the ship sailed from New York on 28 October, but it became clear that the repairs to the propeller were unsatisfactory, as it was unbalanced and fouled the stern post, causing enough damage for it to become unserviceable. The engines were stopped on 8 November and in moderate south-westerly winds all of the sails she could carry were set. The wind freshened to a westerly gale with a high sea, and under reduced sail the ship showed her paces; the log reported, 'Ship scudding and steering beautifully taking spray on the larboard quarter and beam occasionally, but is easier than any ship I ever knew'. She passed a large ship which was hove to because of the weather and overhauled several packets with ease. Her log again reported, 'This is wonderful with our little spread of canvas, and more than I expected well as I thought of her sailing qualities'. After three days of gales the wind moderated but again sprung up to gale force on 14 November for part of the day. She made Liverpool on 17 November, a passage of twenty days, and her passengers presented a surprisingly forgiving

BELOW A stern view of *Great Britain*.

address to Captain Hosken expressing 'the superiority of the *Great Britain* in a heavy gale .... For safety, speed and comfort she is unsurpassed, and during this passage of unexpected length we have not suffered the slightest diminution of comfort and in particular our table has been as good and well supplied as ever.'

A winter refit was used to tackle some of the teething troubles: a new and heavier propeller with four blades was fitted, and the air pumps and boiler fire flues were redesigned, allowing ample steam to be raised without difficulty. In sea trials during April 1846 a speed of 11.8 knots under steam alone was achieved, much better than any earlier performance. The refit also entailed removing the mast immediately abaft the funnel, increasing the size of the fourth mast (now the third) and converting it to square rig to resemble the original mainmast, and fitting topgallant masts over the topmasts. Two trysail masts were fitted to become the new fourth and fifth masts, with gaffs that could slide up and down, replacing the original brailing gear. The aim of this re-rigging was probably to balance the rig so that there was less weather helm. Also, the white band on the hull was painted over so that it became completely black.

The Third Atlantic Voyage

After trials in the Irish Sea the new season began on 9 May when the *Great Britain* sailed from Liverpool with only twenty-eight passengers – the ordeal of the previous voyage had clearly diminished confidence in the ship. Unfortunately the fears were not entirely misplaced, for four days out the guard of the after air pump fractured and the engines were shut down for repairs. The ship continued under sail but it took twenty days to reach New York. After repairs she sailed again on 8 June with forty-two passengers and successfully reached Liverpool in thirteen-and-a-half days, averaging 13 knots on the best day. With 110 passengers on board, the outward passage of the next round voyage was completed in a similar time, despite touching bottom on the Cape Broil Reef, Newfoundland, again due to a navigational error by Captain Hosken. Another mishap occurred on the return passage, which began on 1 August, when a driving chain broke and the engine had to be shut down. The voyage took thirteen days, so the target of thirteen days out and eleven home remained tantalisingly out of reach, even though it was not unrealistic if all went well.

Stranded on the Irish Coast

The next outward passage was to end in disaster. After leaving Liverpool at 11 am on 22 September 1846 the *Great Britain* intended to pass south of the Isle of Man and then turn north to round the northern coast of Ireland. Inexplicably the turn was not made and the ship blundered ashore on the County Down coast of Ireland, in Dundrum Bay, at about 10 pm. This was the third, and most unfortunate, navigational error made by Captain Hosken. For the 180 passengers on board it was a traumatic ordeal. They were just retiring after a concert at which 'all was bright, joyous and happy'. They then heard cries of 'Stop her!', 'Aground, aground!', 'The breakers! The breakers!', accompanied by the sound of the ship grounding and loud screams from the ladies' cabins. According to the *New York Tribune*, 'To add to that moment of woe, the lightning glared, the thunder bellowed portentously from a thick curtain of overhanging cloud, and the rain began to fall in torrents'. A Canadian passenger recalled:

> '... the scene on board was most distressing .... The great majority of the passengers were very ill .... Several passengers who ought to have shown more firmness betrayed lamentable weakness. Captain Hosken continued cool and composed and several times referred to his charts. No one retired to rest – all were full of fears. But it was found next day that one passenger had never awoke until morning'.

In *The Times* a passenger agreed that 'Captain Hosken behaved with admirable self-possession and energy; and immediately after the ship struck went down below, and, by his assurances, quieted the excited apprehensions of the passengers. His efforts were successful ...' So much so that, 'A portion of the passengers returned to their berths and slept until morning.'

A woman passenger gave a vivid account in a letter to a friend:

'We have indeed been in fearful peril. The ship struck the rocks at 10 o'clock. I had just gone to my stateroom and the instant I felt the shock I knew something was the matter. In a moment there was a second shock and all was confusion. Men and women rushed out, the latter from their berths, and some threw themselves into the arms of strangers. We could with difficulty stand. Oh I cannot tell you the anguish of that night. The sea broke over the ship, the waves struck her like the thunderclaps, the gravel grated below. There was the throwing overboard of the coals, the cries of children, the groans of women, the blue lights, the signal guns, even the tears of men and amidst all rose the voice of prayer. [A group of clergymen, led by the Revd S. H. Cox of New York, conducted a service to calm nerves.] The day dawned and we lay between two long ledges of rock while another stretched across our front. 500 yards to the right or left, 200 yards in advance, and the ship [would have] been dashed to pieces. At dawn we were lowered over the ship's side and carried on shore in carts of seaweed manure. We walked through an Irish bog and lay down upon the floor of an Irish cabin. With much fatigue we came on to Belfast and Liverpool'.

Salvaging the Ship

Captain Claxton, one of Brunel's associates, arrived on the scene on 28 September. He found that the ship was settled on two detached rocks on the sand and was taking in a little water. During a gale the following day water was breaking right over the stern of the *Great Britain*. The fabric of the ship was already sustaining damage and Claxton decided to raise the sails and drive her further up the beach. Attempts to protect her by building a wooden breakwater around her stern were frustrated by heavy seas that twice swept the structure away. On 8 December Brunel went to Dundrum Bay and was furious with what he found. He wrote to Claxton:

'I was grieved to see this fine ship lying unprotected, deserted and abandoned by all those who ought to know her value and ought to have protected her instead of being humbugged by schemers and underwriters .... the finest ship in the world, in excellent condition, such that four or five thousand pounds would repair all damage done, has been left and is lying like a useless saucepan kicking about on the most exposed shore that you can ever imagine.'

Brunel sought to reassure the directors of the company that the damage to the vessel was not extensive and was mainly confined to the bottom under the boiler and engines, the boilers having been forced up by about 15 inches. This, he said, 'could easily be repaired if the vessel were in dock.'

Brunel devised measures to protect the ship, including a flexible breakwater of faggots (bundles of wood) secured together with iron rods and weighed down with chains. A protracted salvage operation ensued, in which the ship was lightened and lifted up by mechanical levers and wedges so that the bottom could be repaired, and a trench was dug between the stern and the sea. On 27 and 28 August 1847 she was finally towed clear on the high tide by HMSs *Birkenhead* and *Scourge*, and taken to Belfast Loch to be pumped out before the tow back to Liverpool.

The Great Western Steamship Company was crippled by the costs of the salvage, for the *Great Britain* had been greatly under-insured. *The Times* reported a stormy shareholders' meeting that lasted three days, at which 'a most angry discussion arose as to the directors not having insured the stranded vessel, which cost nearly £120,000, for more than £17,000' and the directors were also blamed for having returned the passage money, and for not having taken immediate and efficient measures to get her off. Both *Great Britain* and *Great Western* were put up for sale and the company was wound up. At first no buyers were attracted to the *Great Britain* and she lay in the Coburg Dock until, on 2 January 1851, a sale to Gibbs, Bright & Co. was completed. The sale price was only £18,000, a fraction of the original £120,000 cost of what was still the largest ship in the world.

ABOVE The replica engine (left) and a replica of the original six-bladed propeller (right).

Conversion to Emigrant Ship

Gibbs, Bright & Co. had interests in the Great Western Railway and also operated the Eagle Line of sailing packets from Liverpool to Australia. The owners knew Brunel and had even been involved in the original discussions prior to the formation of the Great Western Steamship Company. Their interest in buying the *Great Britain* was sparked off by the Gold Rush in Australia, which followed the first discoveries of gold in Victoria in early 1850. The lure of prospecting for gold denuded the workforce in Melbourne and the surrounding rural area, and wages rocketed. Ships were required to convey to Australia the new flood of emigrants attracted by this bonanza. Such ships were at this time still largely dependent on sail because of the length of the voyage and the high costs and uncertainties of bunkering coal en route. So *Great Britain*'s new owners apparently decided to convert her to a sailing vessel with powerful auxiliary steam power, rather than keeping her as a sail-assisted steamship – although this vision was not initially achieved. They also wanted greatly to increase her passenger load and cargo space so that she was a more viable proposition than before. The number of masts was to be reduced to four, although the 27,000-square-foot sail area provided an increase of seventy-five per cent in relation to the original sail plan. However, with No.s 1 and 4 masts fore-and-aft rigged and the others square-rigged it was an unconventional and untried configuration.

John Penn & Co. of London (who were later to build the engines for *Warrior*) manufactured the new, more economical, two-cylinder oscillating engine, with direct gearing to a triple-bladed propeller. The propeller could be disengaged to revolve freely when the engine was not in use, thus reducing drag. Two new boilers were fitted side by side, venting to twin funnels that were also positioned side by side. Transverse wrought-iron beams were fitted at the lower deck levels to strengthen the hull, which would now be worked at deeper draughts to carry increased cargo and fuel. A wooden keel, 17 inches deep and 20 inches wide, was

The Emigrant Passage to Australia

In all, ships such as *Great Britain* and *City of Adelaide* (see Appendix) carried a total of nearly 1.5 million emigrants from the United Kingdom to Australia in the nineteenth century. In this trade *Great Britain* was unusual in having auxiliary steam power, and ships using sail alone dominated until the 1880s.

For many of the estimated 25,000 emigrants who sailed to Australia on the *Great Britain* the passage would have been their first experience of shipboard life. As they boarded the ship it seemed like a small town 'well lit up in all directions'. There was a mêlée in which 'the decks [were] crowded with passengers, some looking for their berths, others searching for a missing box … all wearing an anxious and unsettled look'. Among the passengers were those whose families had forced them to go to the colonies because of a lack of opportunities at home, or because of misdemeanours. In the early days many were seeking their fortune through gold. 'We are a rough looking lot. There is a dash of every nation here … Nearly all the passengers are going to the diggings and I only hope there is gold enough for all', wrote Stephen Perry on the first Australian voyage. As preparations were made for sailing the ship's band played and the sailors sang as they went about their duties.

Once at sea many passengers were seasick, as the ship still had a tendency to roll. As they found their sea-legs the emigrants were able to sample the ship's catering, which varied enormously depending on the class of ticket held. The first-class passengers could take their pick. There was an abundance of fresh meat from the livestock on board: on a typical voyage from Melbourne in 1865 the ship carried 126 sheep, 4 lambs, 30 pigs, 2 bullocks, a cow to provide milk for the saloon passengers, 510 fowls, 286 ducks, 65 geese, 32 turkeys, and 6 rabbits. In addition, large stocks of fresh mutton, beef, lamb, pork and veal were kept in ice-stores. A bakery produced fresh bread and rolls, and soups, nuts and cheeses complemented the main courses, while desserts such as plum pudding were also served. This could all be washed down with copious quantities of beer, spirits and wine. In the other classes food was rationed more frugally. Each passenger received 1lb of oatmeal a week; ½lb of raisins, 6oz each of suet and lime-juice and 21 quarts of water. Ship's biscuit was available, though the passengers sometimes found it impossible to break. According to class there were also varying amounts of beef, pork, treacle, sugar, tea and coffee. The

fitted below the original flat plate keel, and wooden bulwarks more than 4 feet high were fitted right along the sides to keep the weather deck dry. By stripping out the cabin and dining accommodation on the lower tween decks, 57,000 cubic feet of cargo space was added. To compensate for this lost accommodation a 300-foot-long deckhouse was added, containing the first-class dining saloon, the spacious grand saloon, second-class passengers' cabins and the Captain and Chief Officer's staterooms. The upper tween deck contained passenger staterooms and, at the stern, an airy lounging room with transom windows. On top of the deckhouse was a hurricane deck where passengers could promenade. Steerage and intermediate- (third-) class passengers were accommodated in cabins next to the engines where conditions in the tropics were intolerable. As one passenger wrote, 'The fierce sun of the equator has made the iron receptacle that contains us one enormous oven in which we poor are sweating all day and night long. There is no approach to coolness but on deck'. In all, 730 passengers could now be accommodated, including fifty first class.

Entering Service to Australia

Before entering the Australia trade the new owners decided that the *Great Britain* should complete a shakedown voyage to New York, leaving Liverpool on 1 May 1852, which went off without major incident. On 21 August she sailed for Australia and, showing that she was still an object of great interest, once again attracted enthusiastic crowds to see her off. Under the command of Captain Robert Matthews, she was carrying 630 passengers on a voyage to Melbourne that was forecast to last fifty-six days. In light airs the first five days were under steam, until on 26 August sail was set and Cape St Vincent cleared. On the following day there was an accident when the ship was taken aback while attempting to re-engage the propeller, which had to be locked for that purpose. The fore and topmast studding sail booms snapped and the wreckage landed on the deck. Progress through the South Atlantic was fitful, with adverse headwinds and, eventually, when only 700 miles from the Cape of Good Hope, it was decided that the ship should return to bunker at St Helena, 1,100 miles away. From here some passengers wrote letters of complaint to the press, criticising the captain's seamanship and navigation. Captain Matthew's choice of route was not suited to sail, ignoring as it did the established trade-wind route via the coast of Brazil and south to about fifty-five degrees before running west. He had also misjudged the need for bunkering when the ship had first passed within about 200 miles of St Helena. Having returned to that island the passengers now had a week to explore it before sailing on 29 September. After putting in to Cape Town the *Great Britain* finally arrived off Melbourne on 12 November, a voyage of eighty-three days. After five days in Melbourne the ship sailed for Sydney, arriving there to great fanfare on 20 November. The return voyage was also very slow, and the route was questionable: steaming west to Cape Town meant battling against the prevailing winds, and the ship was obviously under-powered for steamer routes such as this. The traditional trade-wind route would have taken the ship eastwards via Cape Horn.

New Rig

By the time of her return to Liverpool in April 1853 her owners realised they had to make more decisive changes to her rig so that she could operate as a true sailing ship, using the trade-wind routes and making less use of her machinery, which would be reserved for those times when there was little wind. The two fore-and-aft rigged masts were landed, and a traditional three-masted ship rig was adopted. Her new rig proved much more successful: leaving Liverpool on 11 August 1853, her next passage to Melbourne took sixty-five days and the return sixty-two, faster than the sailing clippers of this era. On the return voyage she carried nearly 7 tons of gold and twenty-three bales of cotton, the first to be imported from Australia. There was also wool and tin and 15 tons of mail.

At last there was to be some continuity for the *Great Britain*. But for the stranding in Dundrum Bay she might well have become a successful transatlantic liner. Now she became established in the Australian trade, completing thirty-two circumnavigations, and earning a reputation for fast and regular passages. These were interrupted by service as a troopship in the Crimean War between February 1855 and June 1856. She was able to carry 1,850 infantry and thirty horses in service that took her to Malta, Constantinople and Smyrna; in all she transported 44,000 troops. On completion of this charter her owners decided to give her a thorough refit, during which a heavier ship rig was fitted, with new masts carrying a sail area of 33,000 square feet. A new lifting propeller was fitted; this could be disengaged and raised in a stern frame by a block and tackle into the trunk above, thus leaving an unimpeded flow of water below. She also received a new single, wider funnel, and there were various changes to the accommodation. With the work complete the ship sailed again for Melbourne on 16 February 1856. In the succeeding voyages she was to record excellent times, such as the round passage beginning in December 1859, of fifty-five days sixteen hours out and sixty-one days home.

In 1854, before her third Australian voyage, command had passed to Captain John Gray, a Shetlander. He became her most successful and longest-serving captain, until being lost overboard in 1872 – his cabin was found empty with the windows open. He may have taken his own life during a period of ill health (though there was also speculation that he may have been murdered for the money that he kept in his cabin). In 1861 the *Great Britain* took the first England cricket team out to tour Australia. They played twelve matches, winning six, losing two and drawing four – a performance that present-day English teams would envy!

second class also received cheese, pickles, tripe and milk when available.

On deck sightings of marine and bird life provided frequent interest: green turtles off Africa, petrels and albatrosses in the Southern Ocean, porpoise, whales, dolphins and sharks. Shipboard entertainments were mostly organised by the passengers rather than the crew, including concerts, theatricals, charades, music and singing classes. On some passages a ship newspaper was produced by the passengers. On deck in fine weather games such as quoits and Aunt Sally were played and dances held to a fiddle accompaniment. Chess, draughts, dominoes and backgammon provided amusement indoors.

Rosamund D'Ouseley was a Scottish gentlewoman who sailed, probably as a third-class passenger, on *Great Britain* to Australia in 1869 to work as a governess. She found the steerage passengers to be 'exceedingly dirty and ill-favoured in countenance'. On boarding they were inspected by a doctor and an immigration official. Her own attempts to keep clean, using the baths constructed on deck behind screens, were sometimes frustrated: 'Caroline and I were up before 6 a.m. to take a shower-bath, but there were too many gentlemen about – in future we intend trying it before 5 a.m.' Although the food supplied was far more substantial and luxurious than that provided for steerage passengers, she wrote that 'we are savagely hungry, these meals do not half satisfy us … so we have an extra tea at 4 p.m. and supper at 9 p.m. of our own providing or we should not be alive.' As they approached landfall in Australia a banquet was served – roast boiled mutton, pastries and puddings in abundance, raisins and nuts, and two decanters of sherry and one of port, which 'was thankfully received by us starving beggars who have been fed five times a week on salt meat and twice on fresh and that not 'ad libitium'.'

(Adapted from Nicholas Fogg, *SS Great Britain – Brunel's Flagship of the Steam Revolution*, 1996, and Robin Haines, *Life and Death in the Age of Sail*, 2003)

ABOVE Bow detail on *Great Britain*.

Around the Horn

On 1 February 1876 the *Great Britain* completed her final Australian voyage at Liverpool and was laid up. Now obsolete in the passenger trade she was put up for sale by auction in July 1881 while lying in the West Float at Birkenhead, but failed to reach the reserve price. In late 1882 she was transferred to the ownership of Anthony Gibbs, Sons & Co., a company related to Gibbs, Bright & Co, and converted into a sailing cargo ship. The engines, funnel, passenger accommodation and deckhouse were removed, a new wood deck was laid, and the hull was sheathed in pitch pine. She served for four years in the South America trade, taking coal from Cardiff round the Horn to San Francisco and returning with wheat. These were long, arduous passages of up to 160 days in each direction. For what proved to be her final voyage she loaded coal for Panama and sailed from Cardiff on 6 February 1886. Suffering damage in gales and a hurricane off Cape Horn the ship laboured onwards against the wishes of her crew. Eventually the captain agreed to put back to the Falkland Islands, and she arrived at Port Stanley on 26 May 1886. She was found to be beyond economical repair and was sold to the Falkland Islands Company to be used as a storage hulk for wool and, later, coal. In 1914 her coal was used to bunker the British battlecruisers *Inflexible* and *Invincible* before their victory in the Battle of the Falklands.

Salvage and Restoration

The *Great Britain* lay at anchor in her Falkland Islands role until the 1930s. By then her condition had deteriorated so that she could no longer be used for storage and in 1937 she was beached at Sparrow Cove, about three and a half miles from Port Stanley. Even at that time restoration of the historic ship was mooted as a possibility, but it was not until 1968 that the first active steps were taken and a survey was carried out. A difficult salvage operation was undertaken in 1970, and the ship was towed back to Bristol on a pontoon, arriving at Avonmouth on 24 June. She was undocked from the pontoon and on 5 July was towed up the Avon to Bristol. On 19 July 1970, 127 years to the day since her launch there, she entered the Great Western Dock where she was originally built. The formidable task of restoration commenced and was not completed until July 2005.

Approaching the ship in her dock she makes a magnificent sight. Dressed overall, her six masts are framed by lines of brightly coloured flags, the White Ensign flaps from the ensign staff below which her decorated stern is vividly embellished with gold leaf-coated carvings. Visitors can tour the weather, promenade and saloon decks. Much of the accommodation has been reinstated, including the elaborately decorated dining saloon on the saloon deck and the first class cabins, promenade saloon, captain's cabins, galley and steerage accommodation on the promenade deck. The replica engine and stokehold can be seen from both of these decks. The forward hold is accessible, revealing the ship's original structure. The dry dock has been glassed over at the ship's waterline level, beneath which dehumidifiers create a controlled atmosphere to minimise corrosion. Visitors can descend to the floor of the dock to view the propeller and rudder, and the underside of the hull, which corrosion has perforated with many small holes. There is also an excellent museum on the dockside.

Warrior

World's first large iron warship

The frigate that revolutionised warship design, with a heavily armoured iron hull and steam-driven screw propulsion; now afloat at Portsmouth and open to the public

Design and Build

In the half century after Trafalgar, technological change altered the face of naval warfare and *Warrior* was probably the most significant ship to evolve from that process. Some wooden line-of-battle ships, similar in appearance to *Victory*, had been modified or built with auxiliary steam propulsion and screw propeller, while retaining their full sailing rig. However their wooden construction made them extremely vulnerable to the new explosive shells that were replacing roundshot. To help overcome this, iron-cladding could be added to the hulls, as in the French *La Gloire*, the construction of which caused great alarm in Britain. The Royal Navy's response was *Warrior*, the world's first large iron-hulled armoured ship, ordered in 1859. Built by Thames Ironworks, she was launched on 29 December 1860 at Blackwall by Sir John Pakington, the First Lord of the Admiralty. Despite the coldest weather for fifty years, with thick frozen snow covering the shipyard, large crowds assembled to watch the spectacle, but *Warrior* was frozen to the slipway, and – after the naming ceremony – refused to budge. The use of hydraulic rams, braziers burning alongside the hull, and the firing of a heavy gun from her upper deck failed to free her. A line was then attached to a powerful tug, hundreds of hammers made the ways vibrate, while men ran from side to side on her upper deck, trying to rock her free. After twenty minutes she finally slid down into the river.

The Steam Frigate

Warrior was classified as a steam frigate because she only had one main gun deck (she was later to be reclassified as a battleship). The old line-of-battle ship (epitomised by *Victory*) was eclipsed and effectively replaced by the new armoured frigate. On entering service *Warrior's* combination of a long, narrow, iron hull, heavy armour cladding and steam propulsion immediately made all other large warships obsolete including, critically, those of the French. However, *Warrior's* new Armstrong 110-pounder breech-loading guns, designed to fire armour-piercing shells, were found to be less effective than the round cannon balls fired from the 68-pounders that they replaced. In consequence the original ten mounted in *Warrior* were not increased in number as had been originally intended, and the 68-pounders were retained. Although contributing to her elegant appearance, the bow and stern of *Warrior* were similar to those of earlier wooden frigates and, as such, anachronistic, and were soon superseded in later ships by more functional forms.

The central section of the hull was an armoured citadel, 208 feet (63.4 metres) long, built of 4.5-inch (11-cm) wrought-iron plate with 18-inch (45.7-cm) teak backing. The protection thus provided to the guns and machinery was vastly superior to that afforded by a wooden hull.

The iron construction allowed the inclusion of strong watertight athwartship bulkheads to separate the armoured central section from the unprotected bow and stern, which it was also used to subdivide. The size, speed, construction and firepower of *Warrior* made her the most powerful warship afloat. Even so, her type was short-lived, for within five years centre-battery ironclads had evolved as a new battleship form.

'Down Funnels, Up Screw'

Warrior's steam engines (built by John Penn & Sons of Greenwich) though economic by the standards of the day, were rather inefficient, requiring large amounts of coal, with sixty-six stokers toiling in temperatures of around forty-three degrees centigrade. Loading the ship with coal took two days, as teams of seamen and marines filled two hundredweight [cwt] (100 kilograms) wicker panniers aboard the collier alongside. The panniers were hauled through the gun ports, lifted over the deck and emptied down chutes to stokers in the bunkers below. The ship's sixteen-piece band played to help keep up the morale of the blackened crew. Coal dust also blackened the gun deck and took a week to clean up afterwards. Hence it was not surprising that *Warrior* was the first warship to have fitted washing machines. However, she also retained a full spread of sail for cruising. The three-masted rig was similar to that carried by an 80-gun Second Rate ship of the line, even though *Warrior* was a much larger ship. Under sail her telescopic funnels could be lowered and her propeller lifted out of the water to reduce drag. Figures from her two commissions show that she spent one-third of her time under steam alone, the remainder being sail only or sail and steam.

Sea Trials

After partial fitting out *Warrior* was rigged by men from Chatham Dockyard, and commissioned on 1 August 1861 at the Victoria Docks, London. Her first master was Captain The Hon. Arthur Cochrane, then aged 37, who had previously commanded the wooden screw sloop *Niger*. The depth of the basin at Victoria Docks limited the load *Warrior* could carry and a week later she proceeded under steam power along the Thames to Greenhithe to embark 375 tons of guns and ammunition, 500 tons of coal, the balance of anchors, cables and boats, and various stores. The rigging was set up and sails bent. Both funnels were at this time painted black. Charles Dickens visited the ship, describing her as '… a black vicious ugly customer as ever I saw. Whale-like in size, and with as terrible a row of incisor teeth as ever closed on a French frigate.' He sensed that the Navy would be changed for ever: 'Admirals and captains will no longer be the men they once were. Mere dogged bravery and reckless bulldog courage will not do now; we shall want science and more comprehensive schemes of combination.'

On 19 September 1861, the ship sailed for Portsmouth on her first sea passage, arriving there on the following day. Sea trials began on 14 October and three days later *Warrior* achieved a speed of 14.4 knots under steam in Stokes Bay, making her the fastest warship in the world. She was officially accepted into service on 24 October. A shake-down cruise to Queenstown, southern Ireland, followed, accompanied by the flagship of the Channel Squadron, *Revenge*. A westerly gale tested *Warrior*'s new crew – most of the younger ratings were seasick – and some sails carried away. Under both steam and sail the ship's speed was of course faster even than the trial speed under steam alone. It was reported by the *Hampshire Telegraph* that on the return passage between Plymouth and Portsmouth on 23 November, nine of the ten hours were spent at full speed (against a tide that was mostly unfavourable) and 'the maximum speed during the day was 17½ knots under steam and plain sail to royals'.

Warrior left Spithead on 18 January 1862 on another trial cruise, this time to Gibraltar. A storm in the Bay of Biscay inflicted some minor damage to the ship, including a cracked main yard. Cochrane reported that no accident of any kind had occurred and felt that the ship had acquitted herself well. She arrived at Devonport on 5 March for a three-month refit to make good defects and undergo modification, including fitting a shorter bowsprit.

The First Commission

On 10 June 1862 *Warrior* sailed for Queenstown to join the Channel Squadron, covering an area from Gibraltar to Scandinavia. Her deterrent effect contributed to a decline in the aggressive intentions of the French and she was never required to fire a shot in anger.

After working up at Portland in August and September 1862 there was a cruise to Gibraltar in October, accompanied by *Warrior*'s sister ship *Black Prince* and the flagship of the Mediterranean Fleet, *Edgar*. The opportunity was taken for the two new sister ships to race against one another for an hour, and *Warrior* won by 1,000 yards. The ship remained in the Gibraltar and Lisbon area and spent Christmas Day at Madeira. *Warrior* was back at Portsmouth on 21 February 1863 to prepare for a ceremonial duty. Together with *Revenge*, *Defence* and *Resistance* she was to escort the Royal Yacht *Victoria and Albert*, which was carrying Princess Alexandra of Denmark to her wedding with the Prince of Wales (later King Edward VII). The ships left Antwerp on 5 March for Gravesend. For the final part of the voyage *Warrior* took station ahead of the yacht as sole escort. The warship's yards were manned by two hundred seamen in white suits with beribboned hats. On 7 March the Prince came aboard at Gravesend to greet his bride.

On 14 March *Warrior* arrived at Devonport for her annual refit when she was fitted with hydraulic steering gear. On 1 April a new gunnery lieutenant, John Fisher, then aged 22, joined the ship; known as 'Jackie' Fisher he was to go on to achieve the highest office in the Royal Navy – as First Sea Lord he drove the programme for building *Dreadnought* and her successors.

After leaving Spithead on 11 July *Warrior* joined seven other units of the Channel Squadron, for a twelve-week flag-showing tour around Britain, during which she was visited

by 270,000 people in eleven different ports before arriving at Plymouth on 3 October. The cruise was successful in its objective of reassuring the merchant shipping community of the Royal Navy's potency. One visitor to *Warrior* at Liverpool described his tour on board:

> *'Along the broad white deck, which looked like a great broad street, men were seen rope making, carpentering, making hammocks, and hand ropes, etc … Going down the ladder to the main-deck, the ear was greeted with the bleating of sheep, and the cackle of domestic fowls in spacious coops, and the animals seemed quite at home among plenty of clean fodder and food. Large quantities of butchers' meat hanging up ready for cooking. Cooks busy at work in the galley, preparing all sorts of dishes – the smell set up is savoury, and calculated to give one an appetite. It is not yet meal time, yet here and there are seen some of the fine fellows leisurely (it being their watch below, as it is termed) dispatching their 'levener', from the hour 'eleven' at which it is taken; and which, in one instance, was a goodly snack of fried beefsteaks and onions; and another mutton chops and boiled rice; and in both cases plenty of biscuits. While a great many were eating, many were engaged in reading (newspapers mostly) or writing letters; some working hearthrugs by a quilting process, or embroidering pictures. Many lay asleep, having to go on deck at twelve o'clock; some sat wrapt in their own meditation, as if unconscious of what was going on around them; one man, a marine, chaunted a song, with a fine cultivated voice…'*

For the second year running Christmas was spent at Madeira with other ships of the Channel Squadron. The return passage took in Tenerife, Gibraltar and Lisbon, before arriving at Portland on 5 March 1864, where she remained until 30 April – on which day *Warrior* proceeded to Spithead and Fisher left the ship to return to HMS *Excellent*, the gunnery school. The ship continued in the Channel and southern Irish waters for the remainder of the year, except for a visit to Gibraltar in September. She paid off at Portsmouth on 22 November for a long refit in the dockyard. *Warrior* was re-armed with muzzle-loading rifled guns: four 8-inch and twenty-eight 7-inch (eight on the upper deck and twenty on the main deck), while the 40-pounders on the upper deck were replaced with 20-pounders.

A Typical Day at Sea Aboard *Warrior*

At sea the crew was divided into the port and starboard watches, which covered the twenty-four hours in alternating watches of either four or two hours. A typical day at sea under sail in 1862 for the starboard watch began very early: at 0345 the starboard watch and 'idlers' (day men) are woken, mustered at 0400 and set to work scrubbing the decks or manning the pumps below decks. The midshipman heaves the log to record the last hour's distance, and the master takes star sights. At 0700 hands are piped to breakfast for half an hour and this is followed by cleaning the ship. At 0900 hands are piped to divisions for inspection and prayers. Then drills follow with the crew taking up their 'general quarters' stations and conducting training such as 'repel boarders'. At 1020 they resume ship's work.

At 1100 the ship is hove to by counterbracing the yards and the lead is used to take a sounding. At 1200 the master uses the sextant to observe the sun's altitude and report the latitude. Then the crew is piped to dinner of salt pork, cabbage and oatmeal. At 1400 the band practises on the cable deck, with four violins, cello, clarinet, viola and euphonium. At 1415 the commander begins a tour of the ship, inspecting the crew as they undertake a variety of training and maintenance tasks. At 1530 the watch coils ropes down and sweeps the deck. At 1600, with the change of watch on deck, the ship is braced round onto port tack. At 1615 hands are piped to supper – cocoa and biscuits – and have time for recreation.

At 1700 drums beat to evening quarters and at 1715 the off-duty watch is brought on deck; each watch takes its own side to lower the topsail and raise it again on each mast. At 1800 lamps are placed on main deck and time is given for recreation, allowing men to light up their pipes for two hours. (Sunday afternoon was also for recreation.) At 1930 'down hammocks' is piped and the ship's company collect hammocks, sling them on the main deck, and stand by their hammocks. At 2000 lights are extinguished on the main deck. The commander conducts the night rounds and reports to the captain on completion.

(Adapted from Captain John Wells, RN, *The Immortal Warrior*, Kenneth Mason, 1997)

The Second Commission

On 1 July 1867 the ship was recommissioned under the command of Captain J Corbett, with many of the crew transferred from *Black Prince*. *Warrior* then moved to Spithead for the Review of the Fleet by Queen Victoria, together with the Sultan of Turkey and the Khedive of Egypt, on 17 July. Corbett and his crew then transferred to HMS *Mersey*, and Captain Henry Boys took command of *Warrior* on 25 July with a new crew for further service with the Channel Squadron. The ship left Spithead on 24 September for Queenstown where she joined the squadron's cruise to Lisbon for training exercises.

Shortly before Christmas 1867 *Warrior* anchored in Osborne Bay, Isle of Wight, joining *Irresistible* on guardship duty while Queen Victoria was at Osborne House. This was prompted by fears that Irish separatists might mount an attack on the queen.

In April 1868 *Warrior* and three other ironclads escorted the Royal Yacht with the Prince of Wales on board for an official visit to Dublin.

On the night of 14 August 1868, while sailing in line ahead with the Channel Squadron, *Warrior* rammed *Royal Oak* which had lost speed when some of her rigging parted, causing limited damage to both ships. On 12 December the flag of Vice Admiral Sir Thomas Symonds was raised as *Warrior* became flagship of the Channel Squadron. Between December 1868 and April 1869 there were four training cruises to Lisbon, as the new admiral sought to increase discipline and efficiency in his squadron. In July 1869 *Warrior* left her familiar cruising grounds of the Channel and Bay of Biscay and joined her sister ship *Black Prince* to tow a new floating dock from Madeira to Bermuda, the base of the West Indies Squadron. The tow, at an average speed of 4.7 knots, lasted from 4 to 28 July; the arrival of the floating dock established Bermuda as the main base for the America and West Indies Squadron.

Captain Frederick Stirling assumed command on 28 August at Portsmouth, and the year ended with a training cruise in November to Madeira, Tenerife, Gibraltar and Lisbon. Another cruise to Lisbon ensued in late January–early February 1870. The following month Captain Henry Glynn took command and in August the ship joined a combined fleet at Gibraltar. While the fleet was at sea in the Bay of Biscay on the stormy night of 6/7 September the experimental battleship *Captain* capsized. The following day *Warrior* was involved in the search for survivors but found only wreckage; only eighteen survived from the crew of 472, having reached the Spanish coast in a ship's launch.

In early May 1871 *Warrior* left Bearhaven, Ireland, for the squadron's summer cruise to Madeira, Gibraltar and Tangier. She arrived at Portsmouth on 1 September and paid off into reserve and refit two weeks later.

Relegation to Reserve

During the major refit at Portsmouth she was re-boilered and a poop deck, a longer bowsprit and a steam capstan were fitted. However, the ship was to see no further operational service. *Warrior* recommissioned in April 1875 as a ship of the First Reserve, her design by then being obsolescent. At Portland, and then from 1881 on the Clyde, her duties were as a static guardship, a drillship for the Royal Naval Reserve, and a coastguard headquarters. She had a small full-time crew, which was augmented by the Reserve each summer for a five- or six-week cruise. These cruises were largely uneventful, although on the first – when *Warrior* was flagship – *Iron Duke* rammed and sank *Vanguard* off the Irish coast. In May 1883

Technical Details

Overall length:	420ft (128.02m)
Beam:	58ft (17.68m)
Draught:	26ft (7.92m) at full load
Displacement:	9,210 tons
Armour:	Sides 4½ inch over 208ft of the central part of the hull.
Propulsion:	10 boilers, two-cylinder horizontal single-expansion steam reciprocating engines, 5,287 ihp, single shaft
Speed:	14.4 knots (under steam); 13 knots (under sail); 17 knots (steam and sail)
Coal:	850 tons
Range:	2,100 miles at 11 knots (under steam)
Sail Area:	4,490sq m (48,400sq ft)
Total weight of canvas:	Approximately 12 tons
Height:	Of masthead lights from upper deck 169ft (51.48m) [fore], 175ft (53.31m) [main] and 138ft (42.03m) [mizzen]
Armament:	10 x breech-loading 110-pdrs, 26 x muzzle-loading 68-pds, 4 x breech loading 40-pdrs (mounted on the upper deck)
Complement:	705 (including 127 Royal Marines)

Warrior was paid off from the Reserve at Portsmouth. Her engines, boilers and guns were removed and for several years she was laid up in Fareham Creek.

Harbour Service

From May 1901 to July 1902 *Warrior* was used as a storage hulk for torpedoes, and then in July 1902 became the depot ship for destroyers at Portsmouth, flying the flag of the flotilla captain. In April 1904 she became part of the naval torpedo school, HMS *Vernon*, joining two wooden steam battleships in Portchester Creek. Part of her role was to supply steam and electricity to the other hulks that formed HMS *Vernon*. In March 1904 she took the name *Vernon III* to release the name *Warrior* for a new armoured cruiser. In 1923 *Vernon* moved ashore at the Gunwharf, and the ship reverted to her original name, *Warrior*, on 1 October of that year.

She was taken in hand in 1927 for conversion into a mooring hulk for oil tankers at Llanion Oil Fuel Depot, Pembroke Dock. She arrived at her new home on 15 March 1929 to take up a role that lasted until 1978. For this role she was renamed *C77* and during nearly fifty years of such service about 5,000 ships refuelled alongside her. During the Second World War she was also used as a depot ship for motor minesweepers. The hulk was never renamed *Warrior* again by the Royal Navy. Instead the name was taken firstly by an aircraft carrier launched in 1942 and, following the sale of that ship in 1958, by the Fleet Headquarters at Norwood in 1963. It was a happy accident that because of her unglamorous duties the old hulk survived to become a subject for restoration, following the closure of the oil depot in 1978. She was handed over to the Maritime Trust on 20 August 1979 and nine days later left under tow for Hartlepool where she arrived on 2 September to begin the restoration to her 1862 appearance.

Restoration

Warrior's hull was basically sound, having been maintained by the Royal Navy; however, new bulwarks and much new decking were required. The rest of the ship was in a very poor state and almost all of the original equipment and fittings had been removed – only a capstan and two pumps remained. Her top deck had been covered with 200 tons of concrete which had to be removed.

Replicas of the engines and guns were manufactured, often using modern materials – sheet steel instead of cast or wrought iron in the engines, and fibre-glass mouldings for the guns. The lower masts and yards were of steel rather than the original wood (the adoption of which would have been prohibitively expensive). Many aspects of the rebuild were informed by the 1861 journal of Henry Murray, a fourteen-year-old midshipman who had drawn plans and diagrams recording in great detail all the equipment and fittings and their positions. The rebuilding cost £6.5 million, taking eight years to restore the ship to magnificent condition. In June 1987 she returned to her old base, Portsmouth, where the local council had spent £1.5 million on a new jetty and supporting facilities for her. *Warrior's* position near the Hard allows her to be seen to good effect and attracts the attention of visitors and ferry passengers to the Historic Dockyard. At the end of 2004 she was dry docked at Portsmouth so that her bottom could be repainted.

ABOVE The ship's wheel on the gun deck (detail).

Warrior's Layout

Visitors can tour the hold and the upper, main (gun) and lower decks. Aft on the upper deck are: the propeller well (into which the propeller was raised when the ship was not under steam); a stern pivot gun which could be swivelled over an arc (there is a similar gun at the bow); the ship's wheel; the captain's bridge above the armoured conning tower, between the main and mizzen masts, (providing the steering position under normal sailing conditions); racks for storing hammocks; and the two telescopic funnels. The wheel on the upper deck has four linked wheels and was manned by up to eight men in strong winds; beneath it on the main deck is another similar wheel which could be manned by a further eight men. Between the fore and main masts is another bridge, which was used for navigating the ship. On long voyages sheep were kept in pens on the upper deck for fresh meat, with chickens and ducks kept in the boats. Below the main deck beyond the forward bulkhead there was a manger for cows.

There are twenty-two 68-pounders and four 110-pounders enclosed within the armoured citadel on the main deck. Before the citadel are two 110-pounders, and aft of it are four 68-pounders and two 110-pounders. There are also thirty-six messes for 655 men, arranged between the guns. About eighteen men were detailed to each mess, where they ate, slept and relaxed. *Warrior's* four anchors each weighed 5.6 tons and had to be raised manually, an operation that took four to five hours and involved at least 170 men at each linked capstan. The capstans can be seen on the gun deck, as can the galley, the captain's day cabin with his sleeping cabin on the starboard side, and the cabins of the master and the commander.

On the lower deck are the wardroom and fourteen officers' cabins, the laundry, the cells and the issue room where the daily food allowance for each mess was issued and taken to the galley to be cooked by seamen who, due to age or disability, were unable to perform more strenuous duties. In the hold can be seen the replica engine and the ten boilers, each with four furnaces: here stokers toiled for hours in temperatures as high as 110°F (43°C).

BELOW The wheels on the upper deck.

Gannet

Victorian sail and steam sloop

A sloop from among the Victorian Navy's smaller ships that policed the empire's colonies and trade routes; now afloat at Chatham and open to the public

Gunboat diplomacy – defined as the use of warships in peacetime to further a nation's diplomatic and political aims – had a role in the nineteenth century as part of British imperial history. The exhortation 'Send a gunboat' was directed at the smaller vessels of the Royal Navy that might be called upon for these tasks. One such ship, *Gannet*, is representative of the ships of the mid-Victorian era that policed the trade routes and the more remote parts of the rapidly expanding British Empire. The Empire's import and export trade expanded eighteen-fold during the nineteenth century and the demand for protection increased commensurately. This was complemented by policing work dealing with incidents in the many new colonies, often operating with marines, soldiers and anti-slavery patrols.

Design and Build

Gannet was one of fifty sloops that were built between 1873 and 1904 as enlarged versions of the gunboats and gun vessels that had been conceived for the Baltic and Crimean wars in the 1850s. The definition of a sloop in 1875 was a cruising vessel with a crew of between one hundred and two hundred. Sloops were more weatherly ships, and more heavily armed, than the shallow-draught gunboats, making them better suited to deepwater cruising. As such, *Gannet* was capable of operating independently and was able greatly to extend her range through the use of sail power. She saw service in the Pacific, Mediterranean and the Red Sea before succumbing to a series of harbour roles that ensured her survival.

One of the first group of seven *Osprey*-class screw sloops, also classed as colonial cruisers, she had a graceful clipper bow; the second group of seven ships in the class had vertical stems. *Gannet* was ordered from Sheerness Dockyard on 14 February 1876, was laid down in December of that year and launched on 31 August 1878. Humphrey and Tennant & Co manufactured the engines and boilers at Deptford. Her hull was of composite construction – teak planking on iron frames – which lent itself to repair at less well-equipped dockyards, and was copper-sheathed below the waterline. She was barque rigged with three masts, there being four yards on each of the

Technical Details (as built)

Displacement:	1,130 tons
Length:	190ft (57.91m)
Beam:	36ft (10.97m)
Draught:	15 ft 9½in (4.81m) – loaded; 12ft (3.66m) – light
Propulsion:	Two-cylinder horizontal compound expansion steam engine, 1100 shp; single shaft. Three cylindrical boilers
Coal bunker capacity:	145 tons
Speed:	12½ knots (under steam); up to 15 knots under sail
Range (under steam):	2,000 nautical miles at 11½ knots or 3,240 nautical miles at 5 knots
Armament:	2 x 7-in muzzle-loading guns (pivoting), 4 x 64-pdrs (2 pivoting, 2 broadside). Some changes were made to this during her career.
Complement:	139 (including 13 officers and warrant officers, 27 petty officers, 64 seamen etc, 11 boys and 24 marines)

fore and main masts and fore and aft rig on the mizzen. Like *Warrior* she combined the use of both sail and steam, the engine having twin horizontal cylinders athwartships driving a propeller that could be retracted into the stern to minimise drag when under sail, and the funnel was telescopic. Her armament initially comprised two 7-inch rifled muzzle-loading guns and four 64-pounders. Two of the 64-pounders were in fixed broadside positions in the forecastle, and the remaining guns were mounted on the main deck in swivel carriages normally stowed on the centerline of the ship but capable of being moved to either side of the ship as required.

Service in the Pacific

HMS *Gannet* was commissioned on 17 April 1879 for service on the Pacific station, and on 1 May undertook steaming trials on a measured mile. On 3 May she completed a six-hour steaming trial, obtaining an average speed of 10¾ knots by the patent log. Two days later she left Sheerness for working up in the English Channel. On completion of the work up she spent nine days at Spithead taking on stores while the crew painted the ship. Weighing from there on 22 May, she put into Plymouth on the following day to pick up a sub-lieutenant who had been sent to hospital at Sheerness on 3 May.

Gannet sailed from Plymouth on 25 May 1879 for Madeira, arriving there on 1 June to take on stores and coal, and set up the rigging. She was en route to Rio de Janeiro, where she arrived on 30 June. Here she refitted, took on coal and stores, and painted ship. After the crew had taken shore leave she left for Valparaiso via the Straits of Magellan. Off Cape Vigius in southern Argentina she encountered Force 9–10 storms, with a heavy head sea, squalls of rain and snow and vivid lightning. The storms lasted for eight days and must have provided a stern test for her crew at this early stage in the commission. Before navigating the Straits of Magellan *Gannet* sailed into Possession Bay near the entrance to the straits. During the passage through the straits parties were often landed to cut wood for fuel. On one of these stops, at Gray Harbour on 8 August, the crew watched two volcanic eruptions on Hurne Island, observing that the vapour and ash rose to a height of 5,000–6,000 feet. The route through the straits avoided Cape Horn, and *Gannet* then headed north, again experiencing Force 9–10 winds off Juan Fernandez. She entered Coronel Bay on 25 August, where she stayed for four days while hands were employed to coal ship. Finally, *Gannet* arrived at Valparaiso on 31 August.

Her commission was to range along the Pacific coasts of South and North America, as far north as San Francisco, and across the South Pacific, to islands such as Hawaii, Christmas Island and Tahiti, for nearly four years. She shadowed the action during the nitrate war between Chile and the Peruvian/Bolivian alliance and was present off Callao when the Peruvians scuttled their own fleet to prevent it falling into Chilean hands. In 1881 she had a short mid-commission refit. On 27 June 1883 she arrived home at Plymouth, having sailed more than 60,000 miles on her first commission, the majority of this under sail. The sloop then proceeded to Sheerness where she paid off into refit on 20 July.

Service in the Mediterranean

The refit replaced her original flying bridge with a full poop (or quarter) deck, providing space underneath for a commanding officer's cabin and for additional armament, including two 5-inch breech-loading guns forward of the mizzen mast and two four-barrelled Nordenfeldt machine guns. The ship's rig was lightened to compensate for the extra weight added aft. *Gannet* recommissioned on 3 September 1885 for service in the Mediterranean and the Red Sea, which could be reached using the Suez Canal. On this

Gannet's Sailing Qualities

In her first captain's log *Gannet*'s sailing qualities were recorded. 'Sails very well with the wind abaft the beam and very fairly on a wind with smooth water. Carries about half a turn of weather helm on the wind. Works in about 13 points. Stays quickly in smooth water, and wears very quickly. Makes very little leeway. Stayed on one occasion under topsails, jib and spanker in moderately smooth water, Force 4 of wind. Attained a speed of 15 knots on another occasion with the wind on the quarter Force 6 to 8 under single reefed topsails, light sails and courses in smooth water.'

commission she steamed far more often. Much of her time was spent on anti-slavery patrols in the Red Sea, stopping and searching suspicious vessels and rescuing any slaves found on board. In September and October 1888 she was to fire her guns in anger for the only time in her service. On 11 September she was ordered from Malta, where she was undergoing a mid-commission refit, to relieve HMS *Dolphin* at the Red Sea port of Suakin in the Sudan. Here she was to provide support for British and Egyptian troops, and local friendly tribes, commanded by General Graham, who were under siege from rebel Mahdist forces under Osman Digna, a former slave trader. The action was part of a protracted series of attempts by the British to help the Egyptians regain control of the Sudan. The alliance with Egypt was a legacy of British involvement in the Suez Canal, which was of great strategic importance to British trade. *Gannet* arrived at Suakin on 15 September and began shelling the lines of the

BELOW *Gannet* in No. 4 Dock at Chatham.

enemy forces. This continued intermittently into October, with the expenditure of more than 200 shells from her main armament and more than 1,200 rounds from the Nordenfeldts. She was relieved by HMS *Starling* on 15 October, the support of both sloops helping to prevent Suakin falling into rebel hands.

Gannet returned to Malta, where she paid off on 1 November 1888, ending her second commission. She recommissioned on 10 November 1888 for the first of two consecutive three-year commissions of service on the Mediterranean station, where her duties included survey work. The third commission ended in December 1891 and she was recommissioned on 26 January 1892 for her fourth and final commission. This commission again included survey duties in both the Mediterranean and the Red Sea. The ship left Malta for the last time in December 1894 and returned to Sheerness where she paid off into reserve on 16 March 1895.

Drill Ship

Some accounts say that for a short time after this *Gannet* may have been in the sail training squadron at Portland. In the autumn of 1900 she was taken from reserve at Chatham and leased to the South Eastern & Chatham Railway as an accommodation hulk for their ferry terminal at Port Victoria on the Isle of Grain; she was to serve in this role until June 1902. In 1903 she became the drill ship for the London Division of the Royal Naval Reserve in the West India Dock, and was renamed HMS *President* on 16 May to replace as drill ship an old Fourth Rate of that name. In 1909 she was renamed *President II*. This role lasted until 1911 when she was relieved by HMS *Buzzard*.

Training Ship *Mercury*

Her next role was to last fifty-five years, on loan from the Navy to a training school for boys, the *Mercury*, on the River Hamble in Hampshire. Winston Churchill, as First Lord of the Admiralty, supported the project and a lease was agreed in 1913 with Mr C. B. Fry, a famous cricketer, who by then was running the school, assisted by his wife, Beatrice, who had previously been the mistress of the *Mercury*'s owner, Charles Hoare. Although described as a woman of vast intelligence, energy and charisma, Mrs Fry was something of a harridan, a strict disciplinarian with a sharp tongue, and due to her husband's frequent absences she was effectively in charge. She dressed in male attire with bare feet when on board, so that she could lead the boys on their first exercise of the day, up the rigging and over the tops.

Conversion work was carried out at Sheerness Dockyard, adding an additional full-length covered deck above the main deck. In 1914 *Gannet* was towed to Portsmouth by the battleship HMS *Queen* and then taken by tug to the Hamble to join the Training School *Mercury* as a dormitory ship, replacing the former barque *Illovo*. Approximately 100 boys lived aboard at any one time, enduring a harsh regime that prepared them for entry into the Royal and merchant navies. In the 1920s boys were, allegedly for minor misdemeanours, tied to guns and beaten with a cane until blood was drawn, or sent to the top of the school's mast to stand all day without food or water. Beatrice clung to her post until she died, aged 83, in 1946. Fry did not retire until 1950, aged 78. Thereafter the violent punishments were removed, although discipline remained hard. The school closed in July 1968 and *Gannet* was returned to the Royal Navy, leaving the Hamble in 1970 for Southampton and then Fareham Creek.

Restoration

In 1971 ownership was transferred to The Maritime Trust and *Gannet* remained in their care until 1987 when she was chartered to Chatham Historic Dockyard. Extensive restoration was necessary to return her to her original appearance, which was undertaken at Chatham Dockyard where she is now displayed.

A slow restoration programme was initiated, and in 1994 ownership passed to the Chatham Historic Dockyard Trust. After gaining £3 million of lottery funding, work was accelerated, so that by late 2003 she was refloated in No. 4 Dock (which dates from *c*.1840). The largely original hull has been fully conserved and re-coppered, while the upper decks, cabins, masts and spars have been replaced. Some original and replica pieces of ordnance were fitted, and externally she is now in her 1880 appearance. Her internal accommodation is still being restored, but the boiler and engine rooms remain empty.

BELOW A gun on the upper deck of *Gannet*.

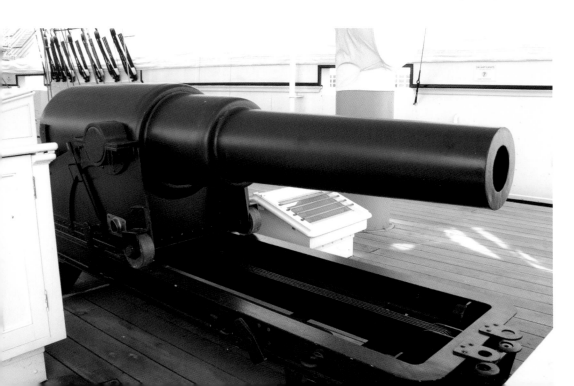

Discovery

Scott's Antarctic exploration vessel

Scott's first polar expedition and research ship; now afloat and open to the public at Dundee, where she was built

Built for Scott's first Antarctic expedition by traditional wooden whaler builders in Dundee, *Discovery* returned to that port in 1986 after a long and varied career as expedition ship, cargo ship, research ship and drill ship. It was a career that took her to icebound waters in both hemispheres, and included three phases on direct or indirect attachment to the Royal Navy. Her heavy construction helped ensure her longevity, as well as providing opportunities for new duties when each role had been exhausted.

At the end of the nineteenth century the Antarctic was largely unexplored and its extent unknown. The Sixth International Geographical Congress, meeting in London in 1895, resolved that 'the greatest piece of geographical exploration yet to be undertaken' was the exploration of the Antarctic regions. The challenge was taken up by the Royal Geographic Society, which launched fundraising activities to provide £45,000 for a National Antarctic Expedition and persuaded the British Government to contribute an equal amount. The expedition ship was to be named *Discovery* – the latest in a long line of ships bearing that name, which had been commanded by Baffin, Cook and Vancouver, among others. She was to be based in McMurdo Bay (now McMurdo Sound) in Victoria Land for exploration and survey work.

Design

The new *Discovery* was designed by W. E. (later Sir William) Smith, the Royal Navy's Chief Constructor, who had been trained in wooden shipbuilding. Born in Portsmouth in 1850 he had begun work at the age of ten in the dockyard ropery, rising to become a shipwright and then naval architect. The starting point for the design – in terms of the general lines and sail area – was the previous *Discovery* (formerly the Dundee steam whaler *Bloodhound*) which had been employed in Arctic exploration. One dominant constraint on the design was that there should be no iron or steel within a 30-foot sphere of the magnetic observatory on the upper deck. This meant that the hull had to be wooden, the auxiliary steam engine and boilers – which were to supplement the sails – had to be situated aft; the fittings on the lower deck and hold were of gunmetal or brass, and hemp cordage was required for the main shrouds. The screw and rudder needed to be easily shipped and unshipped for repairs, be drawn up into the main hull for their protection when in ice-floes, and be protected by a rounded overhanging stern. The funnel was to be hinged so that it could be lowered when the ship was under sail. The hull was to be 10 feet longer than the old *Discovery*, thus allowing the commanding officer's cabin to be moved from its previous position in the counter abaft the engine room. It also enabled larger engines to be fitted. Two water ballast tanks were incorporated to increase stability when the ship was returning lightly laden from the Antarctic in stormy seas.

ABOVE *Discovery* is frozen in for the winter near Observation Hill, 1902.

The hull construction was massive in order to resist crushing by ice when the ship was frozen in during the Antarctic winter and to support the ice-breaking function of the bows. The frames were of 11-inch-thick English oak, with a four-inch inner lining of Riga fir and an outer skin comprising two layers of English elm or greenheart planking, 6 inches and 5 inches thick. There were stout transverse beams, the lower of 11-inches-square pitch pine, at intervals of less than 3 feet. The bows were described by Scott as a 'network of solid oak stiffeners [which] gave this portion of the vessel a strength which almost amounted to solidity.' The bows and stern were protected by steel plates for some 4 feet on both sides, for additional protection when ice-breaking. Glazed brass mushroom vents or 'ankle bashers' took the place of the more usual portholes in the ship's sides, to avoid weakening the hull. They let in light and air to the deck below from where they could be opened and closed. Throughout the ship there were letterbox-shaped slots cut into the sides, which gave access to the space between the inner and outer hulls and frames. These spaces were filled with rock salt, which would mix with any water that entered these areas, to help preserve the timbers.

The expedition's physicist, Louis Bernacchi, in his *Saga of the Discovery* (1938), commented on the strength of the hull: 'The knowledge of its stoutness was a comforting thought when the grinding, crushing ice-floes hammered us in months to come with a force that seemed to have behind it the inhuman determination of a whole ocean bent on our destruction.'

Build

The order was placed on 16 December 1899 with Dundee Shipbuilders Company, which was very experienced in this type of construction through its history of building whalers. Local firms were able to complement the shipbuilding company, making *Discovery* a truly Dundee-built ship: the engines and boilers were by Messrs Gourlay, and the sailcloth by Baxter Brothers. The keel was laid on 16 March 1900 and a year later, on 21 March 1901, the launching by Minna, Lady Markham (wife of Sir Clements Markham, president of the Royal Geographical

Society) took place. Thousands gathered on the dockside and ships in the harbour were decorated with bunting. Lady Minna cut the cord with a pair of golden scissors and a bottle of wine garlanded with flowers was broken on the bows as she named the ship *Discovery*. The ship reportedly cost £34,050 plus £10,322 for the engine.

Scott's Antarctic Expedition

Robert Falconer Scott was appointed to command *Discovery* in May 1900. Then torpedo lieutenant on HMS *Majestic* in the Channel Squadron, Scott had Arctic experience and was promoted to the rank of captain in his new command. Her crew, predominantly Royal Navy, was to comprise seven officers (five RN and two RNR), four warrant officers RN, six petty officers RN, two Royal Marines, five scientists, three other civilians, sixteen seamen (twelve RN and four merchant navy) and six stokers (five RN and one merchant navy). The two RNR officers were both commissioned from the merchant navy for the expedition, one of them being Ernest Shackleton.

After fitting out in the Victoria Dock, *Discovery* underwent sea trials in May 1901. On 3 June 1901 she berthed in the East India Dock at London for two months of preparation and loading. With cheering crowds everywhere, *Discovery* sailed on 31 July and steamed down the Thames, being greeted by every ship with flags, hooters and sirens. At Spithead she was swung for the adjustment of compasses, before anchoring at Cowes where the annual yachting week was in full spate. Here King Edward VII and Queen Alexandra came on board and the King requested that the White Ensign be flown 'if consent can be got from the Admiralty'. On 6 August she left Cowes for Cape Town, calling at Funchal and South Trinidad Island (off Brazil) thus following the trade winds. She entered Table Bay on 3 October for bunkering and was refitted at the Royal Navy's yard at Simon's Town. *Discovery* sailed from the Cape for Lyttleton, New Zealand, in late October and weathered gales and tremendous seas in the high southern latitudes, which were to prove the ship's seakeeping abilities.

The ship was stopped in heavy pack ice in mid-November and bird specimens were captured, and on 22 November during another stop at Macquarie Island the crew caught penguins – penguin was served for dinner that night followed by penguin eggs for breakfast. *Discovery* arrived at Lyttleton on 29 November. Here the rigging was overhauled and refitted, and stores had to be restowed and partly replaced due to a persistent leak (that came to be known as the 'Dundee leak'.) The ship was re-coaled, and a magnetic survey base was established at Christchurch, for simultaneous observations with those on the Antarctic expedition. Deeply laden, she sailed on 21 December to a big send-off, with an escort of 'five gaily-dressed steamers crowded with passengers, with bands playing and whistles hooting'.

LEFT Officers on Scott's expedition; Captain Scott is fifth from the right.

Tragically though, in the excitement, a young seaman named Charles Bonner, who had climbed above the crow's nest to the top of the main mast, fell to his death on the corner of an iron deckhouse.

Coal was taken on at Port Chalmers, and the ship left on Christmas Eve, the crew taking what would be their last view of civilisation for more than two years. On 2 January 1902 the first iceberg was sighted as *Discovery* neared the Antarctic Circle, crossing it the following day. For five days she navigated floes of pack ice. On 8 January land was sighted and the ship anchored in Robertson Bay. She proceeded to explore Ross's 'Great Ice Barrier' (now the Ross Ice Shelf), edging the Ross Sea to King Edward VII Land, and looking for a site for secure winter quarters. These were established in February at the head of McMurdo Sound, later known as Winter Harbour, and the vessel was soon frozen in. *Discovery* was used as the expedition living quarters for the forty-eight men; from April to August there was no daylight but limited scientific work was undertaken, collecting specimens and taking meteorological readings and soundings. From September 1902, in the Antarctic summer, sledging journeys were undertaken over sea ice and inland. Scott led Shackleton and Edward Wilson over the Great Ice Barrier towards the South Pole to latitude 82°16', then the farthest point south reched by any explorer. They were unable to go any further because their remaining dogs were exhausted (and were shot to lighten the sledges of the animal's food). The round journey covered 960 miles in ninety-three days.

A relief vessel, *Morning* (a former Norwegian whaler), arrived in late January 1903 bringing supplies, and Shackleton was to leave with her on 2 March. A second winter was spent in the Antarctic, and in the summer of 1903–04 there were further sledging journeys. In January 1904 *Morning* returned together with *Terra Nova*, a former Scottish steam whaler. At this point *Discovery* was twenty miles inside the ice and attempts to saw through the ice proved futile. *Morning* brought instructions to abandon *Discovery* as there were no funds for a further year in the Antarctic. Although the Admiralty had refused to provide any additional funding for research it did fund the second relief voyage. However, the ice began to recede and by 16 February the ship was released with the help of explosives to clear local ice. But the ship became gale-bound, thudding against the ice-foot broadside on, until the weather eased. *Discovery* arrived at the Aucklands, islands south of New Zealand, on 15 March to rendezvous with her two consorts, and reached Lyttelton on Good Friday, 1 April. *Discovery* and *Morning* then sailed, via the Straits of Magellan, to the Falkland Islands to complete the magnetic survey.

Discovery finally arrived at Spithead on 10 September 1904, just over three years after leaving the Solent, and then made for the East India Dock in London – where she arrived on 15 September. The expedition had yielded the richest results, both scientific and geographic, ever brought from the largely unknown region of the Antarctic, having explored the interior of the continent and many hundreds of miles of coast for the first time.

Service with the Hudson's Bay Company

Discovery was now redundant and in January 1905 was sold for £10,000 to the Hudson's Bay Company for service as a cargo ship between London and Hudson Bay, a route first established by Henry Hudson in 1610–11 in an earlier *Discovery*. The route was navigated by wooden sailing ships for two and a half centuries, serving the Hudson's Bay Company trading posts in the southern part of the bay. It entailed negotiating Davis Strait (between Greenland and Canada), Hudson Strait and Hudson Bay, for which the vessel's strength and ice-breaking capability were essential. She was refitted in Glengale Ironworks' dry dock, at which time the scientific and other surplus equipment was removed. The hold size was increased, partly by taking out cross timber stiffening and bulkheads. Space for four passengers was incorporated. *Discovery* operated on this route from 1905 to 1911 and again in 1918, on the yearly run that delivered supplies and returned with a cargo mainly of furs.

The 1906 voyage may be taken as typical: after loading at the West India Dock the ship left on 14 June and anchored in the Powder Ground off Gravesend to take on gunpowder. She then headed north to arrive on 18 June at Peterhead, to load stores including fowl. She continued northwards into the Atlantic and arrived at Charlton Island in Hudson's Bay on 9 August. Her return voyage began on 24 August and she crossed the Atlantic to enter the English Channel, finally docking at the West India Dock on 5 October. Conditions varied from year to year: in 1908 the passage through Hudson Strait alone took twenty-eight days because of heavy ice.

First World War

In 1912 *Discovery* was replaced by a new steamer, *Nascopie*, and was sold in October 1913 for £9,500. Her buyers intended to use her for the planned British Antarctic Expedition in 1914, but the outbreak of war led to its cancellation; the leader of the expedition later died in the sinking of *Lusitania* in 1915. The sale was never completed and *Discovery* remained in the South West India Dock until joining the Bay Steamship Company, which had been set up by the Hudson's Bay Company to transport supplies purchased by them on behalf of the French government. Additional agreements were entered into with the Romanian, Russian and Belgian governments. The new company was an extensive enterprise with some 300 merchant ships, 110 of which were lost, mainly to enemy submarine action.

Discovery had deteriorated during her period of lay up and after only cursory repairs was given orders in April 1915 for New York. She had to put into Falmouth for repairs with a bad leak in the rudder truck – her crew having refused to continue. Further repairs were necessary in June at New York before sailing for La Pallice, but she still leaked badly on the voyage. At Falmouth on 30 July her captain resigned, apparently because of the state of the ship. She sailed with a new captain, again for New York, without full repairs. Further cargoes were taken to Archangel and other European ports after more repairs at Swansea.

In July 1916 the Hudson's Bay Company lent the ship to the Admiralty free of charge to be sent south to relieve the party of Shackleton's Antarctic expedition that was stranded on Elephant Island following the crushing and sinking of *Endurance*. *Discovery* was commanded by a Scottish whaler captain who was commissioned as a lieutenant commander, RNR, for the

Technical Details

Displacement: 1,570 tons
Gross tonnage: 736 tons
Length: 179ft 2½in (54.65m)
Beam: 33ft 10in (10.31m)
Draught: 15ft 9in (4.8m)
Propulsion: Coal-fired triple expansion steam engine, single screw, 450 ihp; plus sail
Speed: 8 knots
Complement: (for first Antarctic expedition) 7 officers, 38 men, plus 7 scientists and assistants.

voyage. Under tow of the collier *Polesley* she left Plymouth Sound on 10 August, but only sailed as far as Montevideo before news that the men had been rescued caused the mission to be abandoned. The trip was not entirely wasted, however, as *Discovery* loaded grain in Buenos Aires before finally arriving at Plymouth on 28 November. The Admiralty handed her back to the Bay Steamship Company on 18 December 1916 and she resumed her cargo runs, which until April 1918 were mainly coasting between French Atlantic ports, usually in convoys because of the threat of German U-boats.

Final Voyage to Hudson's Bay

In 1918–19 *Discovery* undertook her last voyage to Hudson Bay, under the flag of Sale and Company. She left Cardiff on 6 June 1918 for Charlton Island, but did not arrive until 10 September, having twice become trapped in ice in Hudson Strait under a captain who was inexperienced on this run. She then took cargo to St Johns, Newfoundland, and left Halifax on Christmas Eve for Liverpool. Encountering heavy weather, her decks were strained and she developed leaks, putting in to Queenstown for bunkers and repairs, and finally arriving at Liverpool on 16 January. Other coasting runs followed, before taking supplies to the White Russians in southern Russia at Novorossiysk in 1919 during the civil war. In June 1920 lack of cargoes led to her being laid up again in the South West India Dock. In 1922 she was a temporary headquarters for the 16th Stepney Sea Scouts.

Falklands Service

Discovery was once again reprieved from the ignominy of being laid up when, on 18 October 1922, the Crown Agents purchased her for £5,000, for a project instigated by the Falklands Islands government. The Discovery (Oceanographic) Expedition was to study the whale population of the Southern Ocean as part of a plan to produce a sustainable industry – the whale population had been largely exhausted in the northern hemisphere and the activity had moved to the southern hemisphere. *Discovery* sailed for Portsmouth to be refitted and converted into a research vessel by Vosper. In fact the work was extensive, virtually amounting to a reconstruction. She was re-planked inside and out, the majority of the keel was replaced, new decks were laid and new deckhouses fitted. A wardroom was reinstated, chemical and biological laboratories were built, and a large trawl winch and three powered reels were fitted for towing nets to collect specimens. The engines were rebuilt and she had new masts, yards and rigging; the fore and main masts were moved forward one position in an attempt to improve her sailing qualities. The cost of the work, including purchase price but excluding scientific equipment, was £114,000. Her port of registry changed from London to Port Stanley, and she was designated as a Royal Research Ship, flying the Blue Ensign emblazoned with the coat of arms of the Falklands Islands.

The reconstruction by Vosper took far longer than anticipated and towards the end was very rushed. On 25 July 1925 the ship left Portsmouth for the Bay of Biscay to test experimental echo-sounding gear developed by Admiralty scientists who were on board. In the Channel she met violent storms and aspects of Vosper's work were found wanting. Aborting the voyage, *Discovery* had to put in to Dartmouth for two months of extensive repairs. On 24 September she left Dartmouth and, after conducting the delayed trials, put the scientists ashore in Falmouth. The ship left there on 5 October and sailed into Table Bay on 20 December. The expedition's first southern voyage commenced when *Discovery* sailed on 17 January 1926, and took in Tristan da Cunha, South Georgia and the Falklands Islands, arriving back in Table Bay on 29 June. A three-month refit at Simonstown Royal Dockyard ensued, when bilge keels were fitted and the upper topgallant yards were struck, to lessen the ship's rolling and wind resistance.

The second southern voyage, to Antarctic waters, began when *Discovery* left Simonstown on 27 October 1926. The route included Bouvet Island, South Georgia, Elephant Island, the South Orkney and South Shetland Islands, the Antarctic Peninsula, Cape Horn and the Falkland Islands. Despite the latest modifications, the expedition leader, Dr Stanley Kemp, was rather critical of the ship, and wrote to his committee saying that,

'Square-rigged vessels of the Antarctic type are quite unsuitable for the work we are engaged on and the "Discovery", as I have proved, is worse than any other vessel of her class. Her sailing qualities are inferior, her speed less, her coal consumption greater and her bunker capacity little more than half.'

Difficult winds and the shortage of coal forced the oceanographic work to be cut to the minimum. From Bouvet Island towards South Georgia – the stretch of ocean of greatest interest – the average speed was only 3¼ knots and the scientists were able to do virtually nothing. Useful work was, however, done on later parts of the voyage, but Kemp had recommended that *Discovery* be replaced, and she was to return home on completion of the southern summer. In June 1927 *Discovery* arrived at Capetown from the Falklands and spent three weeks in dock before proceeding up the west coast of Africa into the Gulf of Guinea to investigate the whales' breeding grounds and to pick up relevant information from different coastal whaling stations. She arrived at Falmouth on 29 September, having covered 37,000 miles since leaving the United Kingdom.

Back to the Antarctic

Despite Kemp's reservations about her suitability, *Discovery* was soon in service again for the British, Australian and New Zealand Antarctic Research Expedition led by the Australian explorer Sir Douglas Mawson, and in many respects these were successful voyages. The ship was lent by the British government to the expedition and two southern summer voyages to the Antarctic were made in 1929–30 and 1930–31 to carry out surveying and scientific work. She left London's East India Dock on 1 August 1929, flying the Australian flag at her stern and carrying a Gypsy Moth aircraft (which was to be used for reconnaissance) secured on deck. The ship put in to Cape Town in October for refitting and her main yards were sent down and landed, while the fore topgallant yards were lashed on deck to make the vessel easier to handle with the small crew (especially with the constant tacking in ice packs) and to reduce wind resistance when under sail. She was at the Iles Crozet, a small group of volcanic sub-Antarctic islands, by 2 November. From 31 December *Discovery* was off the Antarctic continent and in the next four weeks discovered MacRobertson Land from the Gipsy Moth and visited Kemp and Enderby Lands, proving them to be connected. The coastline from 45°E to 75°E was roughly charted, and on 13 January a landing was made on Proclamation Island, where the sovereignty of the sector between 73°E and 47°E was asserted. The vessel met the Norwegian *Norvegia* near Cape Ann on 14 January 1930, when the leaders of the two expeditions agreed on longitude 45°E as the boundary between British and Norwegian activities. The season ended at Port Adelaide on 1 April 1930.

The expedition's second season began when *Discovery* left Hobart on 22 November for the south, and anchored off Cape Denison, King George V Land, on 4 January 1931, where sovereignty was proclaimed. Later in January 'Banzare Land' and Cape Goodenough were discovered and 'Sabrina Land' was named, in flights by the Gipsy Moth. Bowman Island was discovered on 28 January. In February Princess Elizabeth Land was discovered and proclamations of sovereignty were made on Murray Monolith and Cape Bruce. At the end of the season *Discovery* returned to Hobart, arriving there on 19 March 1931. The voyages had charted unknown regions of the Antarctic and discovered several islands, and the British Antarctic Survey still use the data gathered on the oceanographic survey. The political and imperial objectives of the expedition had resulted in sovereignty being claimed over a number of areas. After visits to Melbourne and Wellington, where the expedition's successes were fêted, the ship came home via Cape Horn to arrive in the East India Dock, London on 1 August – two years to the day after she had left.

On the Thames for Fifty Years

Discovery was now obsolete and had been replaced by a new steel-hulled *Discovery II*. She remained laid up in the London docks until 1936. There was a desire to keep her from the scrapyard and fundraising was initiated on behalf of the National Maritime Museum at Greenwich. In the event she was offered in October 1936 to the Boy Scouts Association as a training ship for the Sea Scouts and as a memorial to Captain Scott and his comrades. A handing-over ceremony was held a year later, on 9 October 1937, by which time the ship was at moorings in King's Reach alongside the Embankment, the berth that she was to occupy for the next forty years.

After the outbreak of war in 1939 the ship became the headquarters of the River Emergency Service, a river ambulance service, and Sea Scouts aged sixteen and over were used as signalmen. In 1941 this service was taken over by the Royal Navy, and *Discovery* became a Parachute Mine Station. Sea Scouts kept a twenty-four-hour watch for falling parachute mines and telephoned a compass bearing through to a naval unit in the docks. Pre-naval entry courses in seamanship were also held on board and attended by some 2,500 Sea Scouts. During the war *Discovery*'s yards, engine and boilers were all removed, the latter two being broken up for scrap metal. An additional mess room and a gymnasium filled the vacated area.

BELOW *Discovery* at her Embankment berth on the Thames, 1958.

After the war the ship reverted to her Sea Scout training role, but by 1954 the cost of maintaining her had become prohibitive to the Boy Scouts Association. She was given to the Admiralty for use as an additional RNVR drill ship for the London Division and – after repairs and alterations at Blackwall – was commissioned as HMS *Discovery* on 20 July 1955, flying the flag of Admiral Commanding Reserves. Once again she lay alongside the Embankment, with the other drill ships, *President* and *Chrysanthemum*. In addition to her RNVR (later RNR) duties *Discovery* still accommodated some Sea Scout training, served as a naval recruiting centre for a number of years, and was used for training those about to begin their National Service, until its abolition in 1960.

She continued to fly the flag of Admiral Commanding Reserves until late 1976, just before that post was abolished. The Admiralty was by then considering her future because the Reserves were being reduced and she was in need of an extensive refit. On 2 April 1979 *Discovery* was handed over to the Maritime Trust, reverting to the designation Royal Research Ship, and with the support of the National Maritime Museum became a subject for preservation and display. A docking at Sheerness allowed essential repairs before the ship went on display in St Katharine Docks, London, as part of the Maritime Trust's collection of historic vessels. New yards and a new mizzen spanker boom were fitted, greatly improving her looks. This and other restoration work helped return *Discovery* to her 1925 appearance.

Preservation at Dundee

The combined collection of ships at London was not a very viable attraction and it was decided that many of the vessels could be offered to ports that could provide appropriate homes for them. Thus, after seven years in St Katharine Docks, *Discovery* was moved on the floating dock ship *Happy Mariner* to Dundee, her original birthplace. The project was underwritten by the Dundee Heritage Trust and the Scottish Development Agency. In the words of the Maritime Trust's deputy director,

> *'The ship was to return to a prestigious, cold salt water, custom-built dock; a free berth, funds to complete her restoration and an enthusiastic professional team to finish the work started by the Trust in 1979; a £2.6 million project to place a unique part of our maritime heritage in Scotland.... in a revitalised tourist area of a famous and historic port.'*

Discovery left London on 31 March 1986 and entered the Victoria Dock at Dundee on the midnight tide of 3/4 April. A lone RNR piper on board the wooden frigate *Unicorn* heralded her arrival. Since her arrival further preservation work has been progressed, including the replacement of some of the inner and outer planking, the lower masts, and the stem and stern posts. Initially remaining in the ownership of the Maritime Trust, she was sold to the Dundee Heritage Trust for £1 in 1995, and is open to the public daily at Discovery Point in Dundee. Visitors can tour the bridge, engine room (with reproduction machinery), wardroom, mess, laboratory, officers' cabins and storerooms. There is also a good interpretation centre on the quayside which has exhibits relating both to the ship and polar exploration.

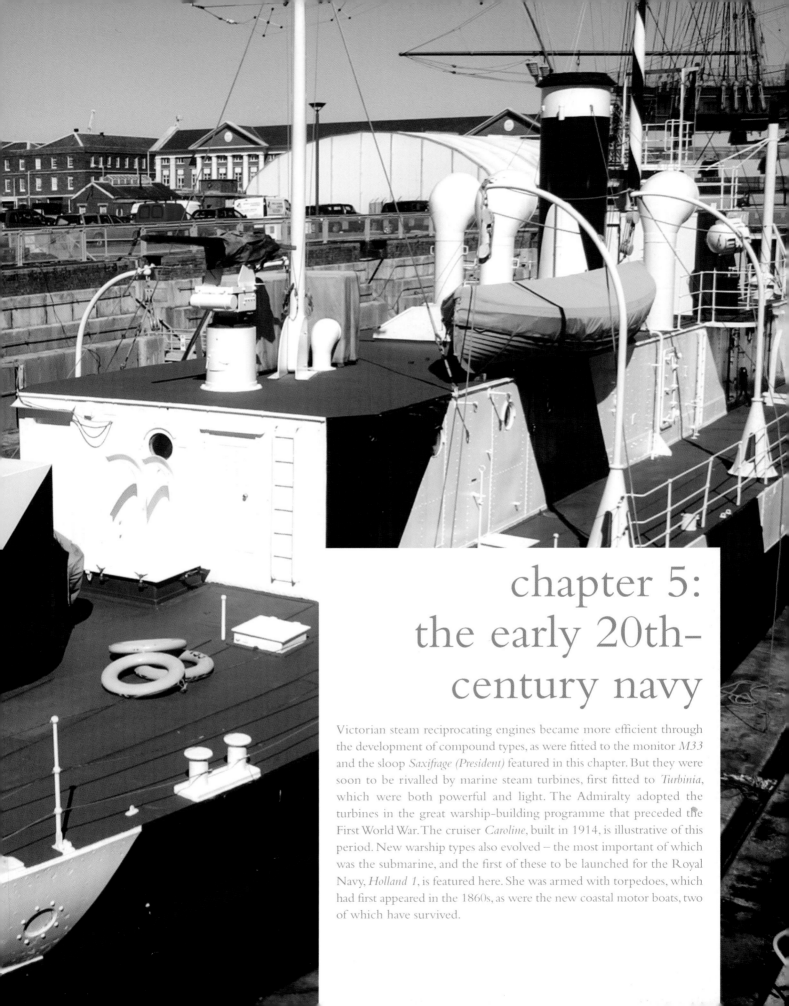

chapter 5:
the early 20th-
century navy

Victorian steam reciprocating engines became more efficient through the development of compound types, as were fitted to the monitor *M33* and the sloop *Saxifrage (President)* featured in this chapter. But they were soon to be rivalled by marine steam turbines, first fitted to *Turbinia*, which were both powerful and light. The Admiralty adopted the turbines in the great warship-building programme that preceded the First World War. The cruiser *Caroline*, built in 1914, is illustrative of this period. New warship types also evolved – the most important of which was the submarine, and the first of these to be launched for the Royal Navy, *Holland 1*, is featured here. She was armed with torpedoes, which had first appeared in the 1860s, as were the new coastal motor boats, two of which have survived.

Caroline

Battle of Jutland cruiser

The only ship now surviving from the Battle of Jutland; this cruiser is still in commission and afloat as a static drillship at Belfast – she can be seen externally but is not normally open to the public

HMS *Caroline* is remarkable in being the only surviving ship from those that fought at the Battle of Jutland in 1916. She is still in commission at Belfast, as a static drill ship for the Royal Naval Reserve, making her the oldest HM ship afloat. While this role is expected to last for at least several more years, she is a long-term candidate for restoration to her original appearance and display as a museum ship.

Design

Built by Cammell Laird at Birkenhead, *Caroline* was the name ship of a class of six light cruisers ordered in 1913. The *Caroline* class was a slightly larger development of the *Arethusa* class, and was designed for North Sea operations against the German navy. These light cruisers could operate as scouts for the Grand Fleet and had the ability to fight destroyers, act as leaders of destroyer flotillas and protect trade routes. In peacetime they were suitable for colonial policing work. By modern standards they were quite small – equivalent to a small frigate – and in heavy seas their decks were awash with water (known as wet ships in a seaway). Resembling the *Arethusa* class, the *Carolines* had three funnels and a tall pole foremast, with a forecastle deck extending as far as the first funnel. The stem was curved and protruded underwater to form a ram.

Their principal armament comprised two 6-inch guns mounted aft of the funnels, and eight 4-inch guns mounted in pairs on the fo'c'sle alongside the bridge structure and amidships (forward and aft of the twin torpedo tubes) in the waist. The 6-inch guns were intended for use when running from a more powerful ship, while the 4-inch were better for chasing destroyers. (However, in the light of wartime experience, the 4-inch guns were to be replaced by two additional 6-inch.) The hull was armoured with 3-inch-high tensile steel plate amidships, tapering to 2 inches at the stern and 1½ inches at the bow, while the upper deck had 1-inch-thick plate amidships and at the rudder head.

The *Caroline* class also included *Carysfort*, *Cleopatra*, *Comus*, *Conquest* and *Cordelia*. *Caroline* was the sixth ship of

Technical Details (original configuration)

Displacement:	4,220 tons (4,733 tons full load)
Length:	446ft (135.94m)
Beam:	41ft 6in (12.65m)
Draught:	16ft (4.88m)
Propulsion:	Four Parsons geared steam turbines, 40,000 shp; eight oil-fired boilers; four shafts
Speed:	29 knots
Armament:	2 (later 4) x 6-in guns; 8 (later 4) x 4-in guns; 1 x 13-pdr anti-aircraft gun (later 2 x 3-in anti-aircraft guns); 4 x 21-in torpedo tubes. *N.B. All armament now removed.*
Armour:	3-inch side amidships, bows 2½–1½ inch, stern 2½–2 inch, upper deck amidships and rudder head 1-inch
Complement:	289

the name in the Royal Navy (including the *Royal Carolines*). The first *Caroline* was a Royal Yacht named in 1716 after Princess Caroline, wife of King George I's son Prince George (later King George II).

Build and Early Service

Caroline was built very rapidly in just over ten months. Having been laid down on 28 January 1914, she was launched on 21 September and commissioned on 4 December 1914. The following day she steamed to the Clyde to carry out speed trials on the measured mile. Then, on 17 December, she sailed to join the Grand Fleet at Scapa Flow. Over that Christmas she undertook a sweep (or patrol) of enemy waters in the Skaggerak, stopping and searching foreign merchant ships for contraband cargo, the first of many such sorties. Just before midnight on Boxing Day a marine, Private James Morris, was washed overboard and lost in heavy seas while he was taking some meat from the beef screen on deck; his ghost is said to haunt the ship to this day. His drowning was to be the only casualty of *Caroline*'s wartime service, and thus she came to be regarded by her crew as a lucky ship.

Initially she was leader of the 4th Destroyer Flotilla of the Grand Fleet, and then joined the 1st Light Cruiser Squadron in February 1915 at Rosyth, also operating from Scapa Flow for part of the time. From April 1916 until the end of the war she was part of the 4th Light Cruiser Squadron, with which she fought at Jutland. During this period up to May 1916 *Caroline* did not make contact with enemy forces, although she was involved in an unsuccessful chase in April 1916 following the enemy's raid on Lowestoft. Most of her time was spent on contraband sweeps and in tactical or strategic exercises in company with destroyers, other light cruisers, or the Grand Fleet as a whole. These activities were carried out in all weathers and usually lasted between thirty-six and seventy-two hours.

The Battle of Jutland

On 31 May 1916 the Grand Fleet and the Battlecruiser Fleet steamed south towards the Skaggerak, to the north of the Jutland peninsula. *Caroline* had left Scapa Flow the previous night, weighing anchor at 9.45 pm and by 0.30 am she was steaming south-eastwards at 18 knots. With her among the 148 British warships that left their Scottish bases that night, were the other members of the 4th Light Cruiser Squadron: *Calliope*, *Comus*, *Constance* and *Royalist*. At 5.13 am *Caroline* took up her station ahead of the fleet, steaming at 15½ knots towards the

PREVIOUS PAGES The monitor *M33* in No. 1 Dock at Portsmouth.

BELOW A broadside view of *Caroline* in 1917.

ABOVE A stern view of *Caroline* at Belfast.

Skaggerak. The Germans were sighted at 2.40 pm, to the west of the northern tip of the peninsula, and at 3.05 pm *Caroline* was cleared for action and increased speed to 19 knots. By 3.30 pm Admiral Beatty and his battlecruisers were in touch with the enemy, who opened fire shortly afterwards.

Caroline and the 4th Light Cruiser Squadron first became actively involved about 5.40 pm when smoke was sighted on the starboard bow. The 2nd and 1st Light Cruiser Squadrons, followed by battlecruisers, came across the bows of the 4th Light Cruiser Squadron, which turned and proceeded after them, in consequence being on the disengaged side of the battlecruisers. At 6.07 pm *Caroline*'s log reported shells falling all around her (these being 'overs' aimed at the battlecruisers), and two destroyers astern of her were hit. Her crew witnessed the battlecruiser HMS *Invincible* blowing up at 6.31 pm, the third British battlecruiser to be lost in this way in the battle. Jellicoe's battleships had joined the fray and in one report *Caroline* was said to have narrowly escaped being rammed by the flagship, *Iron Duke*. The battlefleet opened heavy fire, *Iron Duke*'s squadron firing right over *Caroline*'s squadron. Then *Caroline* moved outwards towards the enemy to stop them launching a torpedo attack, and opened fire on a German destroyer, dodging two or three torpedoes.

At 9.05 *Caroline*'s squadron was stationed two miles ahead of *King George V*, leading the vanguard of the battlefleet, when a line of ships was sighted in the mist. This was in fact the van of the German High Seas Fleet, which became clear when heavy cranes could be seen mounted amidships, a feature not shared by the British ships. The Germans challenged the British ships by flashlight. *Caroline* fired two torpedoes at a *Deutchland*-class battleship, one of a group of three that subsequently fired heavy shells in return, and these fell close to *Caroline* as she turned away at full speed, making smoke to cover herself. Eleven-inch shell fell near her for about eight minutes, one shell passing between the wireless and upper deck, and spray from the splashes fell on the upper deck several times. The cruiser *Royalist*, which was in company with *Caroline*, also fired torpedoes at the German battleships at a range estimated to be just less than three miles. The torpedoes failed to find their targets and the German ships disappeared into the growing darkness. Vice Admiral Sir Martyn Jerram in *King George V* (flagship of the 2nd Battle Squadron) thought that they were Beatty's ships and had at first refused *Caroline*'s request to launch a torpedo attack. As Geoffrey Bennett quotes in *Naval Battles of the First World War*, when Captain Crooke of the *Caroline* repeated that they were the enemy Jerram replied, 'If you are quite sure, attack'. Nevertheless, Jerram remained convinced that they were British ships and did not open fire: this was one of a number of missed opportunities that denied the British any sort of clear victory at Jutland.

At 9.30 pm *Caroline* took up station ahead of *Iron Duke* and was steaming at 18 knots with the battle fleet firing astern. Firing was heard by *Caroline*'s crew until about midnight. At daylight there were no signs of the enemy, which had returned to base, and at 4.30 pm *Caroline* herself stood down from action stations and headed back to her base. Despite having come under heavy fire in the battle, *Caroline* had escaped without even a scratch to her paintwork. She was awarded the battle honour Jutland 1916.

Jutland was the last naval action fought between great fleets in contact with one another. In many ways it was an anti-climax to the great arms race that had centred on the construction of the rival fleets of dreadnoughts by Britain and Germany. A decisive action similar to that of Trafalgar had been envisaged, but the battle was inconclusive. The British lost three battlecruisers, three cruisers, and eight destroyers, totalling 111,000 tons, against German losses of one battleship (an old pre-dreadnought), one battlecruiser, four light cruisers and five destroyers, totalling 62,000 tons. In manpower terms the losses were similarly weighted – the British suffering more than 6,000 killed against slightly more than 2,500 Germans. Jutland has been seen as a tactical victory for the Germans, but a strategic victory for the British – because the German High Seas Fleet was not to venture forth again until its surrender two years later.

Other War Service

Caroline had no further encounters with the enemy before the war ended in November 1918, although there were a number of alarms and excursions in consequence of reported enemy activity. Her routine consisted of exercises with the fleet, the stopping and searching of merchant ships as part of the blockade of Germany, the convoying of merchant ships between Scandinavia, the Baltic and the United Kingdom, gunnery practice and practice torpedo runs in Scapa Flow. In February 1917 *Caroline* entered Fairfield's yard at Govan on the Clyde, for a refit and modifications. A tripod mast replaced the pole mast, and her four forward 4-inch guns were removed and replaced by a 6-inch gun on the forecastle and two 3-inch high-angle guns (one on either side of the upper deck beneath the wings of the bridge). The four 4-inch guns amidships were replaced by a single 6-inch gun (which was removed after the war since it had been found to cause buckling of the deck).

On 27 March, after her return to Scapa Flow, Captain H. R. Crooke, who had been in command since *Caroline* was first commissioned, was replaced by Captain O. E. Leggatt, a pre-war Hampshire county cricketer. On 9 July at 11.36 pm *Caroline* was lying at Scapa Flow when the battleship *Vanguard* blew up as a result of an internal explosion. Witnesses aboard *Caroline* saw the *Vanguard* engulfed by a sheet of flames as the ship seemed to lift out of the water. Flaming wreckage and bursting ammunition lit up the sky for miles around. *Caroline*, being only about a quarter of a mile distant from her, launched her boats to search the floating debris for survivors, but they found none. Many other craft joined the search but only three of the *Vanguard*'s crew survived – one officer and two men, the officer dying soon afterwards.

Another modification to *Caroline* was the fitting of a launching platform above the forecastle deck 6-inch gun, for a Sopwith Camel aircraft. This could take off with its engine at full power when the ship was heading at full speed into the wind. But there were no landing facilities on board so the plane had to land ashore and be brought back to the ship by drifter. The experiment does not seem to have been very successful, and was never used operationally. On 22 October 1918 the ship went into dry dock at Hawthorn Leslie's yard on the Tyne for a refit. She was still there when news of the Armistice came just after 9 am on 11 November. Everywhere flags were hoisted and sirens were sounded, and work stopped for the day in the shipyards. By January the ship was at Rosyth, and

BELOW The drill hall on *Caroline*.

sailed from there on the 23rd for Pembroke Dock where she came alongside on the 29th to pay off. On 5 February 1919 she was reduced to care and maintenance.

Service in the East Indies

With the end of the war many ships were laid in reserve. However, *Caroline* re-commissioned on 26 June 1919 for service on the East Indies Station. Her drab grey wartime paintwork was replaced by the attractive colour scheme then in use on that station – white for the hull and upperworks, and primrose yellow for the funnels, masts and yards. She sailed from Pembroke Dock on 29 June, arriving at Malta on 6 July after a direct passage. Following two days there for shore leave and refuelling she sailed for the Suez Canal and thence to the port of Berbera in British Somaliland, where she arrived on 18 July. Here she showed the flag and hosted celebrations for the Peace Treaty. Then she visited Aden, and continued to Bombay – arriving on 28 July. She spent some time in dockyard hands there and stayed until November when she proceeded to Colombo in Ceylon, and thence to Calcutta where she was visited by the Viceroy of India and spent the Christmas of 1919. In 1919 the East Indies Squadron, based at Colombo, also included the cruisers *Highflyer* (flagship), *Colombo* and *Comus*, and four sloops. *Caroline* continued her service on the station, visiting ports around the Indian Ocean and the Bay of Bengal and exercising with other ships of the squadron until December 1921. In October 1921 the entire crews of *Caroline* and her sister ship *Comus* exchanged ships, with the intention that the crew of *Comus* (who had presumably been on station longer than *Caroline*'s crew) would steam *Caroline* home to Portsmouth. On 21 December *Caroline* duly left Colombo, streaming her paying-off pennant. On arrival at Portsmouth she berthed at the South Railway Jetty and on 24 January 1922 was moved to the Tidal Basin before being officially paid off on 17 February and entering reserve.

Conversion to Drill Ship

After just over nine years of active service the prospect was that she would spend several years in reserve before being sent to the ship breakers. However, in 1924 the new Ulster Division of the RNVR was formed at Belfast and *Caroline* was selected to become its drill ship. She was towed from Portsmouth to Belfast and entered Harland and Wolff's yard for alterations, which included removing her boilers to create workshops for instruction in engine-room procedures and maintenance; the turbines are still in place to this day. Other compartments below decks were converted for instruction in the use and maintenance of torpedoes, wireless telegraphy, signalling and seamanship. A large deckhouse was built over the upper deck abaft the funnels to provide sufficient space for the whole of the division to be mustered. The bridge, tripod mast and foretop were undisturbed, as were the wardroom, gunroom, officers' cabins, sick-bay and main galley. Some of her guns were apparently retained for training purposes.

On completion of the work in September 1924 the ship was moved to the Musgrave Channel and secured to buoys. Recruitment to the new division had already begun and the regular routine of training on two evenings a week was instituted. In 1928 the division contained about 350 officers and men, still some way short of the original target of 500, a figure that increased in the 1930s. In 1937 King George VI and Queen Elizabeth visited the ship and, in 1938, the year of the Munich crisis, the fleet was mobilised along with the RNR and RNVR. On 31 July 1939 the first war appointments of Ulster RNVR officers to ships occurred, and by the time war was declared on 3 September most of the officers and men had left for wartime ships and stations and the Ulster Division ceased to exist for nearly eight years.

The Second World War

During the Second World War *Caroline* remained in commission as the base ship for naval operations at Belfast. Flying the flag of the Flag Officer in Charge, Belfast, she thus re-entered the main section of the Navy List as a Royal Navy, rather than RNVR, unit. She was moved from the Musgrave Channel to the Milewater Basin on the west side of the harbour to provide base support for a group of naval trawlers, drifters and other light craft. Her main function was to supply signal and cipher facilities to those vessels. As the base at Belfast expanded to meet demands arising from the Battle of the Atlantic, so various shore facilities were added, still under the name of HMS *Caroline*. Eventually several thousand ratings were wearing *Caroline* cap ribbons, and *Caroline* herself became the operations centre for a force of destroyers and corvettes. The ship also hosted a school of gunnery instruction, training soldiers, sailors and merchant seamen to serve as gunners on merchant ships that were armed for self-defence. *Caroline* narrowly missed being hit by a land mine that fell into the Milewater Basin during intensive air raids on Belfast in April and May 1941.

Return to RNVR

In April 1946 *Caroline* was handed back to the reformed Ulster Division and was taken in hand at Harland and Wolff for a refit. This included the fitting of new funnels to replace the originals, which were badly corroded. The funnels are a distinctive feature of the ship's appearance and, even though they were long since redundant, the Captain of the Division had successfully fought an Admiralty decision to remove them without replacement. In 1947 a motor minesweeper was allocated to the division to provide seagoing experience for the division's complement. This ship was renamed *Kilmorey* and was later successively replaced by another motor minesweeper, several coastal minesweepers, and finally a fleet minesweeper, HMS *Helford*, before this provision was withdrawn following the 1993 Defence Review. In 1958 the RNVR was merged with the RNR to form a unified Royal Naval Reserve, but *Caroline*'s role was unaffected. In August 1972 an IRA bomb exploded in a shed adjacent to the Gunnery School on Milewater Wharf where *Caroline* was berthed, and the ship received superficial damage to her superstructure but no casualties were suffered. During the Northern Ireland Troubles she was used as a base for special forces and patrol craft.

More recently *Caroline* was moved into the Alexandra Graving Dock on Queens Island, Belfast, where she is afloat and surrounded by high-security fencing. She was opened to the public for the first time on 10–11 September 2005 for Heritage Open Days, but cannot normally be visited. On the rare occasions when access is possible, visitors may be able to view the drill hall, the seamen's galley and heads, the wardroom and its flat, officers' cabins, one of the boiler rooms (now empty), the engine room with its four turbines and donkey boiler, the tiller flat with the secondary steering position, the bridge and a number of RNR training rooms. In 2007 a replica 6-inch gun was manufactured by Kinnegar Engineering and displayed by the aft gangplank; it may be mounted on the forecastle deck at some future date. There is a full-time Royal Navy crew of seven, headed by a lieutenant commander as executive officer, plus two civilians; the current strength of the Ulster RNR Division is about 100. Once most of the RNR divisions had a static drill ship, but now of the fourteen RNR training units only the Northern Ireland unit retains one. *Caroline* is the oldest commissioned HM ship afloat, and the second oldest ship in commission in the Royal Navy (the oldest being *Victory*).

Caroline's Future

It is possible that some time between 2012 and 2014 *Caroline* will be replaced by shore accommodation. Tentative plans are being discussed for her future when she could be released by the Royal Navy, and involve creating a maritime and industrial heritage museum in the area of the Alexandra and Thompson Docks at Belfast. The centerpiece would be a restored *Caroline*, which could be complemented by smaller historic ships, such as *Nomadic* and *Result*, and other artefacts from Belfast's great engineering past such as steam engines and linen looms.

M33

Fought at Gallipoli and North Russia

Built to bombard coastal positions, she is a veteran of the Dardanelles campaign; now on display in a dry dock in Portsmouth Historic Dockyard

Monitors were introduced in the First World War as heavily armed, shallow-draft ships intended to bombard enemy troop positions on the Channel coast of Europe. The largest of them, *Erebus* and *Terror*, displaced 8,000 tons and were armed with 15-inch guns. The nineteen ships of the *M15* and *M29* classes were much smaller, and of these *M33* survives and can be seen in No.1 dry dock at Portsmouth, close to HMS *Victory*.

Design and Build

Ordered on 15 March 1915, *M33* was built in Belfast by Workman Clark under subcontract from Harland and Wolff and launched on 22 May 1915. On the same day *M29* and *M32* were also launched, by Harland & Wolff and Workman Clark respectively. Designed for coastal bombardment, *M33* was one of the *M29* class of five ships. She was fitted with 6-inch guns to a design then in production for the secondary armament of the *Queen Elizabeth*-class battleships. For anti-aircraft purposes a high-angle version of the Hotchkiss 6-pounder gun was mounted. Her construction in just three months was remarkably rapid in order to meet the demands of the Dardanelles campaign in the Eastern Mediterranean – to where she was despatched after being accepted into service on 24 June 1915.

Technical Details

Displacement:	520 tons standard, 580 tons full load
Length:	177ft (53.95m)
Beam:	31ft (9.45m)
Draught:	6ft (1.83m)
Machinery (former):	Twin shaft triple-expansion steam reciprocating, 400 ihp
Speed:	10 knots designed (trials 9.61 knots)
Capacity:	Oil fuel 45 tons
Range:	1440 miles at 8 knots
Armament:	Two 6-in guns, and one 6-pdr HA gun plus two 7.6mm Maxim guns
Range of 6-in guns:	14,700 yards at 17½-degree elevation
Complement:	72 (5 officers, 67 men)

Service in the Mediterranean

The ship arrived in the Dardanelles area on 24 July 1915 to support the Suvla landings. She fired her first shots in anger on 2 August, bombarding the Turkish village of Yeni Shehron on the south side of the Dardanelles. On 6/7 August *M33* was in the squadron that provided counter-battery fire between Anzac Cove and Cape Helles. During this action she only received minor damage from shell splinters and continued to provide artillery support until 14 August when she was relieved by the monitor *Humber*. The recoil of her 6-inch guns had distorted the deck and caused buckling to beams and bulkheads below decks. In consequence repairs were necessary in late August, and her decks were strengthened. She returned to join the other monitors off Cape Helles and Anzac Cove until December.

On 2 December *M33* joined the battleship *Agamemnon* whose 12-inch guns destroyed a bridge on an important

ABOVE *M33* on display in No. 1 dock at Portsmouth, showing the dazzle painting scheme adopted during the Dardanelles campaign.

Turkish supply route while *M33* and *Endymion* provided counter-battery fire. By mid-December she required more deck repairs, which took several weeks and resulted in her being absent during the evacuation of the Dardanelles by the Allies. *M33* was awarded the battle honour Dardanelles 1915–16.

Following the withdrawal from Gallipoli in January 1916 she moved north to Salonika to support the Allied flanks against the Bulgarians. In February and March she patrolled off Stavros and occasionally shelled Bulgarian forces. *M33* was bombed by three aircraft on 29 March but neither the bombs nor the darts dropped by the planes hit her.

In mid-May she was sent to take over from *M30*, which had been damaged by an enemy howitzer. Her crew had been forced to beach her and she had burnt out. *M33* joined the monitors *Earl of Peterborough* and *M32* blockading the Gulf of Smyrna. In the next few weeks the British ships shelled enemy batteries with help from Royal Naval Air Service spotter planes. In July she operated in support of a cattle- and sheep-rustling raid by Greek irregulars, and more counter-battery and blockading patrols followed.

She joined an Anglo-French force to neutralise the Greek fleet in Salamis Bay on 1 September 1916, and then returned to patrols off the Turkish coast until December. The monitor then entered the floating dock at Mudros (a British base established on the Greek island of Lemnos for the Dardanelles campaign) for a refit. Afterwards, *M33* resumed her service in the Aegean, shelling Turkish and Bulgarian positions in May 1917. In late January to mid-February 1918 she was again refitted at Mudros and then patrolled the Aegean islands until July. In August she was at Stavros with Abercrombie and *M32*, bombarding the right flank. At the end of September hostilities ceased on the Salonika front and *M33*'s crew was relieved on 8 October after a thirty-nine-month commission. After being involved in supervising the Turkish armistice the ship returned to Mudros on 20 December and paid off there on 10 January 1919. She was recommissioned on 26 February 1919 and returned home, reaching Chatham on 10 April, to refit and prepare for service in the White Sea with the British Relief Force. Two additional Maxim guns and four Lewis guns were added to *M33*'s armament.

ABOVE *Minerva* (ex-*M33*) as a minelayer, photographed in August 1936.

Service in North Russia

On 12 May 1919 *M33* left Sheerness for North Russia, where she was to join four of her sister ships in the Dvina River Flotilla to cover the withdrawal of Allied and White Russian forces after the Revolution. Arriving at Archangel on 9 June, the force sailed upriver to bombard Bolshevik positions at Seltso and Selemengo Wood. These bombardments continued into August, enabling the Allied forces to make an orderly retreat. On 16 June *M33* was attacked by three Bolshevik aircraft but her anti-aircraft gun fought them off. On 8 July she was hit by a shell in the wardroom, the only occupant of which was the ship's cat – who was thought lost until found clinging to the protruding edge of a plate on the ship's side, having suffered only a burnt tail. The hole in the ship was repaired three weeks later. *M33* was hit again on 7 August when one shell temporarily damaged her steering gear and another entered her engine room via the petty officers' mess, but luckily the shell did not explode. On 18 August she was nearly hit by a mine but it was sunk using one of the Lewis guns.

Throughout the campaign the river depth was unusually low, so in order to return to Archangel at the end of August the guns, ammunition, masts and internal doors, as well as half the fuel, had to be removed and loaded onto barges. *M33* was fitted with dummy guns made from driftwood, pipes and biscuit tins to fool the enemy. Her guns were reshipped and she undertook one further mission upriver to Spaskoe on 23 September, to cover the evacuation of the remaining 500 British troops. Two of her sister ships ran aground on the way back to Archangel and had to be scuttled. *M33* returned to Chatham, arriving there on 17 October 1919 to enter reserve.

Final Service

In 1924–25 she was converted to a minelayer at Pembroke Dockyard and her guns were removed. She was given the name *Minerva* and on 3 February 1925 was recommissioned as a

ABOVE *M33* and *Victory* at Portsmouth.

minelaying training tender to HMS *Vernon* at Portsmouth. As a minelayer she could carry fifty-two mines. In 1937 she was prepared for sale, but was retained, and at the outbreak of war in 1939 was recommissioned as an accommodation ship for naval trawlers at Portsmouth. In 1943 she was reduced to a hulk (with engines, boilers and funnel all removed), as a boom defence workshop, and in the following year was towed to the Clyde. *Minerva* was towed back to the Royal Clarence Yard victualling establishment at Gosport in 1946. Renumbered *C23*, the hulk served as a floating workshop and office for local auxiliary craft until 1984 when she was put up for sale.

Restoration

In 1987 she was purchased by the Hartlepool Ship Preservation Trust and in July of that year was loaded onto the Dutch barge *Goliath*, along with *Foudroyant*, to be taken to Hartlepool for restoration. In the event, because of a failure to secure funds, only the funnel was restored, and in 1990 she was sold to Hampshire County Council who moved her to Portsmouth's No.1 Basin. In 1995 the decision was made to transfer restoration from the Royal Naval Museum to Hampshire County Council Museums Service, which would return the upper deck and external hull to the 1915 appearance. On 23 April 1997 *M33* was placed in No.1 dry dock for extensive work to stabilise hull corrosion; this and subsequent restoration work continued for several years. Two 6-inch guns (believed to have been formerly mounted on the battleship *Canada* at the Battle of Jutland) and a modified Hotchkiss 6-pounder (which dates from 1896) were fitted. In 2007 the ship was repainted in dazzle camouflage. The interior of the ship has not yet been reconstructed and visitors cannot go aboard the monitor, but she can be seen at close quarters from the side of the dry dock.

President

Steam sloop and decoy ship

Built as a decoy ship to lure U-boats under her disguised guns; now afloat on the Thames Embankment as a conference venue; she can be seen externally but is not normally open to the general public

Design

In the twentieth century a number of sailing ship types lent their names to new types of steam-driven warship, such as the corvette, the sloop and the frigate. The last sailing sloops were also steam powered, and of these *Gannet* has survived. The sloop name was re-introduced in the First World War and 112 'Flower'-class sloops were built for minesweeping, patrol and escort work with the Royal Navy. Their construction was based on mercantile practice, allowing them to be built by merchant shipbuilders. Though generally known as the 'Flower' class, there were actually four separate classes, with considerable variations in design. Among these ships were the thirty-four units of the *Anchusa* class. After the war most of the 'Flower'-class vessels were gradually disposed of, though a few survived to see service in the Second World War. Four had by then been relegated to static drill ships for the RNVR, and one of these – *President*, formerly *Saxifrage* – is now a conference ship on the Thames.

Technical Details

Displacement:	1,378 tons (1,670 tons full load)
Length:	277ft 3in (84.51m)
Beam:	35ft (10.67m)
Draught:	14ft (4.27m)
Propulsion:	Four-cylinder vertical triple-expansion steam, two boilers, 2,500 ihp, single screw
Speed:	16.5 knots
Coal bunkers:	260 tons
Range:	3,120 nautical miles at 10 knots (2,445 nautical miles at 15 knots) *Machinery now removed*
Armament *(original, now removed)*:	3 x 4-in guns, 2 x 2-pdr guns, 8 x 7.6mm machine guns
Complement:	119

Q-ship

Saxifrage was built by Lobnitz of Renfrew as a Q-ship, designed to resemble a type of merchant ship known as a tramp. Her armament was disguised so that she could blend in to a convoy, unrecognised as a warship, and apparently surrender herself to a U-boat. As the U-boat approached, the guns and depth charges would be uncovered and used to attack the submarine. She was launched on 29 January 1918, but saw little service in her intended role since the war ended soon after her completion. In December 1919 she was laid up under care and maintenance at Queenstown in Ireland, where many of the Q-ships had been based.

RNVR Drill Ship

Another ship of the *Anchusa* class, *Marjoram*, was allocated to replace the existing London Division RNVR drill ship, *President*, ex-*Buzzard*. However, *Marjoram* was wrecked on Flintstone Head on 17 January 1921 while en route to Haulbowline Dockyard near Queenstown for fitting out. *Saxifrage* was then selected as a replacement; it may have been merely coincidence that the common name for the *Saxifrage* flower is 'London's Pride', since she was not to retain that name. She was renamed *President* on 9 April 1921 and prepared for her new role at Pembroke Dockyard, adopting an unglamorous appearance. Her single funnel was removed, windows were cut into the hull, and a large wooden deckhouse was constructed on the upper deck. Arriving on the Thames on 19 June 1922, she was moved to a berth in King's Reach on the Embankment, which she has occupied ever since. During the First World War most of the men of the RNVR had not gone to sea; due to a capricious decision by Winston Churchill (then the First Lord of the Admiralty) they had become part of the army – he believed that they would not be required for service in the fleet. As the Royal Naval Division they fought in Belgium, Gallipoli and France; at the entrance to the ship's gangway a memorial was constructed to the 179 men of the London Division who died. RNVR training resumed after the war in April 1921, and started aboard the new *President* in September 1922.

In 1926 *President* was dry docked and given a limited refit at Chatham Dockyard. She then had a break from her RNVR role, being instead used at the Royal Albert Dock as a depot ship for the Royal Marines during the General Strike. Further dockings – at Sheerness Dockyard – followed in 1929, 1933 and 1938. Between 1931 and 1938 Navy Weeks were held aboard the ship, during which she was open to the public and displays were staged to demonstrate aspects of naval operations. In 1939 she was joined by her sister ship, *Chrysanthemum*, which had been a fleet target and photographic ship in the Mediterranean, and now became an additional drill ship to help cope with the expanded number of volunteers and training activities in the run up to the Second World War.

The Second World War

During her 1938/39 refit at Sheerness *President* was fitted with two new 4-inch anti-aircraft guns on the upper deck and a high-angle/low-angle director in the bridge structure. This allowed for the training of the London Division to man the guns of four C-class cruisers –

BELOW *President* on the Victoria Embankment, London.

Cairo, *Calcutta*, *Coventry* and *Curlew* – which had been converted for anti-aircraft duties. As a result 226 officers and men of the London Division were afloat in HM ships some days before the declaration of war (the RNVR had been mobilised on 27 August 1939). All four cruisers were sunk by enemy action between 1940 and 1942, though fortunately only eight men of the London Division lost their lives in these sinkings (another two perished in an earlier accident aboard *Curlew*). During that war both *President* and *Chrysanthemum* were used to train merchant seamen and Royal Navy ratings to man guns on defensively equipped merchant ships (DEMS). For this *President* was fitted with a large Dome-Teacher, a lofty corrugated-iron structure.

Post-war Service

On 20 July 1947, *President* went to Chatham Dockyard for a major refit to restore her to drill ship duties, returning on 9 July 1948. Her appearance was transformed with a new funnel, a stump mast in place of the two pole masts, a lower deckhouse for the sake of symmetry, and a new bridge. Inside she had two 4-inch guns with fire-control equipment, well down in the ship where the engine room and boiler room had been, and two Bofors guns. The training accommodation was also greatly improved. She was painted in the colours of the Victorian navy – black hull and white upperworks, with a buff funnel.

In 1947 the practice of attaching small ships to the RNVR divisions for seagoing training commenced, first using fast dispatch boats, then motor, coastal and fleet minesweepers – and for many years these ships adopted the names *Thames* and *Isis*. In 1955 the expedition ship *Discovery* joined as a third drill ship on the Embankment until 1979. In 1958 the RNVR was merged with the RNR to form the new Royal Naval Reserve. *Chrysanthemum* continued to serve until 1987 when she was sold to Inter-Action Children's Charity (and was subsequently sold again for breaking up in 1995).

Staying on the Thames

In 1989 the RNR moved to new shore premises near Tower Bridge – the unit retaining the name HMS *President* – and Inter-Action bought the old *President*. In 2001 she changed hands again and operated as HMS *President* (1918) Ltd, a conference centre. Then in May 2006 the ship was purchased by the MLS Group and major refurbishment commenced, so that she could continue as a venue for corporate and public functions. She remains at her berth on the Victoria Embankment and continues to be known as HMS *President* (1918).

Holland 1

Successful prototype submarine

*The Royal Navy's first submarine; salvaged from the seabed
and restored, she is now on display and open to the public at Gosport*

The First British Submarine

The Royal Navy's first submarines were the five *Holland* class, named after their inventor, John Holland. An Irishman who emigrated to the United States, he produced a number of experimental submarines, selling his *Holland VI* to the United States Navy in 1900. This boat was commissioned as USS *Holland* and is generally thought to have been the first truly successful submarine after 300 years of experimentation by various inventors. The Royal Navy had been sceptical of submarines, regarding them as the underhand weapons of weaker powers. However, in 1901 they decided to assess them more fully and, in the absence of a British design, ordered five Holland boats; they were built under licence by Vickers, Sons and Maxim Ltd. at Barrow-in-Furness, at a cost of £35,000 each.

Design and Build

Holland 1 was launched as the Royal Navy's first submarine on 2 October 1901 and completed in February 1903 (though three of her sisters entered service before her). She had a length of 63 feet 10 inches and a surface displacement of 110 tons. Her engines were both petrol (for surface use) giving a speed of 7.4 knots, and electric (for use when submerged) giving a submerged speed of 7 knots. The sixty battery cells that fed the electric motor were located in two banks, fore and aft, under the internal deck. She was armed with one 18-inch bow torpedo tube and carried two reloads.

With a crew of eight, she had a range of 236 miles, or 20 miles submerged at 7 knots. Fitted with two internal ballast tanks, her hull's uncluttered teardrop shape contributed to her high underwater speed and endurance. The design also allowed the submarine to dive, surface and change depth at an angle, using hydroplanes to pitch the bow up or down (whereas Holland's competitors usually aimed to keep their craft level at all times). This, together with the power available, gave her high manoeuvrability underwater. She was designed to dive to a depth of 100 feet, but it is unlikely that this depth was achieved and the dive limit was more usually set at 50 feet. This was sufficient since the threats of sonar detection and depth charges were not yet present.

Given that the design gave only 4 feet of freeboard the hatch had to be kept closed in any sea other than a flat calm. When on the surface, this made the watchkeeper's position

Technical Details	
Displacement:	110 tons
Length:	63ft 10in (19.46m)
Beam:	11ft (3.35m)
Propulsion:	One 'Otto' 4-cylinder petrol engine (built in USA), 160 hp, single screw; one electric motor, 70 hp
Speed:	7.4 knots (surface), 7 knots (submerged)
Range:	236 miles (surface); 20 miles at 7 knots (submerged)
Armament:	1 x 18-in torpedo tube
Complement:	8

perilous on the nearly flat top of the *Holland*'s exposed casing. The solution, fitted only to *Holland 2*, was to raise the upper hatch by constructing a higher conning tower, which became a common design feature of later submarine classes. Conditions inside the hull were extremely cramped and primitive, though the lack of internal bulkheads allowed the best use of the space. There were a few refinements: unlike Holland's earlier boats, the design incorporated a basic periscope. She also had a WC (or heads), a luxury discontinued in the following sixty-two Royal Navy submarines that followed the *Holland* class, which had only a bucket.

Service History

The *Hollands* were used for trials and training, thus contributing to the development of the new submarine classes that were to serve in the First World War. These larger and slightly better-equipped boats soon entered service with the Royal Navy, while two of the *Hollands* were lost in accidents. On 7 October 1913 *Holland 1* was sold to T. W. Ward Ltd for scrap, but sank under tow near the Eddystone Lighthouse en route to the breakers' yard at Briton Ferry in Wales.

Salvage and Preservation

In April 1981 the minehunter HMS *Bossington* located the wreck and in September 1982 it was salvaged to become a museum exhibit. Initial preservation work was undertaken at Devonport Dockyard, but despite anti-corrosion treatment she rusted badly on display. In 1994 the Royal Navy Submarine Museum at Gosport built a huge glassfibre tank and submerged the hull in 800,000 litres of sodium carbonate. Soaking the submarine in this way removed the chloride ions that were the cause of the uncontrollable corrosion and in 1998 *Holland 1* emerged to be displayed in a new gallery (at the Submarine Museum) with a powerful dehumidification system.

Visitors can now go aboard to explore the interior of the boat, entering via a specially cut door. Although many important pieces of equipment were removed before her final voyage to the breakers yard she still has intact the main components – engine, motor, propeller shaft, ballast tanks and torpedo tube – and new additions of replica equipment. Her hull betrays the evidence of sixty-nine years of corrosion and decay on the seabed.

ABOVE *Holland 1* on display at the Royal Navy Submarine Museum, Gosport.

OPPOSITE TOP The launching of *Holland 1* on 2 October 1901.

OPPOSITE BOTTOM *Holland 1* underway with the crew on deck.

LEFT The 18in torpedo tube on *Holland 1*.

Coastal Forces of the First World War

War-built coastal motor boats

CMBs – Design and Build

Two classes of coastal motor boats (CMB) were built in the First World War to the designs of John I. Thornycroft Ltd. The 40-foot boat carried one torpedo, while the 55-foot version carried two. Their stepped planing hull had been developed by Thornycroft before the war in a series of hydroplanes – probably the world's first planing craft – culminating in *Miranda IV* which reached a speed of 35 knots. The idea to adopt this hull for a torpedo boat originated in the summer of 1915 when three lieutenants in the Harwich Force suggested a fast hit-and-run boat capable of skimming over minefields and attacking German surface shipping in the Heligoland Bight.

A specification was issued for craft to be carried by light cruisers in davits to within sixty miles of their targets, and Thornycroft responded with the 40-foot design, with thirty-nine boats completed. The torpedo was carried pointing forward in a trough on the stern and was launched by being pushed along rails and over the transom by a steel ram powered by

BELOW A 55-foot CMB at speed.

expanding cordite gases. The boat, with a speed roughly equal to that of the torpedo, had to swiftly turn out of the way. Later the larger 55-foot non-hoisting version was added (seventy-three boats), and finally the 70-foot minelaying type (five boats).

Operations

Their two main bases were Osea Island on the River Blackwater and Dunkirk, and the boats' main operations in the First World War were off the Belgian and Dutch coasts. Their first success came in April 1917 when four CMBs attacked German destroyers off Zeebrugge and torpedoed the *G88*. In the spring of 1918 CMBs played

ABOVE *CMB 4* on display at Duxford. The step in the hull chine can be clearly seen on the right of the picture.

a major part in the Royal Navy's attempt to block the harbours of Zeebrugge and Ostend, laying down smoke to cover the approach of the blockships, marking the harbour entrances with flares and attacking German ships and gun positions. Fifteen CMBs were lost in the war: the greatest threat came from aircraft. In August 1918 six 40-foot boats were caught by German seaplanes off the Dutch coast and, in a long battle, three were sunk and the other three driven into Dutch waters where they were interned. In 1919 and 1920 CMBs were used in operations to support the White Russians in both the north (Dvina River, where 55-foot boats were used) and in the Caspian Sea (to where 40-foot boats were transported overland) during the Russian civil war. Examples of both the 40-foot and 70-foot craft have survived, together with one 55-foot boat (*MTB 331*) of much later construction (see Appendix).

CMB 4

40-foot craft which sank a Russian cruiser in a daring raid; now on display at Duxford

The 40-foot *CMB 4* was built by Thornycroft at their Hampton-on-Thames yard in 1916, with a triple-skin mahogany hull and superstructure, and is now preserved in a hangar at the Imperial War Museum's Duxford site. She is a very famous CMB, having sunk the Russian cruiser *Oleg* off Kronstadt in 1919.

Commanded by Lt Augustus Agar, *CMB 4* was one of two 40-foot CMBs tasked with landing two British intelligence agents in Estonia from where they would make their way into Russia. However, Agar decided on a much more daring course of action – to take them directly to the Russian port of Petrograd in the Gulf of Finland through the chain of forts that guarded the approaches. He used Terrioki in Finland – only three miles from the Russian border – as an advanced base. While he was setting up his base the fortress of Krasnaya Gorka rebelled against the Bolsheviks, and warships from the nearby Russian naval base at Kronstadt were sent to bombard the rebels. Agar decided to attack them and on the night of 16/17 June 1919 made his first sortie, which had to be abandoned because the propeller shaft broke on the accompanying *CMB 7*. On the next night Agar attacked using *CMB 4* alone. As he approached *Oleg* the cordite cartridge that powered the torpedo ram was accidently discharged. Agar had to halt for twenty minutes close to the Russian destroyers guarding the cruiser while the cartridge was reloaded. He then changed to full speed and closed to within 500 yards of the target, releasing his torpedo just as her guns began to fire at him. The torpedo struck and *Oleg* turned over and sank in the shallow water, while *CMB 4* made a successful high-speed escape back to Terrioki. Agar was awarded the Victoria Cross for his brave action.

Between 10 June and 26 August 1919 the CMBs made

Technical Details – *CMB 4*	
Displacement:	5 tons
Length:	40ft (12.19m); 45ft (13.72m) over trough
Beam:	8ft 6in (2.59m)
Draught:	3ft (0.91m)
Propulsion:	Thornycroft V-12 petrol engine, 350 bhp, single shaft
Speed:	35 knots
Armament:	1 x 18-in torpedo tube, 2 x 7.6mm Lewis machine guns
Complement:	3

nine trips to Petrograd, successfully landing or picking up agents on six occasions. Seven of these trips were made by Agar himself, all but the last in *CMB 4*. To reach Petrograd Agar had to negotiate minefields and run the gauntlet of the forts and a chain breakwater. The other boat, *CMB 7*, twice came under fire and was scuttled after sustaining serious damage on the final trip. In August 1919 *CMB 4* and six other boats torpedoed two Russian battleships and a submarine depot ship at Kronstadt, causing considerable damage.

After the action *CMB 4* was brought back to Britain and displayed at the Imperial War Museum. She then returned to her build site, Thornycroft's Hampton yard on the island of Platt's Eyot, to be put on display. The boat was passed back to the Imperial War Museum in 1972 following the closure of the yard. Between November 1982 and April 1984 students of the International Boatbuilding Training Centre at Lowestoft restored her extensively.

Technical Details – CMB 103

Displacement:	24 tons
Length:	72ft 6in (22.10m)
Beam:	14ft (4.27m)
Draught:	3ft 6in (1.07m)
Propulsion:	Two Thornycroft Y-24 petrol engines, 750 bhp, 2 shafts
Speed:	36 knots
Armament:	6 x 7.6mm Lewis machine guns; 7 x mines (in troughs) or 6 x 18-in torpedoes
Complement:	5

CMB 103

70-foot minelayer which survived into the Second World War; now being restored at Chatham

CMB 103, the surviving 70-foot boat, is at No. 6 covered slip, Chatham Historic Dockyard, and has undergone some conservation. Built with a triple-skin mahogany hull and superstructure by Camper and Nicholsons at Gosport in 1921, she was one of a class of twelve that had been ordered in February 1918. They were intended as minelayers but could be adapted for alternative armament. Only five boats were completed and they were used for trials, with two boats – including *CMB 103* – surviving into the Second World War. After the war she was displayed for many years on blocks at the foot of Haslar Bridge, Gosport, on the HMS *Hornet* site.

Turbinia

Charles Parsons' radical turbine craft

*The world's first turbine-driven ship, this steam yacht stunned onlookers as she
sped through the lines at Spithead; now ashore as a museum exhibit in Newcastle*

Although not a warship, and never owned by the Admiralty, *Turbinia* had an important role in
naval history as the first turbine-driven ship. Most famously she displayed the capabilities of this
new propulsion at the 1897 Diamond Jubilee Fleet Review at Spithead, before the Royal
Navy adopted the engine design for its destroyers, battleships and cruisers. She was the
brainchild of Charles Parsons who, while working for Clarke, Chapman & Co., of Gateshead
in 1884, had invented a steam turbine engine for driving a dynamo to generate electricity. In
1889 he set up his own business, C. A. Parsons & Co., at Heaton, Newcastle, which was very
successful in the production of turbo-generators.

BELOW *Turbinia* works up to
over 30 knots. Her captain and
lookout, Christopher Leyland,
stands atop the conning tower.

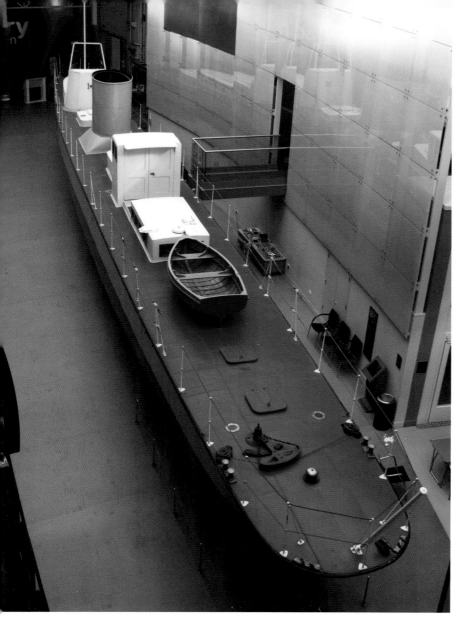

Design and Build

By late 1893 Parsons was designing the first turbine-driven ship, which had a sleek and narrow hull. Constructed of steel by Brown and Hood at Wallsend-on-Tyne, this vessel was launched as *Turbinia* on 2 August 1894. The radial flow steam turbine was manufactured at the Heaton Works but, coupled to a single propeller, gave a disappointing performance of just under 20 knots in the first speed trials of November 1894. Much experimentation with the propeller design was necessary to overcome cavitation (the formation of empty cavities behind the rapidly turning propeller blades) problems, and Parsons later replaced the engine with three parallel flow turbines (with high, intermediate and low pressure respectively) linked to three shafts, each with three propellers. This led to the achievement of speeds of more than 30 knots off the Northumberland coast in early 1897. The maximum speed attained was around 34½ knots. During the trials Parsons himself was normally in charge of the engine room, while the captain and lookout was Christopher Leyland, another director of Parsons' company. *Turbinia* at speed was a very wet ship and her crew and guest passengers were often completely drenched on the trial runs.

The Diamond Jubilee Review

Charles Parsons came up with a spectacular publicity stunt to promote the advantages of his new engine. He steamed *Turbinia* south to Spithead where, on 26 June 1897, Queen Victoria's Diamond Jubilee Review of the Fleet was taking place. After the procession of ships, which included the Royal Yacht *Victoria and Albert* carrying the Prince of Wales as the Queen's representative, had passed through the lines of warships *Turbinia* raced between a line of battleships and cruisers and a line of visiting foreign warships, reaching her top speed before an audience of influential senior officers and visitors.

Aboard one of the visiting warships, Konig Wilhelm, was the German Royal Highness, Prince Henry of Prussia. A second high-speed run was made past the Royal Yacht towards the end of the Review, when the Yacht moved off from her anchorage.

ABOVE *Turbinia* on display at the Newcastle Discovery Museum.

Turbines in the Royal Navy

After the Review, the Admiralty, which had already shown an interest in Parsons' marine steam turbine, was moved to act: they placed an order in 1898 for a turbine-driven torpedo-boat destroyer, *Viper*, the engines for which were built by the newly formed Parsons Marine Steam Turbine Co. Ltd, in their new Turbinia Works at Wallsend-on-Tyne. *Viper* was built by

Technical Details

Displacement:	44.5 tons
Length:	103ft 9in (31.62m)
Beam:	9ft (2.74m)
Draught:	3ft (0.91m)
Propulsion:	Three Parsons steam turbines, 2,100 ihp, three shafts.;three drum double-ended coal-fired boilers
Speed:	34½ knots
Complement:	10

Hawthorn Leslie at Hebburn-on-Tyne and achieved 36 knots on trials in 1900. Although both *Viper* and the second turbine-driven destroyer, *Cobra*, were lost in accidents the turbines were not the cause, and the Admiralty went on to order further turbine-driven destroyers and cruisers, which were followed in 1906 by the revolutionary *Dreadnought*, the first turbine-powered battleship. By this time turbine-driven passenger liners were also being built.

In 1900 *Turbinia* steamed south again and crossed the Channel to Le Havre. Here she entered the River Seine and steamed upriver to Paris, where she was exhibited during the Paris Exhibition. She later made a high-speed demonstration run on the river before an audience of naval architects who were attending an international meeting in the city. In 1907 *Turbinia* was struck and nearly cut in two by the *Crosby*, a ship launched from a yard on the other side of the Tyne, but survived to be repaired.

Preservation

By the First World War she was displayed on a cradle at the Turbinia Works quayside, and in 1926 was offered to the Science Museum in London. However she was too long to be accommodated there and as a simple, if dubious, expedient *Turbinia* was cut in two – seventeen years after the *Crosby* had almost done the same. The 45-foot after section, with engines and propellers, went to the Science Museum at South Kensington, while the fore section was presented to the Newcastle Corporation and displayed in the Municipal Museum of Science and Industry.

When the Science Museum reorganised in 1959 there was fortuitously no room for the after section and it returned to Newcastle to be reunited with the forward end. The complete ship went on display in 1961 at the Municipal Museum of Science and Industry until 1983. At this time she was taken in hand for a thorough restoration of both the hull and engines, and was returned to her 1897 appearance. On 30 October 1994 the vessel was moved into a specially constructed gallery at the Newcastle Discovery Museum and went on display to the public there in March 1996. Visitors cannot go aboard *Turbinia* but excellent views are possible both around and above the hull from elevated walkways.

chapter 6:
coastal steamers and
harbour craft

Steam coasters such as *Kyles* of 1872 and *Robin* of 1890 slowly eclipsed coastal sail until being overtaken themselves by the motor coaster after the Second World War. The first coastal passenger ships were, like *Waverley*, paddle steamers often built for the railway companies as ferries and excursion vessels. *Shieldhall* was one of the last coastal steamers, having been built in 1955, by which time all new coastal passenger ships were diesel-driven. Smaller craft, both naval and commercial, operated in the ports and harbours providing services such as towage, pilotage, moorings and the transport of supplies.

Coastal Steamers

Waverley

Clyde-based seagoing paddle steamer; offers passenger excursions on the Clyde and from ports around the British coast during the summer season

PREVIOUS PAGES Paddle steamers at Ilfracombe, Devon, line up at the pier.

BELOW *Waverley* in the Bristol Channel.

The London & North Eastern Railway (LNER) ordered a new paddle steamer in 1945 to replace war losses. The new ship, *Waverley*, was built for service on the Clyde, and was completed in June 1947. Designed on pre-war paddle-steamer lines, *Waverley* was one of the last traditional paddle steamers to be built. Her main excursion route in the early days was the cruise from Rothesay to Loch Goil and Loch Long, known as the Three Lochs Tour, as most passengers left the ship at Arrochar, at the head of Loch Long, to journey over to Tarbet for a sail on Loch Lomond, rejoining *Waverley* at Craigendoran. Before the cruise she operated the 8.45 am ferry run from Craigendoran to Dunoon and Rothesay, and at the end of the day returned with a ferry service from Rothesay to Craigendoran. Her crew, who had been

working since 6 am, did not finish until about 8.30 pm. *Waverley*'s weekend duties took her into Loch Fyne and the Kyles of Bute. For twenty-seven seasons she continued to operate in the Firth of Clyde and the adjoining lochs, both on excursions and regular ferry services.

By 1971 *Waverley* was one of only two large excursion vessels remaining on the Clyde and, for the first time, was based at Gourock. (The other vessel was the turbine steamer *Queen Mary*, which was withdrawn in 1977 and is now a restaurant and function venue on the Thames.) The continued decline in traffic meant that 1973 was to be *Waverley*'s last season. In 1974 she was sold for a nominal £1 to the Paddle Steamer Preservation Society, thus saving her from the shipbreakers. Rather than becoming a static exhibit, she was refitted for the Waverley Steam Navigation Company, a limited company formed by the enthusiasts who had saved her, and in 1975 reentered service on the Clyde. In 1977 *Waverley* spent a week on excursions from Liverpool, the first time she had ventured beyond the Firth of Clyde, and the success of this led to more than a month being spent on the south coast in the following year. In 1981 she was fitted with a new boiler and embarked on her first full season of Round Britain cruising, with the peak summer weeks spent back on the Clyde. This has extended her season considerably and has helped make her operation viable. In her winter 1990–91 refit the paddle wheels were replaced, and a major two-stage rebuild was undertaken in early 2000 and the winter of 2002–03, at Great Yarmouth, with the support of the National Heritage Lottery Fund. She continues to be maintained in excellent condition and is the last sea-going paddle steamer in Europe. Fully restored and painted in her original LNER colours, *Waverley* makes an exciting sight under steam as she approaches and leaves the many harbours and piers that are included in her crowded itinerary.

Balmoral
Southampton-built motor ship based in the Bristol Channel, offering excursions there and at other ports around the British coast in the summer season

By the 1930s motor vessels were beginning to replace paddle steamers on coastal ferry and excursion work. After the Second World War, when building programmes resumed, they became the norm. *Balmoral* (688 gross tons) was launched on 27 June 1949 for Red Funnel and worked on the Southampton to Cowes crossing and Solent excursions until 1968. She then passed to P. & A. Campbell for excursions in the Bristol Channel, making her last sailing on 14 October 1980.

The Paddle Steamer Preservation Society purchased her in March 1985 for continued work as a cruise vessel, operated by Waverley Excursions and complementing *Waverley*. She spends the main summer season cruising in the Bristol Channel, but also visits the Clyde on key weekends when *Waverley* is away from her home waters, and other ports and piers in the spring and autumn. In winter she is laid up at Bristol.

Kingswear Castle
Small River Dart paddle steamer, now based at Chatham Historic Dockyard and offering excursions on the Medway and Thames

The picturesque River Dart was the cruising ground of three small excursion paddle steamers until the 1960s. One of these vessels, *Kingswear Castle* (94 gross tons), was built at Dartmouth in 1924 and has been fully restored to steaming condition. In 1967 she was bought by the Paddle Steamer Preservation Society and during the 1970s a restoration project gathered momentum, so that by November 1983 she was able to steam again on trials. She carries passengers on afternoon, evening and charter cruises on the Medway and Thames. Further renovation has since involved replacing all the decks and the underwater steelwork, and in spring 2001 she received a new coal-fired boiler.

Technical Details — *Waverley*

Gross registered tonnage:	693
Length:	239ft 6½in (73.03m)
Beam:	30ft 2½in (17.45m)
Draught:	6ft 6in (1.98m)
Propulsion:	Triple-expansion diagonal steam engine, oil-fired, 2,100 ihp
Speed:	14 knots (cruising), 18.4 knots (maximum on original trials)
Passengers:	1,350

ABOVE *Balmoral* in the
Bristol Channel.

RIGHT The decorated
paddlebox of *Kingswear Castle*.

LEFT *Robin*, her masts and
funnel removed, is towed
down the Thames by the tug
Napia in July 2008, en route to
Lowestoft for a major refit.

ABOVE *Maid of the Loch* in Loch Lomond.

LEFT *Kingswear Castle* underway.

Kyles

Small steam coaster that traded for more than 100 years; now a museum exhibit at Braehead, occasionally seagoing

The veteran steam coaster *Kyles* (122 gross tons) was built on the Clyde in 1872 and traded until about 1982, by which time she was the oldest seagoing coaster trading under the Red Ensign. In 1953 her steam engine was replaced by a diesel. In 1984 *Kyles* was purchased by the Scottish Maritime Museum and placed on display at Irvine. In 1996 funding for a full restoration became available and the ship was rebuilt to her 1953 motorised appearance. In 1999 she undertook sea trials and became part of the Clyde-built exhibition at the museum's site on the upper Clyde at Braehead, near Renfrew.

Maid of the Loch

Loch Lomond paddle steamer; now a static exhibit and open to the public at Balloch, Loch Lomond

The last major paddle steamer to be built in the United Kingdom, *Maid of the Loch*, (555 gross tons), sailed on Loch Lomond from 1953 until 1981 and later became a static restaurant and exhibition ship there. Grants obtained in 2000 enabled a restaurant, bar/café and exhibition area to be created on board. Following the restoration of the steam-powered slipway at Balloch she was hauled out of the water in June 2006 (for inspection) for the first time since her withdrawal, as part of her rebuild – the objective of which is to return her to service.

Robin

Last surviving traditional British steam coaster; now on display in the London Docks and used as a training venue – not usually open to the general public

For more than a century steam coasters plied the inshore waters around the United Kingdom, linking ports large and small. When standing on any cliff top or headland it was often possible to see several coasters steaming parallel with the coast in either direction, trailing smoke like the 'dirty British coaster with a salt-caked smoke-stack' of Masefield's poem 'Cargoes'. After the Second World War they were gradually replaced by motor vessels and the growth in size and number of lorries led to a steep decline in their number. Fortunately there is one survivor – the *Robin* (366 gross tons) – which was launched in 1890.

After trading for ten years under the Red Ensign *Robin* was sold to Blanco Hermanos y Cia, of Bilbao, Spain, the beginning of seventy-four years as the Spanish-flagged *Maria*. In May 1974 she was purchased by the Maritime Trust and in June steamed under her own original engine to St Katharine Docks, London. The ship was partially restored at Rochester, renamed *Robin*, and opened to the public as part of the Trust's collection of ships in St Katharine Docks. In 1991 she moved to West India Quay and was subsequently bought by David and Nishani Kampfner who used her hold space for a commercial photography gallery. In 2002 they set up a charitable trust and began running education programmes for disadvantaged youngsters from London's East End. In July 2008 a £1.9 million refit (funded by a loan from Crossrail) began at Small & Co.'s yard at Lowestoft, thus assuring her future for many years to come.

Shieldhall

Late Clyde-built steamer, now based at Southampton offering sea-going excursions and conference facilities

A fine late example of a reciprocating steamer, *Shieldhall* (1,792 gross tons) was built for that most unglamorous of roles – dumping at sea the sludge (treated waste) from sewage works. She was launched in July 1955 at the Renfrew yard of Lobnitz & Co. for Glasgow Corporation. After twenty-one years service on the Clyde she moved to Southampton to continue in a similar role. *Shieldhall* was withdrawn from service in 1985 and handed over to Solent Steam Packet Ltd in June 1988 for preservation in steaming condition. She has a grey hull, red boot-topping, white upperworks, and a buff funnel with a black top, and is based in Southampton Docks. Her passenger-carrying certificate has been renewed, enabling her to operate sea-going excursions (from both Southampton and Weymouth) and charters, as well as being available alongside as a conference and function venue.

Sir Walter Scott

Late Victorian lake steamer still operating excursions on Loch Katrine, Scotland

Since her completion in 1900 the steamer *Sir Walter Scott* (115 gross tons) has graced the inland waters of Loch Katrine and still has her original triple-expansion steam engine. In 2005 a new trust, the Sir Walter Scott Trust, was formed to own and operate her. *Sir Walter Scott*'s usual timetable provides a return trip from Trossachs Pier to Stronachlacher in the mornings and shorter cruises, which do not land, in the afternoon. She was coal-fired until the end of the 2007 season when a two-stage overhaul commenced, which included converting her two locomotive-type boilers to run on bio-fuel.

Wingfield Castle

Pre-Second World War paddle steamer that operated on the Humber crossing; now afloat as a static museum exhibit at Hartlepool and open to the public

For forty years three paddle steamers plied the ferry service between Hull and New Holland across the River Humber until 1974, when they were replaced by a diesel-electric paddle car ferry (which was, in turn, made obsolete by the opening of the Humber Bridge). All three of the paddle steamers have survived: *Wingfield Castle* at the Museum of Hartlepool, *Lincoln Castle* (which was built by Inglis at Glasgow in 1940) as a bar and restaurant ship at Grimsby, and *Tattershall Castle* as a floating pub and nightclub on the Thames Embankment.

Wingfield Castle (556 gross tons) was built in 1934 at Hartlepool and was restored there between 1987 and 1992. She became a floating restaurant and conference centre and was opened to the public as a museum exhibit. By 2007 she was in need of further restoration and a £800,000 refit was undertaken.

BELOW *Wingfield Castle* photographed during her time in service on the Humber.

Harbour Craft

TID Class

Small steam tugs built for war service; see survivors at Chatham in Kent and Maldon, Essex

The TID class tug was a standard wartime type built in large numbers. The Ministry of War Transport ordered the first of these in 1942 to replace war losses and, in all, 182 had been built by 1946 for both government service and charter to commercial operators. One of their roles was to assist with the Normandy invasion preparations along the French and Belgian coasts, towing barges and working with elements of the Mulberry harbours. To minimise the demands on shipyard capacity the design was simplified to allow the construction of prefabricated sections by inland steel fabricators, and utilised a hard chine hull to help in this regard. The sections (of up to 10 tons) were then transported by road and assembled and welded together at a shipyard. During peak production one tug was being turned out every four-and-a-half days. Like the VIC class victualling lighters, they were steam-powered: the first ninety units were coal-fired while the later craft were oil-fired. The origin of the TID acronym is obscure; explanations have included Tug Invasion Duty, Tug Inshore Duties, Tug Intermediate Design, or more simply Tiddler.

Many were assigned to naval dockyards and continued in postwar naval service, some until the mid-1970s. In 1963 sixteen were still in the Port Auxiliary Service at six different dockyards. Two of these – *TID 164* and *TID 172* – have survived to the present day in the hands of preservation enthusiasts, and are based at Chatham Historic Dockyard and Mistley, Essex, respectively.

TID 164 was completed on 28 November 1945 and was in naval service at Port Edgar on the Forth estuary, attached to HMS *Lochinvar*, the minesweeper base. In December 1962 she was placed in reserve at Rosyth and five years later re-entered service attached to the dockyard there. In June 1974 she was sold to the Medway Maritime Museum for preservation.

TID 172 was completed on 13 February 1946. She was allocated to the Nore Command under the Naval Officer in Charge at Lowestoft, and was given the name *Martello*. On 11 July 1946 she reverted to the name *TID 172* with a civilian crew. On 20 October 1946 she was transferred to the Civil Engineer-in-Chief, Chatham, becoming *W92* (which indicates that she was operated by the Ministry of Works). On 1 October 1959 she was allocated to the Port Auxiliary Service at Chatham and reverted to her former name *TID 172*. She was sold to T. W. Ward Ltd, Grays, on 9 July 1973 for demolition, but was reprieved through her onward sale to Mr B. Pearce of Maldon, for preservation, and is now at Mistley in Essex.

Another TID that has been preserved is *Brent*, ex-*TID 159*, which is at Maldon. Built by Pickersgill in 1945, she did

Technical Details – TID Class

Gross registered tonnage:	54
Length:	65ft (19.8m)
Beam:	17ft (5.18m))
Draught:	6ft (1.83m)
Propulsion:	Two-cylinder compound steam reciprocating engine, 220 ihp, single boiler, single screw
Speed:	8½ knots
Bunkers:	8 tons coal or 8.6 tons oil
Complement:	8

not see naval service. In 1946 she was sold to the Port of London Authority, who renamed her *Brent*, and served in the Dredging Department and dock system until she was laid up in 1969. In 1970 she was sold to a shipbreaker but was saved by a private buyer, Ron Hall, in 1971.

VIC Class
Small steamships that transported supplies at naval bases during the Second World War; see survivors at Chatham and Scottish ports

In August 1939 two Clyde puffers, *Anzac* and *Lascar*, were launched. They were small cargo ships of a type used in the Western Isles of Scotland since the late nineteenth century. After the outbreak of the Second World War their design was adopted by the Ministry of War Transport for a class of steam coastal lighters that would service ships at naval bases both at home and abroad, carrying a diversity of cargoes including dry stores, water, aviation spirit, ammunition and coal. Sixty-three of this 66-foot type were built and given VIC names and numbers, an acronym for Victualling Inshore Craft. They had the traditional puffer appearance with the navigating platform (later often enclosed as a wheelhouse) abaft the funnel, a marked sheer to the deckline, a straight stem, countered stern, and a well-cambered hull profile. Most were steam powered with coal firing, so that valuable oil supplies were not needed; however, nine had diesel engines and were used overseas as petrol carriers.

Thirty-five of a larger 80-foot class were also built, two of which were diesel powered while the others were coal- or oil-fired steamers. This type had a utilitarian, slab-sided, hard-chine hull shape with little sheer to simplify the plate work, and the funnel was placed abaft the navigating platform (or later the wheelhouse).

Many continued in government service well into the postwar period: in 1963, for example, the Admiralty's Port Auxiliary Service operated twenty-one of the smaller craft and twenty-two of the larger. By 1978 only *VIC 56* and *VIC 65* remained in naval service, and the last of these, *VIC 65*, was sold in 1980 and scrapped. Others carried on even longer in commercial ownership. Five of the 66-foot vessels and two of the 80-foot have survived in UK waters.

Of the small craft, *Advance* (ex-*VIC 24*) is undergoing restoration at Plymouth. She was built in 1942, sold out of naval service in 1945, and was renamed in 1955. *VIC 32*, completed in 1943, is now at Crinan Ferry, Argyll and Buteshire, in steaming condition, and is used for holiday charters. She was re-boilered in 2006.

Spartan (ex-*VIC 18*) was built in 1940, and was motorised in 1961; she is now at the Scottish Maritime Museum, Irvine, north Ayrshire.

Vital Spark, (ex-*Eilean Eisdeal*, ex-*Elseda*, ex-*VIC 72*), was built in 1944. She was sold out of naval service at Devonport Dockyard (where she had been a stores carrier) in 1968, and was then motorised and renamed *Elseda*. She was in service in the Western Isles until 1994. In 2001 she was brought to Inveraray where she remains, and in 2006 she re-registered as *Vital Spark*, the name of the fictional puffer that appeared in the Para Handy books of Neil Munro.

Auld Reekie (ex-*VIC 27*) was built in 1943 and sold out of naval service at Rosyth Dockyard (where she had been a water carrier) in 1966. She was renamed *Auld Reekie* in 1969 when she became a youth training vessel out of Oban, and in the mid-1990s was used in the filming of the BBC television series based on Munro's books, bearing the name *Vital*

Spark during this time (although not re-registered as such). In 2006 she was moved to Inveraray for restoration.

Of the larger 80-foot design, *VIC 56* – now at Chatham Historic Dockyard – was built in 1945 as an oil-burning steamer. She spent thirty years at Rosyth, first as a stores carrier and later as an ammunition carrier, before being offered for sale in 1978. After her sale for preservation she was converted to coal firing and is still in steaming condition.

VIC 96 – now at Maryport, Cumbria – was built in 1945 and was based at Sheerness Dockyard until 1959, being renamed *C668* in 1949. In 1981 Maryport Maritime Museum purchased her, and then sold her in 1986 to Allerdale District Council, by which time she had reverted to *VIC 96*. Ten years later she was transferred to a charitable trust in a critical state of deterioration. The VIC 96 Trust is restoring the vessel and intends to steam her to Chatham's No.1 Basin where she will be based in seagoing condition.

Cervia

Wartime tug employed in ship towage on the Thames; now a static museum exhibit at Ramsgate in Kent

During the Second World War there was an urgent need for intermediate-sized tugs and about 144 were built between 1941 and 1946 for the Ministry of War Transport and given 'Empire' names, as was the practice for war-built merchant ships in Britain. There were several types varying in size from 129 to 295 gross tons, and their designs were based on successful pre-war tugs. *Empire Raymond* (233 gross tons) was completed in April 1946 and in December that year she was sold to William Watkins Ltd and renamed *Cervia*. She worked on the Thames until 1971 and then on coastal towage until 1983. In July 1985 she was loaned to Ramsgate Maritime Museum, run by the East Kent Maritime Trust. She was refitted and repainted in the Watkins colours, berthed in Smeaton's historic dry dock, and opened to the public. In the mid-1990s her engine was restored to full working order. More recently her condition has deteriorated and the Steam Museum Trust has launched an appeal for her restoration.

Challenge

Large Thames steam tug used for ship towage; seagoing and based at Tilbury Docks, Essex

Challenge (238 gross tons), was built in 1931, and is the last surviving example of a large Thames ship-handling tug. She was one of the Dunkirk Little Ships engaged in the evacuation of Allied troops from France in May and June 1940. After the war she continued in Thames service and was converted from coal to oil firing at Sheerness in 1964. In about 1971 she was laid up at Gravesend, having been the last steam tug to serve on the Thames.

In 1973 *Challenge* was sold for preservation as a static exhibit at St Katharine's Yacht Haven, London. By 1993 her condition had deteriorated badly and the Dunkirk Little Ships Restoration Trust was formed to save her. With support from Sun Tugs and Tilbury Docks *Challenge* was moved to Tilbury Docks and work began on her restoration. She is now returned to steaming condition and was present at the Trafalgar 200 Spithead Review in 2005. Her normal berth is at Tilbury, Essex.

Kerne

Small naval steam tug that later spent many years in commercial service; preserved as a seagoing museum exhibit on the Mersey

Originally to have been named *Viking*, this steam tug (63 gross tons) was purchased by the Admiralty in March 1913 for service at Chatham Dockyard under the name *Terrier*. In 1948 she was sold by the Admiralty and spent twenty-two years in commercial service in the Mersey area. In April 1971 she was laid up for disposal and sold to the North Western Steam Ship Co. Ltd, a non-profit-making organisation, for preservation in steaming condition. She is usually based at the Merseyside Maritime Museum at Liverpool or at the Boat Museum at Ellesmere Port. She has made voyages to the Isle of Man, North Wales ports, Port Madoc and cruises on the Weaver and Ship Canal Systems.

Portwey

Small steam tug that saw service with the US Army during the Second World War; in working order but usually berthed on display in the London Docks

The twin-screw, coal-fired steam tug *Portwey* (94 gross tons) is maintained in steaming condition and is normally to be found berthed at West India Quay, London, astern of the coaster *Robin*. She was launched in August 1927 for barge- and collier-towing duties at Weymouth, and later worked at Dartmouth and Falmouth. In 1967 she was bought for preservation by Richard Dobson of Stoke Gabriel on the River Dart, and in 1982 was sold to the Maritime Trust. In June 2000 she was chartered to the Steam Tug Portwey Trust, which was formed to continue the programme of renovation and operation of the vessel, and is based at West India Quay.

Mayflower

Veteran Bristol steam tug, possibly the oldest in the world; on display as a museum exhibit at Bristol

The oldest surviving British tug (and probably the oldest in the world) is the *Mayflower* (32 gross tons), built of iron in 1861 in Bristol for service on the Gloucester & Berkeley Canal. By the end of the Second World War *Mayflower* had been relegated to light duties as a tender to the canal dredger. In the winter of 1962–3 the canal froze and *Mayflower* was once again used for ship towage on the canal. This was her swansong, for in 1964 she was laid up and was sold two years later. She lay neglected and, in 1977, sank in Gloucester Docks. Refloated in 1981, she was sold to Bristol Industrial Museum for restoration to steaming condition, which was completed by 1987. Since then *Mayflower* has been exhibited outside the museum and has also offered trips under steam in Bristol Harbour, carrying up to twelve passengers. In 2006 the Industrial Museum closed but, after a transformation, is to re-open as the Museum of Bristol. At the time of writing *Mayflower* is undergoing a major refit and should be steaming again when the new museum opens in 2011.

John H. Amos

Last steam paddle tug to be built; laid up on the Medway and not open to the public

The first steam tugs were paddle tugs and although screw tugs largely superseded them, the type continued to be built until 1931 when the last, *John H. Amos* (202 gross tons), was built for towage on the Tees. She was named after an octogenarian Secretary to the Tees Conservancy Commissioners, John Hetherington Amos. *John H. Amos* was completed in February 1931 but it was a further two years before she was finally accepted. In 1968 she was donated to the Middlesbrough Museum Service but a plan to restore her to museum status failed and she was sold to the Medway Maritime Trust. The paddle tug successively occupied several different berths at Chatham, ending up on a disused slipway where she sat on a lump of concrete and her hull was flooded. For many years her condition deteriorated. In 2008 she was lifted onto a pontoon for inspection and restoration, subject to the successful application for grants from the Heritage Lottery Fund.

Daniel Adamson

Steam tug/tender that served in the Mersey area for more than eighty years; now on display and open to the public as a museum exhibit at Liverpool

Tug/tenders were dual-purpose vessels that combined towing capabilities with passenger accommodation. *Daniel Adamson* (173 gross tons), built in 1903 as *Ralph Brocklebank*, is one of only two tug/tenders to survive in the United

Technical Details – Small VIC Class	
Displacement:	124 tons
Gross registered tonnage:	96
Length:	66ft 10in (20.36m)
Beam:	18.5ft (5.64m)
Draught:	8ft (2.44m)
Propulsion:	Steam two-cylinder reciprocating compound engine, 120 ihp, single screw; single vertical coal-fired boiler
Speed:	7 knots
Range:	700 miles
Bunkers:	11 tons
Cargo capacity:	100 tons
Complement:	Two officers and four men

ABOVE *Ralph Brocklebank* (later renamed *Daniel Adamson*) at Liverpool pierhead in 1907.

LEFT *John H. Amos* is lifted onto a pontoon in 2008 by the crane barge *Atlas*, in the first stage of a planned restoration.

RIGHT *Cervia* in service with International Towing Ltd.

BELOW The restored *Mayflower* in steam at Bristol in 2006.

LEFT The preserved *John King* at Bristol.

Kingdom (the other being the *Calshot*), and the only one to retain her original steam power. Designed to operate a barge-towing service between Ellesmere Port and Liverpool, use was made of her passenger-carrying capability on a cross-river ferry and, later, cruises from Manchester to Eastham. She took her present name in 1936. In 1986 she was laid up and berthed at the Boat Museum, Ellesmere Port. By 2004 she was in poor condition and was rescued for restoration and taken to the Clarence Graving Dock. She is now on display in Bramley Moore Dock, Liverpool, and is maintained by the Daniel Adamson Preservation Society.

Calshot
Tug/tender that served the great ocean liners at Southampton; now laid up there and not normally open to the public

The port of Southampton had a requirement for tug/tenders to attend to liners anchored in Cowes Roads, and *Calshot* (684 gross tons) was completed in 1930 to join the fleet of the Red Funnel Line. On 16 December 1940 she was requisitioned by the Admiralty and sent to Scapa Flow to tender the Home Fleet at its anchorage and later went to the Clyde to tender the 'Queens' and other liners, which were on trooping duties. In May 1944 she returned to Southampton for D-Day duties. Her peacetime duties resumed at Southampton and lasted until 1964 when she was sold and motorised for further service at Galway.

In 1986 she was bought by Southampton City Council to be the centrepiece of a proposed maritime museum. This scheme did not proceed and she remained in Southampton Docks. In 1997 the Tug Tender Calshot Trust was set up with the aim of restoring *Calshot* to her 1930s profile, including heightening her funnel. Limited work has been undertaken, but further progress is contingent on successful application for grants.

John King
Small motor tug that served in the Bristol area for sixty years; now preserved as a working exhibit at Bristol

Built in 1935, *John King* (49 gross tons) was a motor tug used by C. J. King & Sons for ship towage on the River Avon and Bristol Docks until 1970. Her last job was to manoeuvre the SS *Great Britain* into the Great Western Dock, but further service ensued under other names and owners. In 1995 she was purchased by the Bristol Industrial Museum. She has been kept in working condition and has operated passenger trips at Bristol, and will continue to be located there as part of the new Museum of Bristol.

Thomas
The navy's first motor tug, later in commercial service; preserved in working order, based at Port Talbot, Wales

Thomas (89 gross tons) was built as *Oner II* in 1937 and was purchased in 1938 by the Admiralty (and renamed *C10*) as their first motor tug, for use on fleet fuelling duties at Portsmouth. In 1958 she was renamed *Destiny*, and was sold in 1961 for commercial service. By 1988 she was owned by Star Tug and Marine Co. Ltd and used for film work. In 1991 she was sold to a Swansea businessman who refitted her and renamed her *Thomas*, and is now preserved at Port Talbot. She was at the 1996 Festival of the Sea at Bristol.

Kent
Small motor tug that served in the Medway area; preserved as a seagoing vessel, based at Chatham

Kent (121 gross tons) was built in 1948 for ship handling at the Medway ports of Rochester, Chatham and Sheerness. She was taken out of service in 1988 and lay on the Medway

Technical Details – Large VIC class

Gross registered tonnage:	145
Length:	80ft 6in (24.51m)
Beam:	18ft (5.48m)
Draught:	8ft 8in (2.62m)
Propulsion:	Steam compound engine, 140 ihp, single screw
Cargo Capacity:	120 tons
Complement:	2 officers and 4 men

in semi-preserved condition. In 1995 the South Eastern Tug Society acquired her for restoration and preservation. She is maintained in working condition, based at No.1 Basin, Chatham, and often attends maritime heritage events. She is a good example of an early postwar motor tug and is of riveted construction.

Freshspring
Steamship that carried fresh water to warships at naval bases; now laid up near Gloucester

Between 1940 and 1946 Lytham Shipbuilding and Engineering Co., Lytham St Annes, Lancashire, built fourteen steam-powered, *Fresh*-class water tankers for the Admiralty. The last of the class to be built was *Freshspring* (283 gross tons), which was launched in August 1946 and completed in February 1947. She became the sole survivor of the class.

Freshspring was based at Malta in the 1950s and early 1960s, and then returned to the United Kingdom to operate on the Clyde and the west coast of Scotland with the Port Auxiliary Service. She was sold on 4 July 1979 to a private owner who towed her to Bristol where she was adapted for the experimental use of alternative fuels to power ships' engines. Some time later she was laid up at Newnham on the Severn and her condition deteriorated, but in June 2007 she was reportedly being gradually restored for youth, educational and leisure purposes.

Lydia Eva
East coast steam trawler/drifter, later in government service; seagoing exhibit at Lowestoft and Great Yarmouth

Steam trawlers, fishing for sole, plaice and other bottom-feeding fish in the North Sea, were built in large numbers from 1881 onwards, replacing sailing trawlers; in contrast, steam drifters — which fished for herring and mackerel in shallower waters — did not eclipse the sailing drifters until the first decade of the twentieth century. In 1913, their peak year, 1,766 steam drifters fished out of Great Yarmouth and Lowestoft alone, together with only a handful of sailing drifters. The steam drifters continued to be seen in large numbers in east coast ports until the Second World War, and one of them — *Lydia Eva* — was later rescued by the Maritime Trust for restoration.

Built in 1930, of 138 gross tons, she fished for herrings for eight years and then entered government service as a mooring vessel, to service buoys and was later renamed *Watchmoor*. She was sold in 1971 to the Maritime Trust for preservation, restored to her original appearance, and from 1973 to 1978 was on display at Great Yarmouth and, from 1978 to 1986 at St Katharine Docks, London. In 1986 *Lydia Eva* was laid up until 1990 when she was chartered to the Lydia Eva Trust and returned to the east coast, at Lowestoft, to be opened to the public, both there and at Great Yarmouth. In 1995 she was sold for £1 to the Lydia Eva and Mincarlo Trust and remained on display until 2000. Following a £839,000 grant from the Heritage Lottery Fund an extensive restoration began in March 2007 by Small & Co. at Lowestoft, allowing the vessel to be returned to sea under her own steam by late 2008.

Edmund Gardner
Ferried pilots out to ships off the Mersey Bar and also led ships across the bar; now museum exhibit at Liverpool, open to the public

Built for the Liverpool Pilotage Authority, *Edmund Gardner*, of 701 gross tons, was launched in 1953 and, with her two sister ships, carried pilots who guided the stream of ships entering and leaving the River Mersey. The cutters had diesel-electric propulsion and a top speed of 14 knots; they were eventually replaced by high-speed launches and in April 1981 the *Edmund Gardner* was withdrawn from service. She was sold in 1982 to the Merseyside Maritime Museum and is now preserved in the Canning Graving Dock, Liverpool.

chapter 7: the second world war navy

In the mid-1930s, as the possibility of war with Germany loomed, the Royal Navy embarked on a significant construction programme. New cruisers were designed to meet arms treaty limitations, and one of these, *Belfast*, was completed just before the outbreak of hostilities. Sloops such as *Wellington* were built, increasingly with anti-submarine warfare in mind, while destroyers were ordered in large numbers, and a standard emergency wartime design emerged: *Cavalier* is featured here. The huge wartime construction programme also embraced submarines such as *Alliance*, midget submarines and coastal forces, examples of which still survive.

Belfast

Britain's biggest preserved warship

Famous British warship that served in the Second World War and the Korean War; she makes an imposing sight at her berth near Tower Bridge, where she is open to the public

HMS *Belfast* is the largest surviving twentieth-century British warship. She has been preserved and exhibited by the Imperial War Museum, and is moored on the River Thames close to Tower Bridge in central London. Providing a valuable example of a principal warship of the Second World War, in the absence of any remaining British battleships she is representative of the final era of the big-gun Navy.

Design

Her design originates in the naval treaties of the interwar period, which attempted to limit the size and number of warships to prevent a repetition of the arms race that had preceded the First World War. In the 1920s heavy cruisers armed with 8-inch guns had dominated the construction programmes of the United States, Great Britain and Japan. The 1930 London Naval Treaty banned any further heavy cruisers and limited the gun calibre to 6-inch. However, the so-called light cruisers, which mounted 6-inch guns, could displace up to 10,000 tons and could thus be as large as the previous heavy cruisers. Furthermore, their lighter shells could be fired much more rapidly than the 8-inch, and more guns could be mounted on a given sized hull, thus providing a broadside which, in weight, was twice that of a heavy cruiser.

This situation was exploited by the Japanese navy, which introduced the *Mogami* class armed with fifteen 6-inch guns, far outgunning the British *Leander* and *Arethusa* classes of the early 1930s, which mounted only eight and six 6-inch guns respectively. The United States followed suit with the *Brooklyn* class and the British, who had favoured larger numbers of smaller cruisers to help police their extensive empire and trade routes, were forced to comply. The result was the *Southampton* class, the first two units of which were included in the 1933 estimates and ordered in May 1934 to a design based on four triple 6-inch gun turrets. To enable two Walrus aircraft to be carried for reconnaissance purposes the design incorporated hangars on each side of the fore funnel with a fixed catapult athwartships between the two funnels. This, together with raked funnels and tripod masts, led to a profile for the British cruiser that was both handsome and distinctive.

The new class was also more heavily armoured than its predecessors, being designed to have some chance of withstanding 8-inch shells – thus enabling the light cruiser, whose guns had a shorter range than the 8-inch, to engage the enemy more closely and deliver a rain of 6-inch shells. Between December 1934 and March 1936 orders were placed for a further six ships, and then in September 1936 the last two ships of the class, *Belfast* and *Edinburgh*, were ordered, incorporating significant modifications that effectively made them a separate class.

They were larger ships, being 22 feet longer than the earlier *Southamptons* and more than 1,000 tons greater in displacement. The design was rather rushed to allow orders to be placed before the impending 1936 London Naval Conference, since it was thought likely that there would be a reduction in maximum cruiser size. The engine machinery was moved further aft and the 4-inch shell magazine was relocated forward. This led to an altered profile: the mainmast was positioned between the funnels, which were further aft, producing a large gap between the bridge/hangar structure and the fore funnel. This gave the ships a less well-balanced look than the earlier *Southamptons*. Initially it was proposed that they would be armed with four quadruple 6-inch turrets to gain parity with the *Mogami* class. The quadruple mounting proved unreliable in trials, however, and rather than accept the delays to construction that further development would take, it was decided to proceed with triple turrets. As a result the potential benefits of the larger design were largely wasted, though the 4-inch gun armament was increased from four to six twin mountings and the deck armour was heavier.

Build

Belfast's keel was laid at Harland and Wolff's Belfast yard on 10 December 1936, as Job Number 1000. On 17 March 1938 Mrs Neville Chamberlain, wife of the Prime Minister, launched the ship and in March 1939 *Belfast* undertook basic sea trials. Speed trials were carried out in late May on the measured mile range off Greenock, and on May 31 she achieved 32.98 knots at full power of 81,140 shp. At this time she was without her 4-inch guns and 6-inch directors and, at 10,415 tons was below her standard displacement. Further trials and final fitting out continued until, on 3 August 1939, she was completed and left Belfast for Portsmouth.

ABOVE HMS *Belfast* in July 1959, shortly after her modernisation.

PREVIOUS PAGES *Alliance* leaving Gosport on 17 April 1952 to lay wreaths at the spot where her sister boat *Affray* was lost exactly a year earlier.

Early Service in the Second World War

On 5 August she was commissioned at Portsmouth as part of the 2nd Cruiser Squadron, Home Fleet, joining *Southampton* and *Glasgow*. She proceeded to the North Sea and Pentland Firth for an exercise and on 3 September was off East Anglia, returning to Portsmouth, when she was ordered to reverse course and head for Invergordon; later that day the outbreak of war was announced. On 31 August she had been transferred to the 18th Cruiser Squadron, which included *Edinburgh*, *Sheffield* and *Aurora*, based at Scapa Flow. In September the squadron was augmented by the addition of *Norfolk*,

ABOVE *Belfast* on display on the River Thames near Tower Bridge.

BELOW The bell on *Belfast's* quarterdeck.

Suffolk and *Newcastle*, while *Edinburgh* left to join the 2nd Cruiser Squadron.

Belfast was deployed between the Orkneys and Iceland as part of the Northern Patrol, a blockade to prevent German raiders entering the Atlantic and to intercept incoming ships carrying supplies to Germany. On 9 October, when fifty miles north-west of the Faroes, she ordered the Norwegian steamship *Tai Yin* to stop and sent her to Kirkwall with a prize crew aboard. Two hours later *Belfast* intercepted the German liner *Cap Norte*, which was disguised as a Swedish ship. The *Cap Norte* was bringing German reservists from Pernambuco in Brazil to Germany, and was boarded and captured. *Belfast's* early success was, however, short-lived. She

was taken off the Northern Patrol and joined *Southampton*, *Glasgow* and *Aurora* to rejoin the 2nd Cruiser Squadron, which was based at Rosyth, on 10 November. On 21 November she weighed anchor at 0917 and sailed down the Firth of Forth for gunnery practice with *Southampton* and two destroyers. At 1058 a violent explosion was felt and extensive damage was sustained. Twenty-one crew members were injured, and one man, painter H. Stanton, died later in hospital. *Belfast* had struck a magnetic mine and was taken in tow by the tug *Krooman*, which had been nearby towing targets (presumably for the gunnery practice). When the ship was dry-docked at Rosyth it was clear that she had broken her back between the bridge structure and the forward funnel. At first it seemed that she might have to be declared a constructive total loss and be scrapped. Although this was averted, *Belfast* was to be out of action for three years.

Rebuilding

Temporary repairs were carried out at Rosyth, but the rebuilding necessary was beyond that yard's capability and on 28 June 1940 *Belfast* left under her own power for Devonport where she arrived two days later. She was docked on 1 August to begin the lengthy reconstruction, which was protracted by the pressure of work at the dockyard and the fact that some of her equipment was cannibalised to keep other ships at sea. The ship was straightened and strengthened, with the addition of heavier armour plating and a bulge to the hull which increased her beam by 3 feet. Among other updating, new RDF (high-frequency direction finding combined with radar) was added. The work took twenty-six months before she recommissioned on 3 November 1942, and then left Devonport for Scapa Flow on 10 December to become flagship of the 10th Cruiser Squadron (Vice Admiral Burnett). While *Belfast* was in dockyard hands her sister ship, *Edinburgh*, had been lost after being torpedoed successively by a U-boat in the Barents Sea on 30 April 1942 and by German destroyers two days later.

ABOVE Twin 40-mm Bofors gun on *Belfast*.

Encounters with German Capital Ships

Belfast's work for the next eighteen months was to escort Arctic convoys to and from Russia and continue the Northern Patrol. Undoubtedly the most dramatic event in these arduous duties was the Battle of the North Cape in December 1943, which led to the sinking of the *Scharnhorst*. The German battlecruiser was intent on attacking two convoys, one eastbound the other westbound, and had left her lair in Altenfjord on Christmas Day. British forces were aware of this and were deployed accordingly. *Belfast*, together with *Norfolk* and *Sheffield*, was part of Force One escorting the westbound convoy and the cruisers made radar contact with *Scharnhorst* at 0834 on Boxing Day, before engaging her with fire fifty minutes later. The battlecruiser was hit by *Norfolk*'s shells, and increased speed and altered course to escape. Burnett made a considered decision to return to protect the convoy. Contact was re-established two hours later when Force One was re-engaged by the *Scharnhorst*, and *Norfolk* was herself hit. The *Scharnhorst* altered course at around 1300 to retreat but her path converged with that of Force Two, led by the battleship *Duke of York*, which had been covering the convoys at a distance. The combined British force subjected *Scharnhorst* to sustained attack by gunfire and torpedoes, crippling the enemy ship. The final torpedoes were delivered by *Belfast* and *Jamaica*, and *Scharnhorst* exploded and sank at 1945, with heavy loss of life – only thirty-six ratings were picked up by British destroyers, and no officers survived, out of a crew of nearly 2,000.

Meanwhile the German battleship *Tirpitz* was under repair at her Norwegian base following the damage inflicted in September 1943 by X-craft, and in March 1944 was reported to have moved up to Altenfjord to ready herself for sea. On 30 March *Belfast* left Scapa Flow with the Home Fleet forces that were to carry out an attack, codenamed Operation Tungsten, on *Tirpitz*. Among those forces were the aircraft carriers *Victorious* and *Furious*, which launched forty-two Barracuda bombers to conduct a successful attack on the German ship. *Tirpitz* was heavily damaged and, unable to put to sea, was sunk later that year by RAF Lancaster bombers.

The Normandy Landings

Belfast's next action was in Operation Neptune, the naval part of Operation Overlord, the Normandy landings of June 1944. Here she was the flagship of Rear Admiral F. H. G. Dalrymple-Hamilton and part of the Eastern Task Force, which was responsible for the landing of three divisions of the British and Canadian Second Army in three sectors: Sword, Juno and Gold. The bombardment group for the Eastern Task Force comprised the battleships *Warspite* and *Ramillies*, the monitor *Roberts*, *Belfast* and four other cruisers and fifteen destroyers. They assembled in the Clyde and sailed on 2 and 3 June to be in position off Normandy for 5 June, the date of the planned landings. *Belfast* weighed anchor at 1100 on 3 June and after a practice shoot with her 4-inch guns headed south. As quoted in the *Mariner's Mirror* vol 94, Lieutenant Peter Brooke Smith, RNVR, aboard *Belfast*, described the scene as the ship entered the Channel: 'From Plymouth onwards we overhauled convoy after convoy of landing craft of all descriptions, loaded with vehicles and crammed with British and American soldiers. We pitied them in those small ships without much shelter from the choppy sea. They must have spent two or three days in extremely cramped confinement waiting for the signal to sail.'

In fact bad weather caused a twenty-four-hour postponement of the landings, but at 0527 on 6 June *Belfast* fired one of the first shells of the invasion, at a German battery at La Marefontaine, at a range of about six miles off Gold

Technical details (final configuration)

Displacement:	11,553 tons standard; 14,930 tons full load
Length:	613ft 6in (187.0m)
Beam:	69ft (21.03m)
Draught:	23ft (7.01m)
Propulsion:	Four Parsons single reduction geared steam turbines, 80,000 shp; four Admiralty 3-drum boilers; 4 shafts
Speed:	32½ knots
Range:	8,000 miles at 14 knots
Armament:	12 x 6-in guns; 8 x 4-in guns; 12 (later 8) x 40 mm guns
Armour:	Side 5in–3in, turrets 2.5in, deck 2in
Complement:	710 (52 officers and 658 men); increased to around 800 as flagship, and 950 in wartime
Pennant Numbers:	35 (to 1948), C35 (1948–71)

Beach. Peter Brooke Smith recalled, 'We were furiously indignant when at 0523 a cruiser to the westward of us, probably HMS *Orion*, opened fire and thus forestalled us the honour of being the first ship to fire a shot in the Second Front. We need not have worried: Rex North, *Sunday Pictorial*'s war correspondent who we had on board, unblushingly gave us that honour.' After two hours of bombardment the assault forces in their landing craft launched their invasion, sweeping past the bombardment force and securing a foothold on the shore.

This was the first of a number of bombardments made by *Belfast* over the following five weeks, punctuated only by two returns to Portsmouth for new ammunition. In the Normandy campaign she fired 1,996 6-inch shells and around 1,000 4-inch shells before finally leaving the area on 10 July for Scapa Flow. She was now in need of a long refit and moved to the Tyne later in July for work by the Middle Dock and High Shields Engineering Company. She re-emerged in April 1945. The refit had prepared her for service in the Pacific, with the fitting of extra light anti-aircraft guns and the removal of the two after 4-inch gun mountings. She had not carried her Walrus aircraft (long-range radar having made them redundant) since mid-1943, so the catapult was removed and the catapult deck converted into a boat deck. One of the two large electric cranes was removed and the other resited. The accommodation was improved to make it more suitable for tropical service.

Post-Second World War Service History

After trials and exercises from Rosyth and Scapa Flow, *Belfast* left Scapa for the Pacific on 17 June 1945 and arrived at Sydney in August, after the Japanese had surrendered. At Sydney she spent a short time in the dockyard so that her anti-aircraft armament could be further enhanced by five 40-mm Bofors guns. In September she became flagship of the 2nd Cruiser Squadron and for the following three months ferried the emaciated survivors of Japanese prisoner-of-war camps between Shanghai and Hong Kong. There followed a series of peacekeeping and flag-flying duties in South East Asia, including a cruise to New Zealand, Fiji and Japan, before a two-month refit at Singapore. In July 1946 she became flagship of the 5th Cruiser Squadron and was soon on the first of two further cruises, both of which took in Japanese and Chinese ports, followed by a visit to Malaya in June 1947.

In August she left the station and arrived at Portsmouth on 15 October to pay off for a long refit. During this refit maintenance to her turbines was carried out and four additional Bofors guns were fitted. *Belfast* recommissioned on 22 September 1948 and shortly afterwards visited the city of Belfast where she was presented with a silver bell to be hung on the quarterdeck, the presentation having been delayed by the war. Also displayed on the quarterdeck are the ship's four battle honours: Arctic 1943, North Cape 1943, Normandy 1944 and Korea 1950–51.

She sailed from Belfast for the Far East on 23 October 1948 to again become the flagship of the 5th Cruiser Squadron, relieving HMS *Sussex*. Her duties took her to Chinese waters to help protect British interests during the fighting that led to the takeover of China by the Communists. This included the rescue of an RAF Vampire jet that had force-landed on a beach in Chinese territory. Tension in the area was high, and for the Royal Navy forces of which *Belfast* was flagship, climaxed with the escape from the Yangtse River of HMS *Amethyst* after bombardment by Communist batteries in April 1949. *Belfast* herself was not directly involved, being in Hong Kong. On the night of 31 October/1 November she went to the assistance of a Chinese Nationalist landing ship that had grounded on a reef in the South China Sea and saved 226 people. Between January and March 1950 *Belfast* underwent a short refit at Singapore.

The Korean War

Three months later, on 25 June 1950, the North Korean army entered South Korea and, under a United Nations mandate, British, American and other nations' forces were sent to repel the invasion. *Belfast* led the Royal Navy's fleet, which also included the cruisers *Kenya* and *Jamaica*,

Operations in Korea, 1950

Belfast's gunnery officer, Lieutenant Commander H. G. G. Ogilvie, recalled the early action of the ship in the Korean War:

'We formed an impressive sight as *Belfast* led the British Fleet into Okinawa. By this time the British government had ordered that our naval forces should at once join up with the Americans and operate in Korean waters in accordance with the United Nations decision to come to the aid of South Korea. The whole fleet sailed shortly afterwards with the US 7th Fleet units towards Korean waters.

Meanwhile we fuzed all the shells with warheads and prepared for war as we steamed north. We carried out the preparations for action so familiar to some of us on board, but a new experience for the young members of our peacetime crew. We were manned with a peace complement and this allowed us to man nine of the twelve 6-inch guns, one turret being unmanned. We worked all the 4-inch twin mountings and half the close-range weapons, but had only skeleton ammunition supply parties. We had a fine, well worked-up ship's company who had been in commission for eighteen months with few changes.

It was, I think, on 6 July 1950 that we went into action for the first time and thereafter we bombarded the advancing North Korean troops for many days and nights, answering calls for fire from the hard pressed army. We carried out indirect bombardments when mostly under way, and the fall of shot was spotted sometimes by forward observers on shore, and sometimes by aircraft. Several times we bombarded at our extreme range of 24,000 yards.

Belfast gained a name for rapid, accurate shooting, and hard hitting. The Americans found it hard to believe that our 6-inch triple turrets were hand worked. We were fortunate in having three fine turrets' crews that had had no changes for a long time, and were trained up to a peak and were keen rivals with each other. As was customary, two turrets were manned by seamen and one by Royal Marines. This made for the keenest competitive spirit. We were able to put the first round of a shoot usually within 200 yards of a target and very soon were pouring in rapid broadsides of fire for effect. The most unusual shoot was our bombardment of moving trains proceeding along the coastal railway. This was an unorthodox gunnery exercise when carried out by the 4-inch batteries controlled by the high-angle fir-control system in low-angle procedure. Sometimes we would illuminate a train with starshell and let fly at it with the 6-inch as it appeared out of a tunnel.

During these operations the ship was always under war routine and closed up at anti-aircraft defence or cruising stations, with always one or two 6-inch turrets manned. *Belfast* was always a happy ship with a proud ship's company. Even when over-crowded and hard-worked, with very little shore-leave as in the Korean War, she was still the happiest of ships, the crew realizing that she was doing a real job and doing it well.'

(Adapted from John Wingate (2004) *In Trust for the Nation: HMS Belfast*, Imperial War Museum)

the aircraft carrier *Triumph*, the 8th Destroyer Squadron and a number of frigates, to rendezvous with the United States 7th Fleet at Okinawa on 1 July.

The two fleets sailed together for Korean waters where they were to conduct an intensive shore bombardment in support of land troops and a blockade of incoming supplies. After approximately one month of operations *Belfast* left the area on 6 August to return to Chatham to recommission with a full war complement, including some reservists and others who were due to have been discharged. After arriving at Sheerness on 6 October she proceeded to Chatham to pay off on 18 October. She recommissioned the following day and sailed from England on 27 October to return to the Far East. En route she worked up at Malta and arrived at Sasebo, the main Royal Naval base for operations during the Korean War, on 31 January 1951. The war had been intensified by the intervention of Chinese troops who had advanced southwards, and *Belfast* resumed her patrols and bombardment between February and April. On 1 June she docked at Singapore for a short refit after which she returned to her patrol area, arriving on 31 August. With occasional breaks for rest and shore leave she remained in this service until the ceasefire in September 1952, which brought the fighting to an end.

In all she spent 404 days on patrol and her 6-inch guns fired 8,000 rounds, necessitating their replacement at Singapore part way through the twenty-seven-month war. *Belfast* was only hit by return fire on one occasion, on 29 July 1952. She was engaging a battery on the island of Wolsa-ri when a 3-inch shell struck forward, killing one Chinese rating (Lau So) and injuring four others. *Belfast* also lost two Royal Marines who were killed while serving on detachment with US landing craft.

Modernisation

The ship returned home, paying off at Chatham on 4 November 1952, and afterwards entered reserve at Devonport. In March 1955 the Board of Admiralty approved a modernisation programme for *Belfast* and this was carried out at Devonport Dockyard between January 1956 and May 1959. There were extensive changes to the ship to upgrade living accommodation, with bunks, showers, air-conditioning, electric galleys (replacing oil-fired arrangements) and centralised messing. An airtight citadel was created, and a pre-wetting system was installed within the superstructure, for better resistance to nuclear and chemical warfare. Externally the most obvious changes to her appearance were the replacement of the tripod masts by lattice masts, the construction of an enclosed bridge, the removal of the torpedo tubes, the replacement of the close-range armament by six twin Bofors mountings, and the fitting of new radar outfits and gun directors. This is the appearance that *Belfast* presents in her preserved state (although it is now complemented by an anachronistic, but eye-catching, wartime camouflage scheme).

Final Service

The ship recommissioned at Devonport on 12 May 1959, once again for service on the Far East Station, and sailed from England on 20 August. On her passage east she worked up at Malta, and docked at Singapore on 16 December. *Belfast* was to spend twenty-seven months on the station – during part of the last decade in which such extended foreign commissions were undertaken by Royal Naval warships. A substantial Far East fleet was still maintained by the Royal Navy, including at least one aircraft carrier east of Suez at all times. *Belfast*'s time was spent ranging over the Pacific and Indian Oceans, on typical peacetime duties including joint exercises with South East Asian Treaty Organisation (SEATO) forces, and visits to Korea, Japan, Australia, Hong Kong and East Africa. She attended the Tanganyika independence celebrations at Dar-es-Salaam in December 1961.

Following a short refit at Singapore at the end of 1960, a new crew (comprising 52 officers and 580 men) flew out on seven chartered flights in time for recommissioning on 31 January 1961, with the old crew flying home on the same aircraft. The impact of air transport had meant that, unlike in 1950, the ship had not had to return to the United Kingdom to recommission, and the length of time spent by crewmembers away from the United Kingdom could more easily be reduced. On 26 March 1962 she sailed from Singapore for the last time, beginning her east-about passage home that was to take in Guam, Pearl Harbor, San Francisco, Seattle, Vancouver, Panama and Trinidad. *Belfast* anchored at Spithead on 19 June 1962 for customs clearance and then proceeded into Portsmouth flying her paying-off pennant.

On 2 July 1962 she recommissioned for Home Sea Service as flagship of the Home Fleet Flotillas. This was a short commission that ended when she paid off at Devonport on 25 February 1963 and entered reserve, but her active service was not quite over. Her final commission was a short spell of seagoing service – on the Royal Naval Reserve's summer cruise as flagship of the Admiral Commanding Reserves. She left Devonport on 16 July 1963 and sailed up Channel to exercise the reserve ship's company by whom she was manned. At Portsmouth she was joined by ten RNR coastal minesweepers and headed for Gibraltar and the Mediterranean for exercises. Finally, on 24 August, she arrived back at Devonport to again be paid off into reserve, though was present at Navy Days a few days later. In May 1966 she was moved to Portsmouth to join the reserve ships off Whale Island, and for four years provided accommodation for the men of the Reserve Ships Division and the offices of the Senior Officer Reserve Ships, replacing HMS *Sheffield*. In May 1971 she was declared for disposal.

ABOVE The forward
steering postion on *Belfast*.

Preservation

In early 1971 a trust was set up to preserve the ship, under the chairmanship of Rear Admiral
Morgan Giles, a former captain of HMS *Belfast*. On 2 September of that year she left
Portsmouth under tow for the Thames, and arrived at Tilbury the following day to be fitted
out as a museum ship. On 14 October she was towed to her berth on the dolphins at Symon's
Wharf in the Pool of London, just above Tower Bridge. She opened to the public on Trafalgar
Day, 21 October 1971, hoisting once again the White Ensign by special permission since she
was no longer in commission. She continues to be regarded as a ship of the Royal Navy but
is administered by the Imperial War Museum. Some 250,000 visitors and around 60,000 school
children tour the ship each year, and are able to explore nine decks from the boiler room up
to the flag deck and gun direction platform. School parties can be accommodated overnight
in bunks on the original mess decks. In 2000 *Belfast* was towed to Portsmouth for dry-docking
and painting, returning to the Thames within a month.

Cavalier

Arctic convoy destroyer

Last remaining Royal Navy destroyer from the Second World War; now afloat at Chatham Historic Dockyard and open to the public

Design

On the day after Britain declared war on Germany in September 1939, the Royal Navy ordered the first of fourteen destroyer flotillas to a new standard design that had been developed from the J class. Each consisting of eight destroyers, the flotillas were ordered between 1939 and 1942 and were generally known as emergency wartime destroyers. First came the O class, then the P, Q, R, S, T, U, V, W and Z classes. The same basic design was used for each, though the hull size increased slightly on the later flotillas and there were variations in armament to suit the availability of weapons. The remaining four flotillas became the C class, each distinguished by the second letter of the name: CA, CH, CO and CR. The CA flotilla was the last to be completed in time to see action, and among this group was *Cavalier*.

Like the preceding Z class the CAs were fitted with four single 4½-inch dual-purpose guns that were capable of an elevation of fifty-five degrees for anti-aircraft fire, two quadruple banks of torpedo tubes, plus lighter anti-aircraft guns. They were powered by steam turbines and offered the classic single-funnel profile of British fleet destroyers first adopted in the J Class.

Build

Cavalier and her sister ship *Carysfort* were ordered from J. Samuel White & Co. at Cowes, Isle of Wight, on 12 August 1942. Originally the ships had been ordered as *Pellew* and *Pique* from Cammell Laird, Birkenhead, in March 1942, the names being among those remaining from a list drawn up for the earlier flotillas. A decision was later taken to give these ships CA names. However, capacity problems at Cammell Laird led to the order being transferred to White's and *Cavalier*'s keel was laid on 28 February 1943. She was launched on 7 April 1944 and after fitting out was handed over to the Royal Navy on 22 November 1944. *Cavalier* was among the first warships to be built with a partially welded hull, with female welders employed on the slipway – though the midships section remained riveted for strengthening purposes. White's were soon afterwards to produce the first all-welded British destroyer, HMS *Contest*.

War Service

On completion, *Cavalier* joined the 6th Destroyer Flotilla, Home Fleet. In December 1944 she went to the aid of the troopship *Empire Javelin*, which had been torpedoed off Cape Barfleur, north-east France, and was involved in the successful rescue of the majority of the passengers and crew. After working up at Scapa Flow, *Cavalier* took part in three operations off Norway in February 1945: Selenium, a strike against enemy shipping; Shred, to provide fighter cover for a minesweeping flotilla; and Groundshoot, an aircraft minelaying strike. She was then sent with the destroyers *Myngs* and *Scorpion* from Scapa Flow to reinforce the escort of the west-bound Arctic convoy RA64, which had left the Kola Inlet, Russia, on 17 February. The convoy had been attacked by U-boats and enemy aircraft, and had become scattered during strong gales with very heavy seas and ice, conditions that were believed to have been the worst weathered in the entire North Atlantic theatre during the war. *Cavalier* joined in the evening of 23 February and helped round up the convoy, which arrived in the Clyde on 1 March having lost only three of the thirty-four merchant ships (a good record for Arctic convoys). Such had been the conditions that all of the destroyers in the escort reported serious defects, and twelve had to be dry docked or refitted. This mission earned *Cavalier* the Arctic 1945 battle honour. She also served as an escort to liners operating as troopships, including the Cunarders *Aquitania*, *Queen Elizabeth* and *Queen Mary*, bringing thousands of American soldiers across the Atlantic Ocean.

Service in the Pacific

When the war in Europe ended on 8 May 1945 the 6th Destroyer Flotilla was detached to the Western Approaches Command and based on the Clyde. On 9 June, during astern angling trials, two of *Cavalier*'s torpedoes collided. One of them then struck the ship and damaged both port and starboard propellers. She was still able to steam but had to dock at Rosyth for repair. In June the flotilla was allocated to the British Pacific Fleet, but by the time *Cavalier*'s repairs were completed, on 18 August, the war with Japan was ending and her flotilla was ordered to relieve the 11th Destroyer Flotilla on the East Indies Station. She left the Tyne on 30 August for work up off Malta, and then proceeded to the Suez Canal. *Cavalier* arrived at Colombo on 29 September and then went to Trincomalee for fifteen days' shore leave. She sailed from there to the island of Java where, on 10 November, together with her sister ships *Caesar* and *Carron*, she bombarded Indonesian extremists' positions at Surabaya, before troops were landed to restore order. On 10 December *Cavalier* arrived at Singapore naval base for the first time. Two days later she was deployed with *Caesar* and *Carron* and the cruiser *Sussex*, to cover a convoy taking the 5th Indian Division to Surabaya.

In February 1946 *Cavalier* was in Force 64 (also including *Cumberland*, *Jamaica*, *Patroller* and *Termagant*) which sailed for Bombay because of a mutiny in the Royal Indian Navy and rioting in the city. Their task was to support British troops in restoring order. *Cavalier* then visited various ports on the west coast of India until 30 April when she sailed from Bombay for Singapore. She left Singapore for the United Kingdom on 20 May 1946, arriving at Portsmouth on 16 June to reduce to reserve. From September 1947 until June 1948 *Cavalier* was at Gibraltar for a refit.

BELOW HMS *Cavalier* arriving at Portsmouth in June 1946 flying her paying-off pennant.

Modernisation and Return to the Far East

Between 1955 and 1957 she was modernised at the John I. Thornycroft yard at Woolston, Southampton, and emerged with a new bridge, and two Squid anti-submarine mortars in place of the X gun, the 4.5-inch gun mounted on the after deckhouse. Her radar and gunnery-control director were also updated, and the after bank of torpedo tubes was removed to allow the shelter deck to be extended forwards. The light anti-aircraft armament was revised to give a single 40-mm Bofors gun on either side of the bridge and a twin 40-mm Bofors on the forward part of the shelter deck.

On 16 July 1957 she recommissioned at Southampton for service with the 8th Destroyer Squadron in the Far East, where she would replace HMS *Comus*. August was spent working up first at Portland, leaving there on 31 August for Malta and further working up. *Cavalier* passed through the Suez Canal on 13 October and, after calling at Trincomalee, arrived at Singapore on 31 October, where she was to be based as a unit of the Far East fleet. Her duties took her to Hong Kong, Saigon, Borneo, Fremantle, Melbourne, Hobart, Auckland and Fiji, before she was assigned for March and April 1958 to the Grapple Squadron off Christmas Island, where atomic bomb tests were taking place and her crew witnessed the explosion. In August *Cavalier* was sent to the Persian Gulf to relieve HMS *Cossack* and arrived at Bahrein on 5 September. She returned to the Hong Kong and Singapore area before paying off at Singapore where she docked on New Year's Day 1959.

Her crew was flown home and a new crew was flown out for the recommissioning ceremony on 4 January 1959. The following month she escorted and exercised with the Royal Yacht *Britannia* in the Malacca Straits during Prince Philip's Pacific voyage. Between March and June 1959 *Cavalier* was refitted in Singapore Dockyard. In August of that year she was guardship at RAF Gan, in the Indian Ocean, because of unrest on the island, and was back there in January 1960. Her normal routine of visits, exercises and short dockings or self-maintenance periods then resumed. This commission ended when she returned to Singapore on 13 May 1960 and her crew was flown home.

On 24 June 1960 she recommissioned at Singapore with a new crew, and from November 1960 to February 1961 the ship was once again in Singapore Dockyard for a short refit. In April she took part in SEATO's biggest exercise, Pony Express, involving sixty ships and 100 aircraft from six nations. *Cavalier*'s fourth commission ended when she returned to Singapore on 4 November 1961 to pay off.

The ship's fifth commission began when *Cavalier* was recommissioned on 11 December at Singapore. She was then involved in Exercise Jet in February and March 1962, followed by a visit to Aden. In June, in company with her sister ship *Carysfort*, *Cavalier* visited Korea and Japan. She was then in refit at Singapore from July to October 1962. On 8 December an armed rebellion against the formation of Malaysia broke out, and *Cavalier* was ordered to steam at high speed to Singapore. Here she embarked 180 troops of the Queen's Own Highlanders, Royal Marines and Gurkhas, plus Land Rovers, trailers and stores, her torpedo tubes being removed to create more space. On arrival in Labuan Bay off Brunei on the morning of 10 December she disembarked the troops and became a forward communications headquarters. Her crew also set up and guarded a prisoner-of-war camp for 400 rebels who had been taken prisoner. After four days the cruiser *Tiger* relieved her with a Royal Marines detachment.

Technical Details

Displacement:	1,710 tons★ (2,530 tons full load)
	★ *later revised to 2,106 tons*
Length:	363ft (110.64m)
Beam:	35ft 9in (10.90m)
Draught (full load):	14ft 6in (4.42m)
Machinery:	Two Admiralty 3-drum boilers, single reduction geared steam turbines, 40,000 shp, twin screws
Speed:	36 knots (32 knots full load) (maximum on original trials)
Range:	2000 miles at 22 knots
Armament:	(As built) 4 x 4.5-in, 2 x 40-mm, 6 x 20-mm guns; 8 x 21-in torpedo tubes; plus four depth-charge throwers
Armament:	(Post 1966 refit) 3 x 4.5-in, 2 x 40-mm guns; 1 x 4 Seacat missile launcher; 2 x Squid anti-submarine mortars
Complement:	186
Pennant No.s:	R73 (until 1948); D73

In January and February 1963 *Cavalier* was engaged as a search and rescue ship accompanying the Royal Yacht for the Queen's tour of the South Pacific. This entailed being positioned on the flight path of the royal aircraft in case of an emergency. On 6 March she left Auckland to return home, visiting Christmas Island, Pearl Harbor, San Diego, Manzahillo and El Salvador before transiting the Panama Canal. Then she was on patrols off the Bahamas and Haiti, crossing the Atlantic to arrive at Portsmouth on 26 May 1963 to pay off.

Further Modernisation and Far East Service

She entered reserve, first at Devonport, and then at Chatham. On 21 May 1964, while being towed by the RFA tug *Reward* from Chatham to Gibraltar for a long refit, *Cavalier* was in collision off Beachy Head with the 18,000-ton Liberian tanker *Burgen*, and was taken into Portsmouth for temporary repairs. Her tour of the royal dockyards continued as she was then towed to Devonport where a new 25-foot welded bow was fitted. Her Gibraltar refit finally began in August 1964. During this refit *Cavalier*'s remaining torpedo tubes and the twin 40-mm Bofors gun were removed and replaced by the Seacat anti-aircraft missile system (only one other C-class destroyer, *Caprice*, was so fitted).

On 24 January 1966 she recommissioned at Gibraltar with a trials crew. On completion of these trials *Cavalier* was then in care and maintenance for five months, the intention being to return her to reserve, but she was hurriedly reactivated on 15 September 1966 at Gibraltar to replace HMS *Jaguar*, which had broken down. *Cavalier* sailed with a passage crew on 22 September 1966 for Portsmouth, where she recommissioned and, after working up at Portland, joined the Home Fleet on 4 November. However, the Gibraltar refit had apparently not been very successful and *Cavalier* entered Devonport Dockyard to correct gunnery problems and many other faults. This docking period lasted until 7 April 1967. She remained in Plymouth until 22 May when she sailed first to Portland and later Portsmouth, where she commissioned for service with the 1st Destroyer Squadron in the Far East.

Leaving Portsmouth on 5 June, *Cavalier* sailed via the Cape of Good Hope because the Six Day War between Israel and Egypt had closed the Suez Canal. On 19 July off Mozambique, the ship began an eleven-day Beira Patrol, and was back again between 16 August and 10 September. These patrols were to reinforce sanctions against Rhodesia following that country's unilateral declaration of independence. She finally arrived at Singapore on 6 October. After a trip to Hong Kong and exercises off Gan with the aircraft carrier *Eagle*, *Cavalier* visited Australian ports in February and March 1968. She then crossed the Indian Ocean for a further Beira Patrol between 12 and 30 April 1968, while en route to the United Kingdom. Devonport was reached on 30 May 1968 and the ship joined the Western Fleet, with which she was engaged in major NATO exercises in the North Sea and the Mediterranean before returning to Devonport early in December 1968. On 3 January 1969 she sailed to take up guardship duties at Gibraltar and on 23 February paid off there.

Final commission

In March 1969 the destroyer began a refit in Gibraltar Dockyard, which was completed on 3 October. After visits to Mediterranean ports *Cavalier* left Gibraltar on 6 January 1970 for Portsmouth. The ship recommissioned at Portsmouth on 6 March 1970 for service in Home and the Mediterranean waters as part of the 4th Frigate Squadron (although *Cavalier* was still classed as a destroyer). On 8 September she was exercising with the carrier *Ark Royal* when she was ordered to stand by the coaster *Saint Brandon*, which was on fire in the Bristol Channel in heavy seas. The coaster's crew had been rescued by a trawler but, because of the weather, it was not until the morning of 10 September that *Cavalier* was able to send a boarding party in a Gemini – still in Force 10 winds – to connect a tow, and the salvaged ship was taken to Milford Haven. After this success, *Cavalier* was involved in a large North Sea NATO exercise, Northern Wedding, with 180 other ships. From 11 to 19 December she was again Gibraltar Guardship and spent Christmas at Malta and in January 1971 was part of Exercise Medtrain off Gibraltar. *Cavalier* was then in home waters, and in June and July was part of the Fishery Protection Squadron, some of her time being spent off Iceland.

BELOW Squid anti-submarine mortar on *Cavalier*.

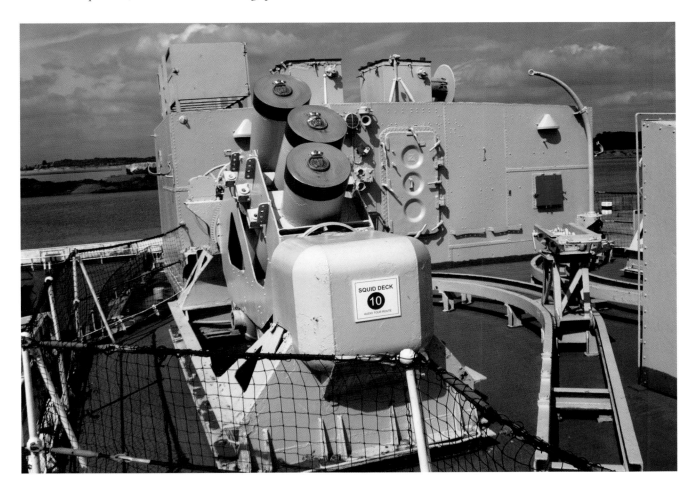

Now *Cavalier* embarked on an unusual adventure, a specially arranged speed trial against the frigate *Rapid*. The latter had also been built as an emergency fleet destroyer, of the R class, but postwar had undergone conversion to an anti-submarine frigate. She still retained her original steam turbine machinery and was thus a potential match for *Cavalier*. The two ships met on the morning of 6 July near the starting line off Peterhead for a race down the North Sea that made the national papers. *Rapid* took a slender early lead but a safety valve blew and *Cavalier* gradually made ground. For a time the two ships were steaming abreast of each other, with each ship creating a massive bow wave and the propellers throwing up great jets of water astern. Then *Cavalier* slowly edged ahead to win by thirty yards, after racing for two hours and covering seventy-four land miles at an average speed of 31.8 knots.

Cavalier returned to Gibraltar as guardship in September 1971 before participating in Exercise Deep Furrow in the eastern Mediterranean and Aegean the following month. Further duties and exercises in home waters ensued before she went back to the Mediterranean for guardship duties, exercises and a visit to Livorno in Italy from 24 April 1972. Her final operational months were spent in home waters, including a visit to Rotterdam until, on 6 July 1972, *Cavalier* sailed up the Medway with her paying-off pennant flying to pay off at Chatham for the last time. She had covered an estimated 564,140 miles during her career.

Preservation

After five years in reserve at Chatham the ship was sold to the HMS Cavalier Trust for £65,000 on 4 October 1977. She left Chatham under tow on 11 October and arrived at Portsmouth the following day. After docking for inspection she was handed over to the Trust on 21 October, and on that day left Portsmouth under tow of commercial tugs for Southampton. Here she was to become a floating museum dedicated to the Second World War destroyer. After repairs and modifications costing £150,000 *Cavalier* was opened to the public in August 1982. This phase was short-lived, however: low visitor numbers and the need to spend substantial further money to fully equip the ship as a museum led to her closure in October 1983. The following month she was towed to Brighton Marina and was again open to the public, but debts mounted and eventually in 1987 she was sold to South Tyneside Council for £70,000. Once again the ship was under tow in search of a viable future.

She languished on the Tyne for ten years as plans for a National Ship and Shipbuilding Exhibition Centre faltered. Some £205,000 was spent on maintenance work during this period. On 20 August 1997 South Tyneside Council accepted a bid from a Malaysian company, Star Cruises Properties, who wanted to display *Cavalier* alongside other warships in the Far East. For her UK supporters it was fortunate that this sale fell through, and on 20 January 1998 the National Lottery Memorial Fund came to the rescue with a grant of £830,000 so that the destroyer could be acquired, made seaworthy again, and taken to Chatham Historic Dockyard for preservation and exhibition. The HMS Cavalier (Chatham) Trust paid £43,350 to South Tyneside Council to take possession, and major renovation work was undertaken by Cammell Laird on the Tyne. On 14 May 1999 *Cavalier* left Tyneside under tow of the tug *Sun London* and arrived at Chatham two days later, her future now hopefully secured. She subsequently entered No. 2 dry dock, the site of the construction of HMS *Victory*.

Further support has been forthcoming from the Heritage Lottery Fund, Medway Council, public donations and Destroyer beer (which is brewed within Chatham Dockyard). Visitors can now tour the ship afloat in the dock, on a route that takes in many parts of the ship, including the weather deck, bridge and Squid deck, as well as many internal compartments such as messes, galleys and the operations room. As with all preserved ships there is a constant battle to maintain the ship in good condition.

Wellington

Imperial sloop that went to war

Built to serve in New Zealand but became a convoy escort in the war; now afloat on the Thames Embankment and open to the public on a few selected days each year

Design and Build

In the interwar years First World War sloops such as *Saxifrage* were replaced with new ships. The first of these was *Bridgewater*, one of fourteen sloops ordered for the Royal Navy between 1927 and 1931. They were intended for minesweeping duties in wartime but it became apparent that anti-submarine and anti-aircraft capabilities would also be required. Thus the *Grimsby* class, eight of which (including *Wellington*) were ordered for the Royal Navy between 1932 and 1935, were 16 feet longer to accommodate additional armament. The succeeding classes grew even larger, culminating in the very successful *Black Swan* class, of which *Whimbrel* has survived at Alexandria, Egypt, following her service as the Egyptian Navy's *Tarek*. These sloops were built in very modest numbers during the 1930s, because the emphasis was placed on fleet destroyer construction, a policy which contributed to the shortage of anti-submarine escorts at the outbreak of the Second World War.

Wellington was ordered in 1933, but unlike the other ships in the *Grimsby* class was named after a New Zealand coastal town rather than a British one, out of courtesy to the country where she was intended to serve. The *Grimsbys* had a heavier armament than the preceding sloops, most of them shipping two 4.7-inch low-angle guns (fore and aft), and the bridge was moved further aft to allow a shelter deck forward for a 12-pounder anti-aircraft gun. A multiple anti-aircraft machine gun (12.7mm) was also mounted, and during the war a second was added. Subsequently 20-mm Oerlikons replaced these anti-aircraft guns, and a Hedgehog anti-submarine mortar was mounted forward in place of the 12-pounder. As built, *Wellington* was fitted with minesweeping gear, but at the outbreak of war this was replaced by depth-charge rails and throwers.

The *Grimsbys* were built in Royal Dockyards and *Wellington* was one of four ordered from Devonport Dockyard. Laid down on 25 September 1933, she was launched on 29 May 1934 and began trials on 7 December.

Technical Details

Displacement:	990 tons (1,300 tons full load)
Length:	265ft (80.77m)
Beam:	34ft (10.36m)
Draught:	17ft 3in (2.21m); 10ft (3.05m) full load
Propulsion:	Single reduction geared steam turbines, 2,000 shp, two shafts; two Admiralty 3-drum boilers
Speed:	16½ knots (16 knots full load) (maximum on original trials)
Armament:	2 x 4.7-in guns, 1 x 12-pounder gun (later replaced by Hedgehog anti-submarine mortar), 4 x 12.7-mm AA guns (later replaced by six 20-mm AA guns); 2 x depth-charge rails and throwers (replaced original minesweeping gear)
Range:	5,700 nautical miles at 10 knots
Complement:	100 (wartime 131)
Pennant No.:	L65 (until 1940), U65

ABOVE *Wellington* in February 1935, showing her appearance as completed, with minesweeping gear aft.

On the New Zealand Station

On 24 January 1935 *Wellington* was commissioned at Devonport for service on the New Zealand Station, for where she left Devonport on 5 February. Her voyage to New Zealand was a leisurely one, calling at Gibraltar, Malta, Alexandria, Ismalia, Aden, Colombo, Singapore and Sydney, before arriving at her name port for a four-day visit in May. Finally she berthed at Devonport Dockyard in Auckland Harbour on 20 May. Also in harbour were the other three ships then serving on the New Zealand Station: the cruisers *Dunedin* and *Diomede* and the sloop *Leith*.

The station was probably the most popular overseas posting in the Royal Navy and the annual calendar for each ship included cruises around New Zealand and the South Pacific islands in the spring, summer and winter. *Wellington* left Auckland on 15 July 1935 for the first of these, a ten-week winter cruise, taking a circular track around the western part of the vast ocean. At her first port of call on Efate Island of the New Hebrides, she was directed to deal with a problem on the neighbouring Malekula Island: a mission teacher had been clubbed to death and, at the request of the district police, a party was landed at night to arrest the local chief and seven others. Following this incident the rest of the cruise to Naura (just south of the Equator), the Gilbert Islands, the Phoenix Islands, the Ellice Islands and the Fiji Islands, was less eventful. Duties at the various ports of call involved 'flying the flag' at public ceremonies, and engaging in harmless pursuits such as football matches with the islanders, inspection of a Boy Scout troop, and attending specially organised entertainments. Islanders made frequent gifts of fruit to the ship's company. On 21 September *Wellington* arrived back at Auckland, having covered 6,880 miles, with thirty days at sea and thirty-nine days in port during eleven calls at eight islands. A four-week spring cruise around New Zealand's North Island began on 2 October 1935, and on her return to Auckland the ship was dry-docked for her first annual refit.

Wellington's first summer cruise was a complete circuit of both North and South Islands of New Zealand, leaving Auckland on 6 January 1936. The cruise lasted 114 days, of which 100 were spent in port, and the ship returned to Auckland on 29 April. Her second winter cruise, for which she departed on 17 June 1936, concentrated on Fiji and those Pacific islands to its north and east, including Samoa, Cook, and Society Islands, before heading towards the Equator to visit eight more remote atolls. The most distant of these were the Fanning and Christmas Islands, both north of the Equator. After heading south again the sloop visited Danger Island and the Tokelau Islands, the Fiji Islands again, and finally the Tonga Islands. She arrived back in Auckland on 1 October, having steamed 9,992 miles during forty-five days at sea with a further fifty-five days in port. The spring cruise followed, from 21 October to 12 December, visiting seven ports in North and South Islands.

The 1937 programme began in January with a visit to Coromandel, near Auckland, and after seven weeks back in Auckland the ship undertook four weeks of port visits in New Zealand and exercises with other ships on the station, including the newly arrived *Achilles* (which had relieved *Diomede*). *Wellington*'s third cruise to the South Sea Islands began on 4 May 1937 and involved taking a party of scientists from Suva, the capital of Fiji, to Canton Island, just south of the Equator, to observe the eclipse of the sun at the beginning of June. The scientists were then returned to Apia, the capital of Western Samoa, and the sloop proceeded to visit the Tokelau Islands, the Cook Islands, and Moorea and Tahiti in the Society Islands. She arrived back in Auckland on 31 July and was dry-docked for her annual refit and bottom cleaning and painting, these latter two tasks being undertaken by the crew. *Wellington* left Auckland on 20 August for her name port where she received a new crew, which had arrived from the United Kingdom on a scheduled sailing of the New Zealand Shipping Line's *Rangitane*.

ABOVE *Wellington* as the headquarters ship of the Honourable Company of Master Mariners on the Thames Embankment.

The Second Commission

Wellington was recommissioned in Wellington on 26 August 1937 for further service on the New Zealand Station. After a period of working up and local courtesy visits the ship embarked on her spring cruise (virtually a repeat of that carried out in 1935), on 26 October, returning to Auckland on 25 November.

In January 1938 a visit was made to Canton Island, a round trip of 2,240 miles, to exchange radio operators at the shore station there, and *Wellington* also landed stores at Hull Island for the only European resident. Once back in Auckland the ship completed a short refit and in March was on minesweeping exercises with *Leith*. In the following month there was gunnery practice with the cruisers *Achilles* and *Leander* (which had replaced *Dunedin*). This burst of warfare activity was perhaps associated with the worsening international climate, which threatened to end the idyllic existence of the New Zealand Station's ships. On 27 April *Wellington* and *Leith* left Auckland for Cockatoo Island dockyard at Sydney, where worn shaft bearings were replaced on both ships. From there both vessels sailed direct on their planned winter cruises in the south-west Pacific islands, with *Wellington* leaving on 13 June for Suva. She sailed north to the Phoenix Islands, and a wireless transmission mast was erected on Hull Island, where a hole was blasted in the coral reef to allow ships' boats to enter the lagoon and land supplies. Heading for remote atolls the sloop crossed the Equator to visit Washington, Fanning and Christmas Islands, and then – south of the line – Malden and Starbuck Islands, before returning to Suva on 17 July. In the second part of the itinerary visits were made to the Santa Cruz Islands and the Gilbert and Ellice group. Returning to Fiji the sloop called en route at the isolated Rotumah Island, where the crew watched a dance in the morning, followed by a talk, a football match and lunch with the native islanders. *Wellington* berthed at Auckland on 9 September, ending a cruise of eighty-eight days, having covered 10,360 miles and visited twenty-one ports in six different groups of islands. The spring cruise from 25 October to 28 November took her clockwise around South Island, followed by eleven weeks alongside at Auckland.

In 1939 the normal summer cruise was foregone for a return visit to Cockatoo Island, arriving there on 24 February, where – once again with *Leith* – the shaft bearings were checked. The two sloops then engaged in anti-submarine exercises with ships of the Australian Station. After their return to Auckland on 6 April the two sloops spent a week on gunnery practice in the Hauraki Gulf and a further week of sea training with a detachment of the Royal New Zealand Navy Volunteer Reserve (RNZVR). Despite the international tension engulfing Europe, a twenty-week winter cruise was planned to cover New Caledonia, the New Hebrides, Solomon Islands, the Gilbert and Ellice group, Fiji, Eastern Samoa, and the Society, Friendly and Cook Islands. *Wellington* left Auckland on 18 May and covered the western section of the cruise to arrive in Eastern Samoa in mid-August. She left there on 19 August, heading east-north-east on the four-day passage to Penrhyn Island. Two days into that voyage she received orders to return to Auckland 'with despatch', and arrived on 30 August (some five and a half weeks earlier than originally planned). She was to be redeployed to the Atlantic for convoy escort duties, but first proceeded to Singapore.

Atlantic Convoy Escort

Leaving Auckland for the final time on 3 September 1939, *Wellington* arrived at Singapore on 19 September to spend six weeks with *Leith* patrolling the Malacca Straits. She left Penang on 2 November for Freetown, Sierra Leone, passing through the Suez Canal on 23 November. Eight days were spent at Malta for boiler repairs before reaching Freetown on 16 December, from where she left two days later escorting a homebound convoy (SL13). On 3 January 1940 *Wellington* attacked a submarine contact off Ushant, without a conclusive result. On 7 January she docked at Cardiff for depth-charge rails and throwers to be fitted on the quarterdeck, replacing saluting guns and the minesweeping gear, and to be camouflage painted; ASDIC was also probably fitted at this time. As part of the Western Approaches 1st Escort Division she then spent four months escorting convoys in the east Atlantic and south to Gibraltar. The shortage of suitable ships meant that she was sometimes the only escort for a convoy. In June she assisted with the evacuation from France of the British Expeditionary Force, taking troops from the beach at Veulette and the harbour of St Valery-en-Caux. Fire was exchanged with shore batteries and tanks, during which *Wellington* sustained some minor damage.

After one further Gibraltar convoy duty the ship was redeployed to Liverpool to join the Western Approaches Sloop Division. For thirteen months from July 1940 to August 1941 *Wellington* operated from her Gladstone Dock base, again escorting Gibraltar and east Atlantic convoys. On 1 October she picked up 169 survivors in ship's boats from the torpedoed Royal Mail liner *Highland Patriot*, which had been returning independently from the River Plate. On 8 November 1940 *Wellington* was damaged in collision with the SS *Sarastone* while escorting Convoy HX43 and was under repair at Liverpool until the end of that month. A refit at Dundee in February and March 1941 probably included the fitting of radar. On 6 June of that year she rescued the complete crew of Hogarth's *Baron Lovat*, torpedoed by an Italian submarine off Cape St Vincent. On 14 July the sloop left Liverpool for the last time, escorting a convoy to Freetown; on her return she was detached to Londonderry to join the Londonderry Sloop Division on 27 August 1941.

Wellington was based at Londonderry for the next twenty-three months until 14 July 1943. The relentless programme of convoy duty continued and, although unable to confirm a submarine sinking, the ship was a constant deterrent to the U-boats and aircraft that shadowed or attacked her convoys, fighting them off in a series of exhausting encounters, coping with false alarms, and surviving the worst weather that the North Atlantic could throw at her. Until October 1942 she remained on the United Kingdom-to-Freetown convoy route, with a refit break for nearly two months at Belfast in March to April 1942, when the more modern Type 291 radar replaced the Type 286, and 20-mm guns were added. On 18 July 1942 she rescued the crew of the torpedoed merchant ship *Lavington Court* and carried out a depth-charge attack on the U-boat without result.

In October 1942 the Freetown convoys were suspended for five months so that the escorts could be used to support Operation Torch, the landings of British and US forces in North Africa. On 14 October *Wellington* joined the 42nd Escort Group, based at Londonderry, which at that time also included the sloops *Weston* and *Folkestone*, the frigate *Waveney*, the cutters *Gorleston* and *Totland*, and the corvette *Azalea*. *Wellington* was part of the escort for two North Africa convoys in each direction to and from Algiers. On 1 February 1943 she arrived at

Convoy Duty

Griff Williams joined *Wellington* at Cardiff in January 1940 as an ordinary seaman, after six months' new entrant training at HMS *Drake*, Plymouth. He described their first convoy duty, in which *Wellington* was the only escort.

Over thirty merchant ships assembled at Falmouth and when *Wellington* arrived they 'were milling around, squeezing into pre-arranged positions, hooting angrily at each other and belching smoke. Before dark, this mass of shipping, strung out over five miles of sea, was on the move. In the lead, like Christ leading his flock across the desert, was the *Wellington*. There was not another warship in sight. We looked at each other uncomfortably, the same unspoken thought on everyone's mind. Someone seemed to have more faith in us than we did ourselves.'

With the convoy arranged in five lines astern of the sloop the ships steamed out into the Atlantic. It was early in the war and none of them seemed to know anything about station keeping or darkening ship. 'After much cussing and pointing, the *Wellington* abandoned her role as head scout and steamed down between the lines of ships, using her loud hailer to pointedly tell each of them which lights she was showing.' The convoy steamed on at 7–8 knots, supposedly the speed of the slowest ship. As dawn was thought to be the most dangerous time *Wellington* went to action stations well before daylight. 'Everyone aboard was involved in that, which was hard luck on those who had completed the middle watch and had only just turned in.' As dawn broke it could be seen that some ships had fallen well behind, showing only their smoke above the horizon astern. The convoy then started zig-zagging in response to flags hoisted by the convoy commodore.

The ASDIC was constantly pinging and there were many 'contacts', usually false alarms ... then came one dead ahead and *Wellington* responded. 'Up went her attack flag, a large black flag that could not possibly be mistaken for anything else. Her siren, a screeching devil of a thing that would start low and finish on a higher note with each blast, would warn the convoy of what was about to happen ... When the commodore fired his signal rockets they would turn away from the danger area, leaving it clear for the warship to attack.' *Wellington* by then had both engines full ahead and was at action stations. A diamond pattern of five depth charges was dropped. Before the final charge had rolled over the stern the first would be exploding. 'The ship would jump like she had been kicked up the backside. Showers of soot would burst out of the funnel and galley chimney. To those below deck each explosion sounded like a mass of sledge hammers pounding on the ship's side ... and we would hear crashes as anything that wasn't secured carried away.'

'Only the people on the bridge and the gun crews would see any of this action, as the depth charge party, usually the anti-aircraft gunners, would be far too busy feeding charges to the dropping point on the rails, or struggling to reload the throwers in time for the next pattern ... Sometimes, at full speed and full rudder, she would lean over so far that the low side of her quarterdeck would be forced under water. Foaming sea would boil over everyone and, as it subsided, there would be a quick head count to make sure that no one was missing as the work of reloading was resumed.'
(Adapted from: G. J. Williams, *HMS Wellington, One Ship's War*, The Self-Publishing Association, 1992)

Sheerness for her annual refit, during which a Hedgehog anti-submarine mortar replaced the 2-pounder gun, and additional 20-mm guns were added to strengthen her anti-aircraft capability. By now – to deal with the additional armament and other equipment – her complement had increased to eleven officers and 120 ratings, making her accommodation even more cramped. After recommissioning with a Chatham crew she left Sheerness on 10 April for Londonderry, and helped escort two more North Africa convoys in each direction.

Coastal Convoy Duty

By 1943 large numbers of more modern escorts had joined the fleet and *Wellington* was redeployed to West Africa coastal convoys, leaving Londonderry for the last time on 19 June. En route she escorted a convoy bound for the assault landings in Sicily, before detaching at Gibraltar to take a small Freetown convoy south. On 14 July she arrived at Freetown and was assigned to the West Africa command for the next eighteen months; her main duties during this period were to escort coastal convoys between Freetown and Lagos, Nigeria, sometimes calling at Takoradi (in the Gold Coast). On 18 August 1943 she attacked a U-boat with depth charges and claimed a sinking but this was not confirmed, and postwar records show that the U-boat must have escaped.

An annual refit at Bermuda between 8 May and 29 July 1944 provided a welcome diversion for the crew, after which the sloop returned to West Africa coastal convoys until being assigned to the Mediterranean Fleet in December 1944. Leaving Freetown on 30 December she escorted the floating dock AFD24 under tow to Gibraltar before joining the 55th Escort Group, based at Gibraltar, on 8 January 1945 for a period of six months. On 9 May, five days after the German capitulation, she received the surrender of *U541* at sea and escorted the U-boat into Gibraltar. As a rather obsolete escort *Wellington* was not destined to serve in the Pacific war, and arrived home at Devonport on 17 June. After de-storing at Liverpool she arrived at Pembroke Dock on 6 August 1945 to join the reserve fleet, and remained there for eighteen months. She had steamed 66,367 miles in four years of peace and 248,586 miles during her war service, escorting 103 convoys.

Headquarters Ship

On 6 February 1947 she was transferred to the Honourable Company of Master Mariners, which had purchased her to become their headquarters ship or livery hall. She was converted at Chatham Dockyard for this role: her engines and boilers, armament, ship's boats, radar etc, were removed and the interior altered substantially. A Court Room and Lounge now occupied the engine and boiler room space, while the commanding officer's accommodation on the fo'c'sle deck became a committee room and clerk's office. On the lower deck a museum and reception area was created, and this contains many fine ship models, pictures and other merchant-ship artefacts such as the wheel and bell from *Ohio*, the first tanker to enter harbour after the siege of Malta. A library and writing room were formed on the upper deck. A magnificent teak staircase over two decks was saved from the Isle of Man steam packet *Snaefell*, and the Court Room oak panelling came from Shaw Savill Line's *Themistocles*. Externally the ship was painted white with a primrose-coloured funnel.

On 9 December 1948 *Wellington* berthed at Temple Stairs on the Victoria Embankment, where she still lies – just upstream of *President*. Flying the Red Ensign, she is known as HQS (headquarters ship) *Wellington* and is maintained in very good condition: she has left the Embankment on three occasions to be dry-docked and refitted. Her livery hall role is augmented by commercial activity as a conference venue and office facility. Each year the ship is open to the public on a number of days. In 2004 she was granted World Ship Trust status and in 2005 became part of a charitable trust, The Wellington Trust, to help secure her long-term future as a permanent maritime memorial.

Alliance

Submarine built for the Pacific War

Last remaining large British submarine of First World War design; open to the public as a museum exhibit out of the water at Gosport

Design and Build

The A-class submarines were designed in the First World War for the war in the Pacific, but were completed too late to see action. Larger than the preceding wartime classes, they were faster on the surface and had a longer range. A deeper diving depth – of at least 500 feet – was required and, to help achieve this, the pressure hull was circular throughout its length. The first boat completed, *Amphion*, dove to 600 feet with no problems. Also to suit the Pacific conditions, the class was fitted with an air-conditioned compartment, which drew air from the rest of the pressure hull and recirculated it after it had been reduced in temperature and humidity, and – if necessary – adjusted for carbon dioxide and oxygen content. To speed up construction they had an all-welded hull which was prefabricated in sections and welded together on the ways. This significantly reduced the number of man hours involved when compared with the construction of the earlier T class. Forty-six boats were ordered in 1943 but only eighteen were launched before the war ended; of these, two were scrapped incomplete and the other sixteen were all completed and commissioned.

Alliance was ordered from Vickers-Armstrong at Barrow on 7 April 1943, and launched on 28 July 1945. She was completed on 14 May 1947 and later that year undertook a record dive, staying submerged for thirty days and covering 3,193 miles between Gibraltar and Freetown, Sierra Leone. This was accomplished with the use of her snort – a tube which drew air into the hull from the surface, allowing the use of her diesel engines and obviating the need to surface to recharge her batteries. She was thus able to stay submerged at periscope depth for as long as her stores lasted, which was about two months.

The snort was developed from the schnorkel that had been fitted to German U-boats. One of the A class, *Affray*, left Gosport on 16 April 1951 with seventy-five men aboard and reported at 2115 that she was diving south of the Isle of Wight, but was not heard from again. Two months later she was found lying in forty-three fathoms of water, thirty-seven miles south of St Catherine's Lighthouse. The snort was salvaged and was found to have fractured, leaving a 10-inch hole in her pressure hull, but the cause of the fracture was not discovered.

Originally *Alliance* was fitted with ten torpedo tubes (six bow and four stern), a 4-inch gun forward of the conning tower and a 20-mm gun on the rear end of the conning tower. Mines (which were torpedo shaped for exit through the tubes) could be carried instead of, or as well as, torpedoes. When she was modernised in the late 1950s the guns were removed and the number of torpedo tubes reduced to six. Her appearance was greatly changed: the hull was streamlined, a larger streamlined conning tower was constructed of aluminium, and a large sonar dome was fitted above the bow. The new shape improved her underwater speed by

2 knots and made her much quieter. A higher battery capacity gave the boat more endurance when fully submerged: patrolling at 2½ knots, she could remain submerged for up to thirty-six hours before the batteries needed recharging and the air became foul.

Early Service History

During the era of *Alliance*'s service the Royal Navy maintained a worldwide submarine presence, with squadrons in Malta, Halifax (Canada), Sydney (Australia) and Singapore, as well as at the home bases of Gosport, Devonport and Rothesay (later relocated to Faslane). *Alliance* served in five of these locations. Her first commission was with the 3rd Submarine Flotilla at Rothesay. During this commission she completed her epic underwater trial in the tropical waters between the Canary Isles, off which she submerged on 9 October 1947, and Sierra Leone, surfacing off Freetown on 8 November. The purpose of the cruise was to obtain information about the living conditions on a submarine during an extended snort patrol. On 13 December *Alliance* arrived back at Portsmouth for shore leave.

She was paid off in December 1948 to refit at Chatham and recommissioned in September 1949, joining the 2nd Submarine Flotilla at Gosport. She was based at Gosport for the next seven years, from July 1951 being part of the 5th Submarine Flotilla (which was renamed the 5th Submarine Squadron in January 1952). During this period, which included three refits at Portsmouth in 1950, 1953 and 1955, her service was in home waters, with occasional visits to the Mediterranean.

On 5 September 1956 she left Gosport to join the 6th Submarine Squadron at Halifax, Nova Scotia, replacing *Ambush*, and served there until February 1958. *Alliance* arrived home at Gosport on 5 March 1958, rejoining the 5th Submarine Squadron there for three months before entering reserve at Gosport in the following June.

Modernisation and Later Service

In September 1958 she was taken in hand at Devonport for her major refit and modernisation. She recommissioned in April 1960 for the 3rd Submarine Squadron at Faslane, transferring to the 2nd Submarine Squadron at Devonport seven months later. In February 1962 she started a twelve-month refit at Chatham, returning to Gosport in February 1963 as part of the 1st Submarine Squadron based there.

This stay at Gosport was short, for she left on 28 May 1963 for Singapore, via Dakar, the Cape of Good Hope, Durban and Aden, to join the 7th Submarine Division – arriving there on 10 October. This was an active period of confrontation with Indonesia to prevent incursions into Malaysia, and the Royal Navy's forces in Singapore were considerably augmented. In 1965 she was used to test a new camouflage paint scheme in the Far East. *Alliance* left Singapore on 9 June 1965, having been replaced by *Oberon*, and after calling at Aden, Malta and Lisbon, arrived at Devonport on 15 July. There she was taken in hand for a refit which was completed in August 1966, when she rejoined the 1st Submarine Squadron at Gosport for a full commission.

On 12 January 1968 when returning to her base from exercises in the English Channel she went aground on the Bembridge Ledge, off the Isle of Wight, at 2000. It was a clear night with good visibility, but her navigating officer apparently confused the brighter light on one navigation buoy with the duller light on a nearer buoy that he should have been aiming for. Some of the crew were taken off by helicopter. The boat was refloated thirty-six hours later by tugs and salvage vessels, and was undamaged. In February 1969 she entered Chatham Dockyard for her final refit, emerging in April 1970 for sea trials before being commissioned at Chatham on 9 May to join the 2nd Submarine Division at Devonport. Between October and December 1970 she was in the Mediterranean, and took part in Exercise Lime Jug. In August and September 1971 she visited Norway and exercised with the aircraft carrier *Ark Royal*. On 29 September 1971 *Alliance* was damaged by a battery explosion while alongside at Portland; one chief petty officer lost his life and fourteen other ratings were injured. She returned to Devonport for repairs. Her final service was in NATO exercises in the North Atlantic and Mediterranean in January and February 1973, when she also visited Lisbon, Funchal (in Madeira), Gibraltar and Tangier, before returning to Gosport on 14 March to pay off.

Preservation

From November 1973 until December 1976 she replaced *Tabard* as the static harbour training submarine at HMS *Dolphin*, Gosport, being subsequently replaced herself by *Grampus* in December 1976. On 28 February 1978 she was transferred on permanent loan to the Royal Navy Submarine Museum at Gosport and an appeal was launched for her preservation. In August 1979 she was towed to Southampton to have her hull strengthened by Vosper Ship Repairs Ltd prior to preservation. On a high spring tide on 17 March 1980 the submarine was floated on to concrete blocks, which were then raised a few feet by vertical hydraulic rams, permanently lifting her out of the water. Preservation work was then undertaken and *Alliance* became the centrepiece of the museum when, on 24 August 1981, she was opened to the public.

Visitors can walk through the length of the hull on a guided tour which gives an excellent insight into life aboard a Cold War conventional submarine of the 1960s and '70s, in conditions similar to those experienced by crews in the Second World War. Alongside *Alliance* is a memorial to the 4,334 British submariners who lost their lives in both world wars and to those officers and men lost in peacetime submarine disasters. *Alliance*'s main significance is as the sole surviving RN submarine (apart from midget submarines) of Second World War design, albeit incorporating postwar modifications. The last opportunity to preserve a British submarine in near original war-time condition had been lost in 1967 when *Tally Ho!* (which had an impressive war record) left Portsmouth Harbour for the breakers.

Technical Details

Displacement:	1,120 tons standard, 1,380 tons full load (surface), 1,620 tons submerged
Length:	281ft 9in (85.88m)
Beam:	22ft 3in (6.78m)
Draught:	16ft 9in (5.11m)
Machinery:	Two sets Vickers-Armstrong 8-cylinder supercharged diesel engines, 4,320 bhp (total) giving a surface speed of 19 knots; two sets English Electric electric motors, 1,250 shp (total), powered by 224 battery cells, giving a submerged speed of 8 knots (10 knots following modernisation); twin screws
Range:	12,200 nautical miles at 10 knots surfaced; 16 nautical miles at 8 knots, or 90 nautical miles at 3 knots fully submerged.
Safe diving depth:	500ft
Fuel capacity:	215 tons
Armament:	(After modernisation) Six 21-inch torpedo tubes (four forward and two aft); carried ten reload torpedoes
Complement:	68 (5 officers and 63 ratings)
Pennant No.s:	P417 (to 1948), S17 (to 1961), S67 (1961 onwards)

X-craft

Second World War midget submarines

Attacking *Tirpitz*

The X-craft were designed to penetrate protected harbours in order to place explosive charges and limpet mines against the hulls of enemy vessels. In one of the most famous exploits *X6* and *X7* inflicted heavy damage to the German battleship *Tirpitz* in a fjord in Northern Norway, and the remains of *X7* can be seen alongside the postwar midget submarine *Stickleback* at Duxford. Two other X-craft, *X24* and *XE8* have survived intact.

For operations X-craft were manned by a passage crew and towed to the vicinity of their target area by a larger submarine. For most of the passage the X-craft remained submerged, only surfacing to ventilate the boat at regular intervals. Then, when approaching the vicinity of the target, the operational crew – comprising captain, first lieutenant, engineer and diver – would take over. The craft had a wet and dry chamber allowing for the egress and recovery of the diver to clear or cut through obstructions (such as defensive nets) and attach limpet mines to the side of the enemy vessel. The boats also had large curved side charges (bombs with time fuses) attached to their hulls that could be released from inside the hull to be set on the seabed under the target ship's hull. Each charge contained nearly two tons of explosive. The craft then withdrew to rejoin the mother submarine. Many X-craft crews received decorations for gallantry, including four Victoria Crosses – but losses were high.

OPPOSITE *XE8* and *XE9* alongside in 1949 (when they had apparently been taken out of reserve for exercises).

X24

Mini-sub that penetrated German defences and disabled a floating dock; on display ashore at Gosport

X24 is a Second World War midget submarine that carried out two successful operations on the Norwegian coast.

Built in 1943–44 as one of the six units of the *X20* class, *X24* was in action the following year in Operation Guidance and was the only unit of her class to undertake a mission in enemy waters. After carrying out dummy attacks on the Scapa Flow defences she left Balta Sound in the Shetlands on 11 April 1944 under tow of the submarine *Sceptre* to attack the Lakesvaag floating dock at Puddle Fjord, near Bergen. This dock was regularly used by U-boats and was believed to be capable of taking the crippled *Tirpitz*. After diving off Kalvenhoes Light at 0230 on 13 April, *X24* laid charges at what was thought to be each end of the floating dock,

Technical Details – X24

Displacement:	(Without charges) 27 tons (surface), 29.5 tons (submerged)
Length:	51ft 7in (15.73m)
Beam:	5ft 9in (1.75m)
Draught:	5ft 9in (1.75m)
Propulsion:	One Gardner diesel engine, 42 hp, and single electric motor, 30 hp, single shaft
Speed:	6½ knots (surface, with charges), 4½ knots (submerged)
Range:	With charges: 1,320 nautical miles at 4 knots (surface), 80 nautical miles at 2 knots (submerged); without chaarges: 1,860 nautical miles at 4 knots (surfaced)
Bunkers:	1 ton of oil fuel
Armament:	2 x 3,570 lb. charges of Amatol high explosive, plus limpet mines
Complement:	4

however she was actually beneath the freighter *Bahrenfels* which was lying nearby. The freighter was sunk and the adjacent coal wharf badly damaged, remaining out of action for the rest of the war. *X24* successfully withdrew, though since she had been submerged for nineteen hours her crew was in very bad shape, suffering from lack of oxygen and carbon-dioxide poisoning; even when they surfaced and fresh air rushed into the boat, two of the crew were violently sick – as is not uncommon under these circumstances.

During the summer King George VI visited Scapa Flow and carried out an inspection of *X24*. The attack on the Lakesvaag floating dock was repeated under Operation Heckle later that year, with *X24* leaving Rothesay on 3 September 1944 – again under tow of *Sceptre*, with the small submarine depot ship *Alecto* in company – and arrived at Balta Sound on 6 September. *Sceptre* left there the following day, towing *X24*, for the Norwegian coast. The weather deteriorated until, on the night of 8 September, a full gale was blowing and *Sceptre* and *X24* went down to 120 feet. Unfortunately, *X24*'s sub-lieutenant was lost overboard during the passage and a substitute had to be transferred to her. The X-craft entered Puddle Fjord on the morning of 11 September and commenced her attack at 0810. This time *X24* inflicted major damage to the floating dock, destroying four of its six sections, and also damaged two ships. In each of these actions the respective commanding officers of *X24* were awarded the Distinguished Service Order (DSO) while *X24* herself was awarded the battle honour Norway 1940–45.

Like *Alliance* and other conventional submarines *X24* was powered by diesel and electric engines; the same Gardner diesels also powered London buses. Although cramped and uncomfortable, these boats were quite sophisticated, with most of the features found in regular-sized submarines. Many of the X-craft were prefabricated inland by a precision engineering firm with no shipbuilding experience. In *X24*'s case this was Marshall, Sons & Co. Ltd, in Gainsborough, after which she was assembled at Barrow early in 1944. After trials she joined the 12th Submarine Flotilla at HMS *Varbel*, Port Bannatyne, Kames Bay, in Bute, and was given the unofficial name *Expeditious*. Training for the first operation was undertaken from Edrachilliz Bay, Sutherland, where the depot ship *Bonaventure* provided specialist support for X-craft. On 22 March 1944 she was at Scapa Flow and on 9 April *Alecto* escorted *Sceptre* as she towed *X24* to Balta Sound for Operation Guidance.

Technical Details – *XE8*

Displacement:	30.25 tons (surface), 33.5 tons (submerged)
Length:	53ft 3in (16.23m)
Beam:	5ft 9in (1.75m)
Draught:	5ft 9in (1.75m)
Propulsion, armament and complement: as *X24*	

X24 was in reserve before the end of the war, and was placed on the disposal list in 1950 at HMS *Dolphin*, Gosport. She was later moved to a more sheltered site to await a verdict on her future. Following surveys it was decided in January 1972 to restore her for display at *Dolphin* as a memorial, and on 14 February 1973 the craft was transported by road to Portsmouth Dockyard where she was fully restored before returning to HMS *Dolphin* for display. In 1987 she was transferred to the Royal Navy Submarine Museum, Gosport, and is the only X-craft on display anywhere that saw operational service in the Second World War. In 2004 she was renovated for exhibition as the centrepiece of the new Fieldhouse Building at the museum.

XE8

Mini-sub built for Far East service; now on display ashore at Chatham

Also Second World War-built, XE8 was one of twelve craft designed for operations in the Far East. For this reason she had air-conditioning and was slightly larger than *X24* and the other earlier X-craft. She was prefabricated by Thomas Broadbent & Sons, Huddersfield, and assembled at Barrow in 1945. Many of the X-craft were given unofficial names by their crews; *XE8* was known as *Expunger*. On completion she undertook acceptance trials and working up, even though by then it was clear that she would not need to be deployed to the Far East. A number of her class did see action: *XE3* and *XE1* severely damaged the Japanese cruiser *Takao* in the Johore Strait, and *XE4* cut seabed telegraph cables in Saigon harbour.

XE8 was the last X-craft at HMS *Varbel*, which paid off on 14 May 1945. On that day *XE8* moved to Rothesay Bay where she joined the 7th Submarine Flotilla for a week and was then taken by rail to HMS *Dolphin* at Gosport to be laid up alongside four other units of her class. In 1953 she was deleted but was used in the 1955 film *Above Us the Waves*, as an X-craft in the attack on *Tirpitz*. Later she was used as an underwater target off Portland. Raised in 1972, she was taken to the Imperial War Museum site at Duxford. After restoration *XE8* was loaned to Chatham Historic Dockyard in 1990, where she is on display under No.6 Covered Slip.

BELOW The preserved *X24* on display at Gosport.

Coastal Forces
Motor torpedo boats, motor gunboats and motor launches

By 1936, with the increasing prospect of war, the Royal Navy was again investing tentatively in coastal forces and a number of motor torpedo boats (MTBs) were built by the British Power Boat Co. (BPB) at Hythe, on Southampton Water. Vosper, at Portsmouth, responded by building as a speculative venture an experimental MTB of 68-foot length, which, before being armed, achieved 48 knots on trials. Once fully armed and loaded she achieved 44 knots, and proved her seaworthiness in winds of Force 7. This led to her being purchased by the Admiralty as *MTB 102*, and signalled the start of the extensive programme of MTB development and construction by Vosper during the Second World War. The Admiralty ordered some seventy-five Vosper 70- or 71-foot MTBs in 1939 and 1940. A further sixteen were ordered in 1942, followed in 1943 and 1944 by around twenty-eight of the slightly larger and improved 73-foot design. Meanwhile BPB concentrated on motor gunboats (MGBs) and built 113, mostly 70- and 72-foot; some of these were completed as MTBs.

Technical Details – MTB 102

Displacement:	32 tons (loaded)
Length:	68ft (69ft 6in including trailing rudders)
Beam:	14ft 9in
Draught :	3ft 3in
Machinery (original):	3 shaft, Isotta-Fraschini petrol motors, 3,450 bhp. (As built was also fitted with two Vosper V8 auxiliary petrol engines, for manoeuvring at slow speed)
Speed:	43¾ knots
Armament:	1 x 20-mm gun (later varied), 2 x 21-in torpedo tubes
Bunkers:	990 gallons of petrol
Range:	240 nautical miles at 35 knots, 1,100 nautical miles at 9 knots
Complement:	10 (2 officers and eight ratings)
Pennant No.:	102

MTB 102

Prototype motor torpedo boat that served at Dunkirk; restored as a seagoing vessel, based at Lowestoft, often open to the public at various maritime festivals

Two of the Vosper MTBs have been restored. One of these is *MTB 102*, the original Vosper prototype, which had been launched in May 1937 and was commissioned into the Royal Navy on 26 May 1938. Her petrol engines were built by Isotta-Fraschini of Milan, Italy, and developed more than twice the power of the Napier Lion engines used in the early BPB craft. Originally *MTB 102* was fitted with a single torpedo tube in her bow, which was subsequently supplemented by a frame for stern launching a second torpedo, but following trials this combination was replaced by two 21-inch tubes on the side decks at a seven-and-a-half-degree angle to the centreline. In early 1938 she carried a trial 20-mm Oerlikon gun abaft the superstructure, and later (after her return from Dunkirk) a twin 12.7-mm machine gun was mounted in this position. In 1941 light 7.6-mm machine guns were added, mounted forward on stanchions.

After purchase by the Admiralty she was attached to HMS *Vernon* at Portsmouth for further torpedo trials and modification, and this experience provided the basis for the design of the torpedo-launching equipment on all of the Royal Navy's wartime MTBs. In August 1939 the boat was at the Reserve Fleet Review in Weymouth Bay. In March 1940 *MTB 102*, with *MTB 100*, was being used at HMS *Hornet*, Gosport, as the 3rd MTB (Training) Flotilla, providing basic sea training for the early intakes of supplementary reservists appointed to coastal forces. On 26 May 1940 *MTB 102* received orders to proceed to Dover at all speed. At this time she had no gun mounted, so the crew borrowed four Vickers 7.6-mm machine guns from HMS *Vernon* and rigged them aft of the superstructure in a turret between the torpedo tubes. After arriving at Dover at 0700 on 27 May the boat was ordered to Dunkirk, and during the evacuation of the British Expeditionary Force *MTB 102* crossed the Channel eight times. She towed boats packed with soldiers off the beach to destroyers and other ships lying offshore, rescuing several hundred from the coast towards La Panne. When the destroyer *Keith* was bombed by a Stuka, the commander in charge of naval operations, Rear Admiral Wake-Walker, was transferred to *MTB 102* along with his staff officers and two wounded crewmembers. Wake-Walker used her as his flagship for the last two nights of the operation, directing the incoming and outgoing vessels at Dunkirk from the bridge. A rear-admiral's flag was improvised from a dishcloth and red paint, and *MTB 102* was the third to last vessel to leave the scene when, on 4 June, the admiral directed the last of the evacuation from the bridge of the boat.

By late 1942 *MTB 102* was obsolete and on 21 January 1943 was transferred to the Army for target towing and named *Vimy*. Operated by the Royal Army Service Corps (RASC), she was based at the Gunwharf, Portsmouth. In 1944 she carried Winston Churchill and General Eisenhower on their review of the ships assembled on the south coast in preparation for the D-Day landings. She was returned to the Royal Navy at Poole on 14 March 1945 and was listed for disposal on 25 October of that year. In 1948 she was sold to become a motor cruiser

ABOVE The restored *MTB 102* on her way to Ramsgate in 2005 with other Dunkirk Little Ships, after celebrating the 65th anniversary of the evacuation.

ABOVE *MTB 71* on display at Duxford.

on the east coast. Then, in 1973, while under conversion to a houseboat, she was acquired by the Blofield and Brundall Sea Scouts at Lowestoft and converted into a static headquarters ship. Luckily, she was to find a role in the 1976 film *The Eagle has Landed*, for which she underwent restoration to full seagoing state, before being returned to the scout group. The hull and decks received further repairs and reinforcement in 1983 and 1990. She has been re-engined with diesel engines four times, most recently in 2002. In April 1996 she was handed over to the MTB 102 Trust and is now based at Lowestoft, but frequently attends maritime heritage and similar events at other ports during the summer.

MTB 71

Motor torpedo boat that was engaged in North Sea and Channel skirmishes for three years; now a museum exhibit ashore at Duxford, Cambridgeshire

MTB 102's original success led Vosper to gain orders for MTBs from Romania, Greece, Norway and Sweden, though with the outbreak of war the Admiralty requisitioned most of the craft under construction. They included *MTB 71*, a 60-foot boat that had been ordered by the Royal Norwegian Navy as their *MTB 7*, the keel having been laid down by Vosper on 28 July 1939. As fitted out for the Admiralty she was armed with two 18-inch torpedoes and twin machine guns, and also had Isotta Fraschini engines – giving a top speed of 39 knots. Completed on 2 July 1940, she joined the 11th MTB Flotilla at HMS *Wasp* in Dover. The flotilla's work included night-time anti-E-boat patrols and crash-boat duties (picking up ditched fighter pilots and survivors from merchant ships sunk by the enemy). Two months later she was damaged during a heavy air attack on Dover, suffering a fire

Technical Details – *MTB 71*

Displacement:	25 tons
Length:	60ft
Beam:	15ft
Draught:	3ft 6in
Machinery:	2 Isotta-Fraschini V-12 petrol motors, 2,200 bhp, 2 shafts
Speed:	35 knots
Armament:	2 x 12.7-mm machine guns, 2 x 18-in torpedo tubes
Complement:	10 (2 officers and 8 men)
Pennant No.:	71

in her wheelhouse, and repairs at Whitstable took four months. In June 1941 she was slightly damaged in action with enemy escort vessels off Étaples and her petty officer stoker was killed. The next month, in further action off Berck Buoy, she was holed below the waterline and was out of action for two months while under repair on the Thames.

In November 1941 she recommissioned with a Royal Norwegian Navy crew – to join the 1st MTB Flotilla at HMS *Beehive* in Felixstowe – and had a skirmish with E-boats off Kwinte Bank. In February 1942 she reverted to a Royal Navy crew and was in the Dover Straits, participating in the search for the German *Scharnhorst*, *Gneisenau* and *Prinz Eugen* during their daring Channel Dash on 12 February. *MTB 71* was recorded as being damaged that day by shellfire and was then under repair at Brightlingsea for six months. In September 1942 she transferred to the 4th MTB Flotilla at Felixstowe and was in action off the Hook of Holland two months later.

In June 1943 she paid off and, like *MTB 102*, was transferred to the Army. She was laid up by the RASC at Portsmouth and cannibalised for spares for her sister ship *MTB 72*, which had also been taken over by the Army. Then, in September 1944, she was returned to the Navy at HMS *Hornet*, Gosport, and sold the following year for use as a houseboat, *Wild Chorus*, at Birdham. Following the death of her owner, Mr Pudney, in 1992 she was acquired by Hampshire County Council in conjunction with the MTB 71 Group Charitable Trust. She underwent partial restoration within Portsmouth Dockyard and was on display there at the 1999 Festival of the Sea, before being moved to the British Military Powerboat Trust's yard at Marchwood for further restoration as a static exhibit. In April 2005 she was taken to the Imperial War Museum's site at Duxford, Cambridgeshire, where she is displayed in a hangar. Another former Vosper boat, *MTB 219*, is a houseboat at Chelsea.

MGB 81

Motor gunboat involved in combat operations for nearly three years; now based at Buckler's Hard, Hampshire, and seagoing; not open to the public

The British Power Boat Company (BPB) at Hythe near Southampton also became a prolific builder of motor torpedo boats and motor gunboats during the war. Initially they concentrated on MGBs and one of these, *MGB 81*, has been restored to seagoing condition. Her design was produced by BPB in collaboration with the Director of Naval Construction. Like the Vosper craft she was a 'short' boat, with a hard-chine hull form using double diagonal mahogany sides and a triple diagonal mahogany bottom. She had a hogged sheer deck and a streamlined wheelhouse, bridge, chartroom and wireless office on deck, unlike later boats that were more like the Vosper MTBs in superstructure.

Ordered on 27 November 1940, *MGB 81* was not laid down until 16 December 1941, the delay probably being due to capacity at the yard. She was virtually complete at launching on 26 June 1942 as she underwent trials on 8 July, achieving a speed of 38.63 knots on Southampton Water. Later on BPB trials, following the fitting of underwater exhausts, a speed of 43.43 knots was made. Her Packard petrol engines were manufactured in Detroit.

She was accepted and commissioned on 11 July 1942 and then worked up at HMS *Bee*, Weymouth, before joining the 8th MGB Flotilla at Dartmouth in August 1942. Between then and September 1943 *MGB 81* was involved in six actions. Off Guernsey on the night of 13/14 August 1942 she

Technical Details – *MGB 81*

Displacement:	46.6 tons
Length:	71ft 6in
Beam:	20ft 6in
Draught :	5ft 9in
Machinery (original):	Three shafts, Packard petrol motors, 3,750 bhp
Speed:	40 knots
Bunkers:	2,733 gallons of petrol
Range:	475 miles at 35 knots, or 600 miles at 15 knots
Armament:	1 x 2-pounder AA gun, 2 x 20-mm AA guns, 2 x 7.6-mm machine guns, two depth charges (2 x 18-in torpedo tubes added as *MTB 416*)
Complement:	12
Pennant No.s:	81 (to 1943), 416

engaged in a close-range gun attack on two enemy armed trawlers, with one trawler sustaining severe damage. The next month the flotilla moved to Felixstowe, and *MGB 81* was soon in action off the Hook of Holland on 14/15 September, when two enemy motor vessels were damaged by gunfire and four armed trawlers were hit, with no damage to the MGBs. In another action off Holland on 2/3 October four enemy armed trawlers were engaged, and one of the flotilla, *MGB 78*, was lost. On 27/28 February 1943 the MGBs fought the escorts of a German convoy off the Hook, resulting in the sinking of *MGB 79*, and damage to *MGB 81* caused by a shell hitting the engine room. In April 1943 the flotilla returned to Dartmouth, though *MGB 81* was refitting at Brightlingsea from 29 April to 20 May. In June 1943 she was damaged in collision with *MGB 115* and was repaired by BPB at Poole. On 11/12 September she again sustained damage when fired on by shore batteries at Cap la Hague and spent the rest of that month being repaired at BPB's Poole yard.

In late September 1943 the boat was renumbered *MTB 416* and her designated armament was increased to reflect her new role, with the addition of two 18-inch torpedo tubes. Even though they were given the MTB classification, a number of the former MGBs were not fitted with torpedo tubes, and it is not certain if this was the case on *MTB 416*. Her flotilla became the 1st MTB Flotilla, which was redeployed to Ramsgate for a short period in October 1943 before returning to Dartmouth. *MTB 416* was refitted at Poole by BPB between 5 January and 2 March 1944. Her first recorded action as an MTB was in Lyme Bay on 21/22 April when she engaged enemy E-boats and sustained action damage. Repairs were again made at Poole but she was back in action for the Normandy landings, where she was involved from 6 to 30

June 1944. During that time her base became Gosport. On the night of 23/24 June she was involved in an attack on a German convoy leaving Cherbourg. Although *MTB 416* was only backing up this operation one of her crew was killed. On the night of 18/19 July she obtained hits on German R-boats off Cap d'Antifer but her hull was damaged by gunfire and she returned to Poole again for repairs. In September 1944 the flotilla's base changed to Lowestoft and her next action was on 14 February 1945 at Ostend.

On 5 March 1945 a decision was made to lay her up in Category C reserve at Poole and she paid off there on 27 April to be taken in hand by BPB for de-equipping. On 2 October 1945 she was approved for disposal and was later sold. Little is known about her subsequent history until 1958, when her crew were arrested by customs officers at Shoreham while on a smuggling operation. She was sold by the Admiralty Marshal to a Gosport scrap dealer who removed her engines and running gear. Later she was used as an accommodation ship for a sailing school at Hardway, Gosport, and named *Jolly Roger*. In 1964 she was sold to become the houseboat *Cresta*, also at Hardway. In 1984 she was towed to Bursledon on the River Hamble, and in 1988 was bought by Guy Webster to be restored to her wartime appearance. On 17 September 1998 she was bought by Phil Clabburn for the British Military Powerboat Trust at Marchwood, where she was reconstructed between 1999 and 2002. Three 1,000 BHP V12 MAN turbocharged diesel engines were fitted, giving an estimated top speed of 45 knots. *MGB 81*'s base is now Buckler's Hard, near Lymington.

In 2007 another BPB craft, *MTB 486*, was the subject of a restoration project. She was on the River Itchen as the houseboat *Sungo* and was acquired by the Coastal Forces Trust to be shipped to Lake Ontario for restoration. Her wartime service had been with the Royal Canadian Navy.

HSL 102

Fast RAF air-sea rescue launch that rescued ditched airmen from the sea; now based at Lymington, Hampshire, and seagoing, she is sometimes seen at maritime festivals and similar events

In 1935 the first motor torpedo boats were ordered by the Admiralty from the British Power Boat Co. at Hythe, and a similar hard-chine planing hull was used for a class of twenty-two air-sea rescue launches ordered for the Royal Air Force from BPB. The RAF's Air-Sea Rescue Service, in which these boats served, was to be credited with saving the lives of 10,000 airmen during the Second World War – from ditched aircraft, both Allied and German. In such work, speed was of the essence, since the airmen in the sea were vulnerable to hypothermia and were often wounded.

HSL 102, the only survivor of this BPB class, was launched in 1936 and entered service the following year. Of mahogany double diagonal construction, she was powered by three Napier Sea Lion petrol engines. During the Battle of Britain she was mostly based at Blyth, Northumberland. In two months in 1941 she rescued thirty-eight aircrew from the North Sea, including the crews of two German bombers. As a result King George VI and Queen Elizabeth inspected the ship in July 1941. When working off Calshot she was damaged by a Messerschmitt 109 and her radio operator was killed. In 1943 she was transferred to the Royal Navy for target towing, and paid off in 1946.

She became a houseboat in Mill Creek at Dartmouth and was in a sorry state when acquired by Phil Clabburn for restoration. The extensive work needed was carried out by Powerboat Restorations at Fawley between 1993 and 1996. Three six-cylinder 420 bhp Cummins diesels were installed, giving a top speed of about 38 knots. On 5 July 1996 Queen Elizabeth the Queen Mother relaunched *HSL 102* at Fawley. The vessel is now based at Lymington, Hampshire.

Technical Details – *HSL 102*

Displacement:	46.6 tons
Length:	71ft 6in (21.8m)
Beam:	20ft 6in (6.25m)
Draught:	5ft 9in (1.75m)
Propulsion (as built):	3 x 500 BHP Napier Sea Lion petrol engines, three shafts
Speed:	40 knots
Fuel bunkers:	950 gallons (4,300 litres)

ML 1387 (Medusa)

Versatile small ship that took part in the D-Day landings; based at Southampton and sometimes open at maritime festivals elsewhere

A large class of harbour defence motor launches (HDML) was built in the Second World War for patrol work in harbour, estuarial and inshore waters. The Admiralty design was for a round bilge 72-foot launch, and was kept simple so that they could be built by small yards at home and abroad. They proved sea-kindly craft and the success of the design led to them being used worldwide in every theatre of operation. One vessel, *HDML 1387*, has survived to be restored to seagoing condition, after her service as a survey launch had extended her Royal Navy career into the 1960s.

The HDML hull was constructed of double diagonal mahogany planking on stringers with oak frames. The decks were double diagonal larch (or mahogany on earlier vessels) and the superstructure was of marine ply. They were diesel powered and carried an armament of light anti-aircraft guns and depth charges. The choice of guns was often dictated by availability, and variously included 3-, 2- and 1-pounders, 20-mm Oerlikons and 7.6-mm machine guns. Four hundred and ninety-four boats were ordered, but thirty-two were cancelled and twenty were lost while under construction due to bombing or the fall of Singapore.

Laid down by R. A. Newman at Hamworthy, Poole, on 27 July 1943, *ML 1387* was launched on 20 October and commissioned on 29 December of the same year. On completion she joined the HDML (Foreign Service) pool at Poole, but rather than serving overseas she was involved in convoy escort in the Western Approaches before joining the 149th HDML Flotilla at Portsmouth in spring 1944. She took part in Exercise Fabius 1, a practice assault carried out by the Americans at Slapton Sands in Devon. In June 1944 *ML 1387* was present at the D-Day landings, arriving off Omaha beach the night before and staying on station as a navigational marker for Approach Channel 4. In October 1944 she transferred to the 185th Auxiliary Minesweeping Flotilla based at Sheerness. Early in 1945 she was at the Dutch coastal town of Ijmuiden where she took the surrender of the occupying German forces. From Ijmuiden she navigated the North Sea Canal to Amsterdam, the first Allied ship to do so.

In September 1945 she was refitted at Shoreham. In 1946 she was renumbered *FDB 76* (fast despatch boat) and attached to the Cardiff University Naval Division for training. Then in 1947 she was transferred to Severn Division RNVR for two years, providing seagoing training. In 1949, renumbered *SDML 3516* (seaward defence motor launch), she was moved to London Division RNVR in the same capacity and then took the name *Thames*, the first in a line of vessels to take this name as a seagoing tender to that division. In November 1950 she was refitted and offered to the Persian government to replace another launch that had been damaged beyond repair en route to Persia, but the offer was refused.

In 1952 she was refitted at Chatham to become a survey motor launch, but retained the same number. Between 1952 and 1955 she was attached to the Survey Training Unit, Chatham. In 1956–57 the launch undertook independent surveys on the west coast of the Uniyed Kingdom, and between 1958 and 1960 was part of the East Coast Survey Unit. In March 1959 she was in collision with a Dutch coaster off Ramsgate in fog, which required a three-month refit. In March 1960 *SDML 3516* transferred to the Plymouth Command for surveys on the west and south coasts, and in 1961 was renamed *Medusa*. On 30 November 1965 she paid off for disposal at Devonport and while in reserve suffered fire damage.

Technical Details – *ML 1387*

Displacement:	46 tons standard (54 tons full load)
Length:	72ft
Beam:	16ft
Draught:	4ft 9in
Propulsion:	Two Gardner diesel engines, 320 bhp, two shafts
Speed:	12 knots
Bunkers:	1,650 gallons
Armament:	1 x 2-pounder and 1 x 20-mm Oerlikon guns (later two 20-mm Oerlikon guns), twin 7.6-mm Vickers machine guns, up to eight depth charges *(Now mounts two 20-mm Oerlikons)*
Complement:	12
Pennant No.s.:	ML1387 (1943–45), FDB 76 (1945–49), P3516 (1949–61), A353 (1961–68)

ABOVE The restored
ML 1387 leaving Portsmouth
in May 1991.

Sold on 29 May 1968 to Mr Mike Boyce, she was restored – retaining her survey motor launch appearance – at Portland between 1972 and 1985, but remained seagoing for much of this time. In 1986 she was moved to the Solent area to become a museum ship and was refitted to her original HDML appearance. Based at Southampton, she is now under the care of the Medusa Trust and is operated in seagoing condition by volunteers from the Medusa Support Group. In 2006–08 *Medusa* underwent a major restoration and refit at Hythe Shipyard on Southampton Water, with the support of a £1m grant from the Heritage Lottery Fund. The vessel was stripped down to bare frames, some of which were replaced. The hull was re-planked with triple teak, replacing double mahogany, and the vessel was re-decked. The engines, which date from 1940 and 1942 (having been fitted in a 1963 refit), were completely overhauled. However, in a fire at the shipyard on 30 October 2007 various valuable equipment and irreplaceable artefacts were lost and the engines severely damaged, delaying completion of the work. The hull of *Medusa* was nearby in a temporary shelter and was not damaged.

A number of other HDML have survived in private ownership to be listed in the National Register of Historic Vessels (May 2007), their names and locations being: *Lewina* (ex-*ML 1305*), at Faversham; *Vincent* (ex-*ML 1300*), at Belfast; *Pride of the Dart* (ex-*ML 1396*), at Torbay; *Morning Wings* (ex-*ML 1309*), at Upton on Severn; *Sarinda* (ex-*ML 1392*) at Liverpool. *Medusa*'s sister ship as a survey launch, *Meda*, formerly (*ML 1301*), was still extant in 2007 – being for sale at Gibraltar under the name *Gibel Tarik*. Around thirty others probably survive worldwide, according to data from the Medusa Trust. Of all the surviving HDMLs only about six are seaworthy.

chapter 8: the postwar navy

Reconstruction of the Royal Navy after the Second World War began in the 1950s, and was largely dictated by the Soviet threat of the Cold War period. The large Russian submarine fleet was to be countered with boats such as the *Oberon*-class patrol submarines and the nuclear submarine *Courageous*. Midget submarines such as *Stickleback* were even designed to lay nuclear mines as a riposte to a similar development by the Soviets. Also surviving from this era are the guided-missile destroyer *Bristol*, intended to protect new large aircraft carriers that were never built, and the Royal Yacht *Britannia*.

HMS Bristol

Prototype large destroyer

Guided-missile destroyer that served in the Falklands; afloat and in commission as a static training ship in Portsmouth harbour; not open to the public

Anchored off Whale Island in Portsmouth Harbour, *Bristol* is still in commission and serves as a Harbour Training Ship with a crew of about forty-three officers, ratings and civilian staff.

Design and Build

A Type 82 destroyer, *Bristol* was the prototype of a class designed in the mid-1960s to escort a new class of aircraft carriers. Due to defence cuts the new carriers were never built, and three planned *Bristol* sister ships were also cancelled. *Bristol* was ordered in October 1966 from Swan Hunter at Wallsend-on-Tyne, laid down on 15 November 1967 and launched on 30 June 1969. At the time she was the largest ship classified as a destroyer to be built for the Royal Navy, though she has since been eclipsed in size by the new Type 45 class. She acted as trials ship for her new weapon systems and radar for the first three years of her career. The new Sea Dart air-defence missile system was the centrepiece of the ship's armament, while for anti-submarine warfare she carried the Australian Ikara missile-borne torpedo system and a Limbo mortar. She had a 4.5-inch gun for shore bombardment. A landing deck (but no hangar) was provided aft for a small Wasp helicopter.

Like the preceding 'County' class she was powered by combined steam and gas turbines, the former venting through her forward funnel and the latter through the twin after funnels. This machinery was, however, larger than in the Counties – thus losing any benefit of standardisation. The bridge structure was to be topped by the massive dome of the new Anglo-Dutch Type 988 radar, but this was supplanted at the design stage by the 'double bedstead' Type 965, with which she entered service. Later this gave way to the somewhat smaller Type 1022. Two domed Type 909 radars were provided fore and aft for Sea Dart target tracking.

Service History

Bristol was accepted into service on 15 December 1972. During early trials her steam plant failed and for many

Technical Details

Length:	507ft (154.5m))
Beam:	55ft (16.76m)
Draught:	17ft (5.18m)
Displacement:	6,300 tons
Propulsion:	Two AEI steam turbines in tandem with two Rolls Royce Olympus gas turbines, giving combined maximum output of 74,600 shp, twin screws
Speed:	30 knots
Range:	5,000 miles at 18 knots
Original Armament:	One twin Sea Dart anti-aircraft missile launcher, one Ikara anti-submarine homing torpedo launcher, one 4.5-in gun, one Limbo anti-submarine mortar. Two 20-mm and two 30-mm guns were later added. Now disarmed.
Original Complement:	407 (29 officers and 378 ratings)
Pennant No.:	D23

months she operated on gas turbines alone. On 1 November 1974 at Milford Haven she was damaged by fire in the stea-turbine and boiler compartment. During a refit between 1976 and 1978 her steam plant was repaired and two 20-mm anti-aircraft guns were fitted. Her first operational commission commenced in 1980 when she became flagship of the 3rd Flotilla. Equipped to act as a Flagship and Command and Control headquarters for a Task Group, she served as such in the later stages of the Falklands War in 1982.

Leaving Portsmouth on 10 May 1982, she led the first reinforcement group, which included the destroyer *Cardiff*, the frigates *Active, Avenger, Andromeda, Minerva* and *Penelope*, and the RFA's *Olna* and *Tidespring*. They reached Ascension Island on 18 May and joined the Carrier Battle Group off the Falklands on the night of 25/26 May, by which time the Falklands had been retaken. On 1 July *Bristol* replaced *Invincible* as flagship of the Task Force, until relieved in this role by *Illustrious* on 27 August. Although not directly engaged in the war, *Bristol* was awarded the battle honour Falklands Islands 1982. She arrived back at Portsmouth on 17 September and at the end of 1982 entered Portsmouth Dockyard for a refit when two 30-mm guns were shipped.

Bristol was at sea again in 1983, spending short spells overseas – including Canada and the United States in May 1984. On 17 July 1984 the ship suffered a boiler explosion while in Plymouth Sound and three sailors were injured. Shortly afterwards she was taken in hand at Portsmouth for a major refit, during which her now obsolete Ikara anti-submarine missile system was removed. In February 1986 the ship started post-refit trials at Portsmouth, and in March and April was working up at Portland. On 5 May 1987 *Bristol* entered No. 15 Dock at Portsmouth for conversion to a cadet training ship. She was fitted with a deckhouse to accommodate 100 cadets and replaced the 'County'-class destroyer *Fife* as flagship of the Dartmouth Training Squadron, offering sea training for officer cadets. *Bristol* remained available to act as a flagship during exercises and for her primary air-defence role if required.

Static Training Ship

She paid off in July 1991 and her guided-missile systems and guns were removed. On 7 May 1993, *Bristol* recommissioned to replace the 'County'-class destroyer *Kent* as a harbour training and accommodation ship at Portsmouth for the Royal Navy, RNR, National Cadet Forces and youth organisations. Built to a very high standard, her wide passageways and roomy mess decks are ideal for the large number of trainees who pass through her every year. The mess decks (dormitories) and cabins can sleep about 460 and in a typical year (2001) more than 5,000 RN personnel and 12,000 youths were trained aboard her.

ABOVE HMS *Bristol* arriving at Portsmouth from the Falklands in September 1982.

PREVIOUS PAGES
The Royal Yacht *Britannia* overtakes HMS *Surprise* (in the foreground) leaving Tobruk for Malta, 1 May 1954.

Oberon Class: Ocelot and Onyx

Cold War submarines

Patrol submarines that served in the Falklands War and the first Gulf War; now on display and open to the public at Chatham and Sassnitz (Germany)

OPPOSITE *Ocelot* is launched at Chatham, 5 May 1962. This was Cup Final day but the launch still attracted a large crowd.

These two submarines were members of the *Oberon* class, one of the most successful conventional submarine designs produced since the Second World War. Thirteen boats were built for the Royal Navy, as well as three for the Royal Canadian Navy, six for the Royal Australian Navy, three for Brazil and two for Chile. Most boats of the class gave very long service, the Royal Navy boats lasting until the early 1990s: the first boat to be completed, *Orpheus*, served for thirty-two years in the Royal Navy, and the Chilean boats were not paid off until about 2005. By the time the boats were decommissioned the warship preservation movement had become established, and submarines are always popular exhibits. In consequence no fewer than seven boats have been preserved. Of the British boats, *Ocelot*, *Onyx* and *Otus* have survived as museum ships, as have HMAS *Ovens*, which is at Fremantle in the Western Australian Maritime Museum, HMAS *Onslow* at the National Maritime Museum in Sydney, HMCS *Onondaga* at Rimouski, Quebec, and the Brazilian *Riachuelo* at the Submarine Museum in Rio de Janeiro.

Design

The Royal Navy's postwar submarine building programme began in earnest with the eight boats of the *Porpoise* class (though two earlier experimental boats had been built). The design was based on experience gained with the rebuilt boats of the T and A classes, such as *Alliance*, war-built boats that had undergone streamlining and modernisation in the 1950s. The *Oberon* class was a closely related development of the *Porpoise* class, and differed in having glass reinforced plastic panels as part of the conning tower (or fin) construction. Both classes were notable for being exceptionally quiet, much quieter than their American contemporaries. In most respects the design was evolutionary rather than especially innovative. Diesel engines and electric motors provided the propulsion, while the armament comprised eight torpedo tubes, though some boats were later modified to fire the sub-surface-launched Harpoon anti-ship missiles.

The *Oberons* were able to dive to significantly deeper depths than the *Porpoises*, due to improved steel quality for the pressure hull and refinements to the design. Both classes were products of the Cold War, during which the Soviet Navy built up a huge submarine force. Anti-submarine warfare was therefore the primary intended role of the British submarines, though they could also be used as minelayers and for attacks against Soviet merchant ships in the Arctic

and possibly the Baltic and Black Seas. Other roles included reconnaissance and supporting covert special-forces operations, while in peacetime they were mainly engaged in training surface forces in anti-submarine warfare.

The first twelve of the Royal Navy's *Oberons* entered service between 1960 and 1964. The thirteenth boat, *Onyx*, was transferred to the Royal Canadian Nay while under construction, becoming HMCS *Ojibwa*. A replacement British boat was ordered, taking the original name of *Onyx*, and was not completed until November 1967.

Ocelot

Ocelot was laid down on No. 7 Covered Slip at Chatham Dockyard on 17 November 1960, the fifty-fourth submarine to be built there and the last for the Royal Navy. Her pressure hull was built in large prefabricated circular sections, which were welded together on a set of middle-line keel blocks. On 5 May 1962 the ship was launched by Lady Saunders, wife of Admiral Sir Thomas Saunders, Director General, Dockyards and Maintenance. *Ocelot*'s diesel engines were also built at Chatham Dockyard, while her electric motors, like those of the other Royal Navy boats in the class, were by English Electric.

She was commissioned on 31 January 1964 and joined HMS *Maidstone* and the 3rd Submarine Squadron at Faslane on 1 February. *Ocelot* was in home waters until leaving Faslane on 30 July for the Mediterranean, including Gibraltar and Malta, returning to Faslane on 30 September 1964. From late October to early November she was back in Gibraltar, carrying out test torpedo firings. In January 1965 she took part in Exercise Tight Lines with eleven other RN submarines, and in May of that year was involved in Exercise Red Knight with five other RN submarines, including *Dreadnought*. After further service in home waters she again went to the Mediterranean between September and December 1966.

In February 1967 *Ocelot* entered Rosyth Dockyard for a refit that was to last until March 1968. On 29 March 1968 she recommissioned at Rosyth for the 1st Submarine Squadron at Gosport, but first went to Faslane for working up and exercises in the Clyde area. She arrived at Gosport on 13 June 1968, and served there, remaining largely in home waters, until March 1972. During January 1971 she joined seven other RN submarines, including *Warspite*, in Exercise Vendetta. While alongside *Artemis* at Gosport on 1 July 1971 the A-class boat began to sink, trapping three ratings on board. A successful rescue operation was mounted, involving the submarines *Ocelot*, *Otus* and *Walrus*, the mooring vessel *Goldeneye* and the tug *Boxer*, and all personnel were recovered without injury.

On 4 April 1972 *Ocelot* re-entered Rosyth Dockyard for a long refit, emerging in January 1974 to rejoin the 1st Submarine Squadron, Gosport. After working up at Faslane from 28 February she arrived at Gosport on 20 June 1974, and remained within home waters for ten months. From April to July 1975 she was on Exercises Trainex and Marcot in the North Atlantic and Caribbean, and visited Bermuda, Halifax (Nova Scotia) and New London (United States). The remainder of 1975 was spent in home waters, except for a visit to Haugesund, Norway, in September. In June and July 1976 she was at Gibraltar for exercises, but the rest of that year was spent in home waters, with the exception of one visit to Aarhus, Denmark.

There are then gaps in her service history. On 28 June 1977 *Ocelot* and nine other *Porpoise-* and *Oberon*-class boats attended the Silver Jubilee Fleet Review at Spithead. On 7 May 1985 she started a refit at Rosyth. In late 1989 she was

Technical Details – *Oberon* Class

Displacement:	1,610 tons (standard), 2,030 tons (surface), 2,410 tons (submerged)
Length:	295ft 3in (90.00m)
Beam:	26ft 6in (8.08m)
Draught:	18ft (5.49m)
Propulsion:	Two 3,680 bhp Admiralty standard range diesels, two 6,000 bhp electric motors
Speed:	12 knots (surface), 17 knots (submerged)
Range:	9,000 miles at 10 knots (surface), 40 hours at 4 knots (submerged)
Diving depth:	800–900ft
Armament:	8 x 21-inch torpedo tubes (6 bow, 2 stern); 24 torpedoes carried. Boats serving in the Far East carried one deck mounted 20-mm Oerlikon gun
Complement:	69 (7 officers and 62 men)
Pennant Nos.:	*Ocelot* S17, *Onyx* S21, *Otus* S18

with the 3rd Submarine Squadron, Faslane, and was involved in some unnamed operations, after which she visited Chile, the Bahamas and Florida, returning to Rosyth in January 1990 for docking and repair of essential defects. In February 1991 she again crossed the Atlantic, visiting St Thomas and St Croix in the Caribbean and then Bermuda before returning to the United Kingdom. *Ocelot* was finally paid off on 6 September 1991, and was sold to Chatham Historic Dockyard Trust for £90,000 on 5 May 1992. She is now on display there in No. 3 Dry Dock, and is open to the public.

ABOVE *Onyx* at Birkenhead, alongside the frigate HMS *Plymouth*, as part of the Warship Preservation Trust Collection. Astern of her is the minehunter *Bronington*.

Onyx

Onyx, the last conventionally powered submarine to be built for the Royal Navy, was laid down on 16 November 1964 by Cammell Laird at Birkenhead, and launched on 18 August 1966. She was commissioned on 29 November 1967 for service with the 3rd Submarine Squadron (and its depot ship *Maidstone*) at Faslane, where *Onyx* arrived on 2 December. During her first commission she visited twelve foreign ports in seven European countries and fourteen ports in the United Kingdom. In April 1968 – after visiting Lisbon, Portugal – *Onyx* conducted trials with the standard submarine immersion escape suits in Loch Fyne, during which five experienced divers escaped from the boat while she was moving through the water at a speed of 3 knots, and then fourteen volunteers from her crew successfully escaped while *Onyx* was on the bottom at 150 feet. Previous tests conducted in the Mediterranean had already proved that escapes from a depth of 500 feet were possible but there were worries that it might not

be possible to escape from a submerged submarine if it sank in a strong tideway. These concerns might have been prompted by the loss of HMS *Truculent* in 1950 when many of her crew escaped from the submarine but were swept away on the strong ebb tide and drowned.

Between June and September 1968 *Onyx* was involved in Exercises Polar Ice, Russle and Silver Tower. She also carried out live test firings of the new Mark 24 Tigerfish guided torpedo before it entered service. The following year was spent in home waters except for a brief visit to Gibraltar in August. In September she took part in Exercise Peacekeeper with the carrier *Eagle* and two other submarines, while November brought Exercise Vendetta with six other RN submarines. A similar pattern continued for 1970, with visits to Fredrikshavn and Aarhus in Denmark, Gibraltar, and Kristiansand, Norway, and Exercises Danish Blue and Vendetta. On 3 January 1972 she commenced a refit at Portsmouth Dockyard.

Her second commission began in October 1973 when she joined the 1st Submarine Squadron at Gosport. In June 1974 she was in Exercise Square Dance with four other British submarines, and in October was in the Mediterranean in an unspecified covert operation. The following year was fairly routine and spent mostly in home waters, except for a visit to Gibraltar in February following Exercise Springex. In June and July 1976 *Onyx* was in the United States for the bicentennial celebrations and visited ports in Portsmouth and Portland (United States) and St Johns (Canada). This commission ended in October 1976 when *Onyx* entered Portsmouth Dockyard again for a refit, which lasted until 30 January 1978.

Her third commission was with the same squadron at Gosport, and she again saw some

ABOVE *Ocelot* on display in No. 3 Dock at Chatham Historic Dockyard.

Oberons in Trouble

13 June 1969: While submerged two miles off the Ayrshire coast HMS *Onyx* is caught in the nets of the trawlers *Wisteria* and *Watchful*. *Onyx* surfaces to inspect her conning tower and periscope, but they are undamaged. The trawlers' nets are damaged beyond repair.

5 Sept 1969: The French trawler *Pointe de Barfleur* catches HMS *Onyx* in its nets about 20 miles north-north-east of Cherbourg. The trawler faces some resistance when hauling up its nets. A flare is seen shooting up and then the submarine breaks the surface. After some explanation the two boats go on their own way.

Early August 1970: HMS *Ocelot* is carrying out practice torpedo firing in the Clyde exercise area when one of her torpedoes goes astray and skids up a beach, stopping short of a green on the Bute golf course, Kingarth, with its motor still running.

3 July 1979: HMS *Onyx* requires assistance to free herself from the fishing nets of a stationary trawler off Holy Island in the Firth of Forth.

13 May 1980: HMS *Onyx* runs aground in Portsmouth Harbour, it takes a tug twenty minutes to pull the boat free.

16 July 1988: The 78-foot racing yacht *Drum* collides with the partially surfaced HMS *Otus* in the middle of the night as it makes its way round the Mull of Kintyre. The *Drum* suffers a serious gash on the port side, but is able to make it to Crinan at reduced speed. *Otus* makes contact on the radio twenty minutes after the incident offering assistance.

service in the Mediterranean. In 1981 she supported the anti-submarine training of surface warships at Portland and in the following year she sank the old frigate *Rapid* as a practice target. Next, *Onyx* was deployed to the Falklands as the only conventional submarine in the task force that was sent to retake the islands from the Argentinians.

After her return from the Falklands *Onyx* resumed the usual routine of exercises, Portland training of anti-submarine forces, 'Perisher' courses for trainee commanding officers, and showing the flag – this time in Denmark and Holland. In 1983 she sank another old frigate, *Hardy*, as a target. Then in August 1983 she entered Rosyth Dockyard for a refit. Recommissioning on 23 November 1985, she returned to the 1st Submarine Squadron at Gosport. In 1987 *Onyx* returned to the Falklands for South Atlantic patrols, part of a five-and-a-half-month deployment. During this deployment she rounded Cape Horn to Valparaiso for a six-day informal visit. Then the submarine went north and through the Panama Canal to the Caribbean. In 1988–89 she was refitted at Portsmouth. In 1990 *Onyx* was operating out of Halifax, Nova Scotia, helping to work up Canadian and American warships off the Canadian coast, returning to Gosport in December of that year. She was at sea for just one more week, supporting training at Portland, before berthing at Gosport for the final time on 14 December 1990 to pay off.

Onyx was now surplus to requirements and in October 1991 was sold to the Warship Preservation Trust for display at Birkenhead where she arrived in November. In February 2006 this Trust went into liquidation and the ships at Birkenhead faced a very uncertain future. However, fortuitously the backers of the proposed Submarine Heritage Centre at Barrow-in-Furness had been looking for a suitable submarine to exhibit. In 2004 they had unsuccessfully tried to raise funds to have *Olympus*, a former RN *Oberon*, brought back across the Atlantic from Canada, where she had been used as an alongside training boat for the Royal Canadian Navy. *Onyx* therefore provided a cheaper option, and possession was transferred from the Mersey Docks and Harbour Company to Marine Technologies Ltd and its Barrow-born managing director Joe Mullen, who intended to display her on their Barrow Island site. The tow to Barrow took place on 13 June 2006, since when work to prepare the submarine for display in a graving dock has commenced.

The third Royal Navy *Oberon*, *Otus*, is on display and open to the public at Sassnitz, Germany. For all twenty-eight years of her operational life she was based at Gosport, and she reportedly landed special forces in occupied Kuwait during the first Gulf War.

Stickleback

ABOVE *Stickleback* at sea in 1955.

Technical Details

Displacement:	32 tons standard, 39 tons full load (submerged)
Length:	53ft 11in (16.4m)
Beam:	6ft 3½in (1.9m)
Draught:	7ft 6in (2.3m)
Propulsion:	One Perkins 6-cylinder diesel engine, 50 bhp, and one electric motor, 44 shp, single shaft
Speed:	6.5 knots (surface), 6 knots (submerged)
Range:	1,000 nautical miles at 5 knots (surface)
Armament:	Two x 2-ton side charges, plus limpet mines
Complement:	5
Pennant No.:	*X51*

The Re-emergence of X-craft

The use of X-craft was revived during the Cold War as part of the highly secret Operation Cudgel, a plan for them to lay nuclear charges in the approaches to Soviet naval bases, apparently in response to a similar development with which the Russians were experimenting. Four new craft were built for the Royal Navy for this purpose by Vickers-Armstrong, Barrow. The first was launched as *X51* on 1 October 1954, and in December was given the name *Stickleback* (keeping *X51* as her pennant number). *Shrimp*, *Sprat* and *Minnow* followed, though *Stickleback* seems to have seen most service, with the other units spending most of their time in reserve, except when *Sprat* was loaned to the US Navy from June to September 1958. Even so, *Stickleback* was sold to the Swedish navy on 15 July 1958 and was renamed *Spiggen*. She was used as a target during anti-submarine exercises and to train harbour defences against enemy midget submarines (at the time there were regular incursions into Swedish waters by Russian submarines). The idea for the nuclear mine had fizzled out and the other three Royal Navy boats were scrapped in 1965–66. The Swedes decommissioned their craft in 1970 and *Stickleback* was donated to the Imperial War Museum in 1976. She is now on display in a hangar at the museum's Duxford site in Cambridgeshire.

Courageous

Nuclear 'hunter–killer' submarine

Built for the Cold War to hunt other submarines, and served in the Falklands; the only nuclear submarine on display in the United Kingdom, open to the public in a dry dock at Devonport

Design

Conventionally powered submarines, such as the *Oberon* class, had a limited range and needed to surface or use their snort masts to recharge their batteries. After the Second World War other forms of propulsion were considered for submarines, and nuclear power emerged as vastly superior to diesel/electric propulsion. Nuclear-powered boats had an almost unlimited fuel source and could generate oxygen through the electrolysis of fresh water that they were able to distil from seawater. Their submerged range was limited only by the amount of food they could carry and the endurance of their crew, and it was not unusual for them to stay submerged for a month or more. Their deep diving depths and low noise signal made them very difficult to detect.

Following the lead of the United States Navy, the Royal Navy commissioned its first nuclear submarines in the 1960s, starting in 1963 with *Dreadnought*, after which came the *Valiant*, *Resolution*, *Swiftsure*, *Trafalgar*, *Vanguard* and *Astute* classes. The first two units of the *Valiant* class were *Valiant* and *Warspite*, and the three later boats, *Churchill*, *Conqueror* and *Courageous*, were sometimes known as the *Churchill* class, although their differences were only minor. *Courageous* is now decommissioned as a static exhibit at Devonport Dockyard.

Whereas *Dreadnought* had an American propulsion plant, those in the five *Valiant* class were British. This meant that the after section of *Valiant* differed to accommodate the British machinery; the fore end was similar to *Dreadnought*, although the fore planes were moved a little further aft to reduce interference with the sonar. The diving depth was slightly increased to the limits of the new machinery – a diving depth of 300 metres has been quoted. A retractable propulsor, driven off a 112-cell battery with a diesel generator and electric motor, was fitted for reserve power in the event of a main-machinery failure.

The *Valiant* class were armed with Tigerfish guided torpedoes for both anti-ship and anti-submarine purposes. They were guided by wire for the first part of their passage and by a homing device for the final attack sequence. The Sub-Harpoon anti-ship guided missile was also fitted, and was launched from the torpedo tubes.

Build

Courageous was laid down on 15 May 1968 by Vickers Shipbuilding and Engineering Ltd at Barrow-in-Furness, and

Technical Details

Displacement:	4,300 tons (surface), 4,800 tons (submerged)
Length:	285ft (86.87m)
Beam:	33ft 2½in (10.12m)
Draught:	27ft (26.7m)
Propulsion:	Pressurised water-cooled nuclear reactor. English Electric geared steam turbines, 15,000 shp, single screw
Speed:	28 knots submerged
Armament:	6 x 21-in torpedo tubes (32 torpedoes carried, or mines), Sub-Harpoon missiles
Complement:	116 (13 officers, 103 ratings)
Pennant No.:	S50 (not displayed)

Decommissioning of Nuclear Submarines

Many of the early nuclear submarines have been decommissioned after operational lives of around twenty to twenty-five years, but none of them has been disposed of, because of problems in finding a safe and satisfactory way of dealing with the radioactive material that they contain. The reactor cores and some non-radioactive equipment were removed, and the cooling circuits emptied, before the hulls were stored afloat at Devonport and Rosyth dockyards. In 2001, partly in an attempt to allay public fears about the safety of these vessels, it was decided that one of the boats, *Courageous*, should go on display in a dry dock and be open to the public at Devonport. She was moved into No. 3 Dock on 8 March 2002 and was first open to the public on Navy Days, 24–26 August 2002. She is open to visitors touring HM Naval Base, Devonport.

The other nuclear submarines laid up awaiting disposal are *Dreadnought, Churchill, Resolution, Renown, Repulse, Revenge* and *Swiftsure* at Rosyth and *Valiant, Warspite, Conqueror, Splendid, Spartan* and *Sovereign* at Devonport. They are painted with anti-corrosion paint, partially sealed and then laid up. They are inspected daily and receive annual maintenance, plus extensive maintenance every six years. After twelve years they are dry-docked for full inspection and repainting.

was originally to have been named *Superb*. In about September 1969 she was renamed and was launched as *Courageous* on 7 March 1970 by Mrs Morris, wife of Mr John Morris, Labour MP for Aberavon and Minister of Defence (Equipment). Contractor's sea trials commenced on 22 May 1971. She was commissioned on 16 October 1971 and, after leaving Barrow on 2 November, worked up in the Clyde area from her base, Faslane, where she became part of the 3rd Submarine Squadron. Many aspects of her service history remain classified, and involved frequent Cold War patrols mostly in the North Atlantic, but some details are available.

Service History

In mid-December 1971 *Courageous* was at Gibraltar, possibly for test torpedo firings. In April 1972 she was at Aberporth, mid-Wales, and then proceeded to Portland for exercises. In late May of that year *Courageous* participated in Exercise Windy Trumpet in the Gibraltar area. In late November a visit was made to Haakonsvern, Norway. January 1973 saw the boat taking part in Exercise Vendetta, with Exercise Dawn Patrol following in June, and she was at Gibraltar in late June. In January and February 1974 she took part in Exercises Joint Conquest and Stem Turn. On 26 April of that year she arrived at Devonport for docking and essential repairs, remaining there until 2 September. In January 1975 she was again at Gibraltar, and exercises in that year included Rubbing Strake and Serang. In February 1976 *Courageous* took part in Exercises Glendale and Gratitude, and was back at Gibraltar in late April. Most of

May was spent on trials, except for a visit to Corfu, and in June the boat was again in Gibraltar. In September 1976 she was prepared for a major refit, which commenced at Chatham on 1 November and lasted until January 1978 (or August 1978 according to one source).

From May to July 1979 there was another Mediterranean deployment, including visits to Gibraltar, Corfu and Haifa. By August the boat was at Charleston, South Carolina, for a maintenance period and she visited Bermuda in the following month. In April 1980 *Courageous* was at Chatham for an interim docking, and visited Kiel in September. In 1981 she visited Autec, Florida, for the testing of the Sub-Harpoon missile: in total eight firings were made to check the compatibility of the missile with the *Trafalgar*-class submarine. Between 12 May and 13 August 1982 *Courageous* completed ninety-three days in Operation Corporate and was based at San Diego. She conducted the first operational deployment of the Royal Navy's Sub-Harpoon missile over what is believed to be one of the longest periods in which a fleet submarine has remained continuously under way. On 7 October 1982 she sailed from Faslane for the Falklands Islands area and, after a stores and personnel transfer off Ascension Island,

passed thirty-five degrees south, on 23 October. By this time the Falklands War was over, but *Courageous* carried out her first patrol in the area. On 6 December she commenced her transit north, leaving the Falklands area on the 8th, and arriving at Faslane on 23 December 1982. Despite not being directly involved in the conflict *Courageous* was awarded the battle honour Falklands Islands 1982. During the conflict another of the *Valiant* class, *Conqueror*, sank the Argentinean cruiser *General Belgrano*. On 3 March 1984 *Courageous* sailed from Faslane for her fourth and last patrol in the South Atlantic. She returned on 31 May, having spent fifty-four days on station.

On 7 September 1984 she docked at Devonport prior to entering refit there on 1 October. The submarine returned to operational duties in January 1987. In July 1988 *Courageous* was in collision in the North Sea with the yacht *Dalraida*, which sank: four people aboard the yacht were rescued by the frigate *Battleaxe*. The *Valiant* class was paid off for disposal in 1990–92, following the end of the Cold War. Cracks had been found in their primary cooling circuits; although these could have been repaired, their remaining life under defence cuts made this uneconomic. In April 1992 *Courageous* was paid off at Devonport, de-fuelled and was listed for disposal.

ABOVE *Courageous* on display in dry dock at Devonport, by Geoff Hunt RSMA.

OPPOSITE HMS *Courageous* arriving in Portsmouth when in commission.

Gay Archer

Sole surviving fast patrol boat

Built in the 1950s this patrol boat became a victim of cuts in coastal forces; restored and seagoing, based at Watchet; not open to the general public

BELOW HMS *Gay Archer* in commission with MGB armament.

Twelve *Gay*-class fast patrol boats were ordered in 1951, following the outbreak of the Korean War. They were direct descendants of the wartime Vosper 70-foot motor torpedo boats, also incorporating experience from the postwar prototypes *MTB 538* and *539* – but the design was an interim one, pending the development of the diesel-powered *Dark* class. The double diagonal mahogany hull was similar to that of *MTBs 538* and *539* but an altered centre of gravity gave the *Gay*-class boats a marked stern trim and contributed to their difficulty getting up onto a plane when carrying a full load of fuel. They also suffered some structural damage due to the waterline pressure on the middle of a compartment when planing. Transom flaps had to be fitted to cure these problems, and on trials speed increased to 44 knots due to improved propeller efficiency. The fast patrol boat designation meant that they were interchangeable as MTBs or MGBs, depending on the armament mounted. Four boats were built by Vosper at Porchester, including the first of the class to be launched – *Gay Archer*.

Gay Archer was launched on 20 August 1952 and was commissioned in May 1953 for service at HMS *Hornet*, Gosport. A fuel tank was split during acceptance trials and the boat had to be towed out into the Solent to pump out the bilges, the coach deck then being lifted off to replace the tank. Vosper's ferry crew managed to put a hole in her port side on the delivery voyage to *Hornet*. On 7 May 1953 *Gay Archer* sailed for the Baltic and, on the passage north, a propeller was damaged on some driftwood and had to be replaced in Copenhagen. By 17 May

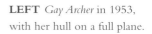

LEFT *Gay Archer* in 1953, with her hull on a full plane.

the boat was alongside at Aarhus in a raft of four fast patrol boats: *Gay Archer* was the outside boat and immediately inside of her was *FPB 1023*, which suffered an engine-room explosion and fire and subsequently sank. *Gay Archer* was extricated from her position but was quite badly damaged. She had to stay in Aarhus for nearly two weeks of repairs before leaving on 29 May to be escorted by *Gay Fencer* back to Chatham for de-fuelling. *Gay Fencer* then towed her to Sheerness for de-storing and her crew left her. As a result, although listed in the programme for the Coronation Fleet Review at Spithead on 15 June, *Gay Archer* was not able to attend. The boat later had yet another mishap when she struck a submerged boom defence pylon off Southsea and her hull was pierced. Taking in water she began to settle by the stern but was taken in tow by an Admiralty tug and returned to *Hornet*. With the run down of coastal forces she was laid up at HMS *Diligence* at Hythe, until being sold on 24 July 1963 to Messrs Cottness Iron Co., Wishaw, Lancashire.

Gay Archer has survived after many years as a yacht or houseboat, and was restored to her original appearance at Northwich in Cheshire by Mr Paul Childs. She was re-engined with two 650-bhp Detroit diesels, giving an estimated speed of 30 knots, and was fitted with a 40-mm Bofors gun and two reproduction 21-inch torpedo tubes. This work was completed in late 2005 and in spring 2006 the seagoing boat moved to Watchet in Somerset to be used for corporate hospitality and private charters, as well as providing accommodation for the owner.

Technical Details

Displacement:	50 tons (standard), 65 tons (full load)
Length:	75ft 2⅓in (22.92m)
Beam:	20ft 1in (6.13m)
Draught:	4ft 2⅓in (1.28m) – light (without full load of fuel and ammunition)
Propulsion:	Three Packard 4M-2500 petrol engines, 4,500 bhp, three shafts 40,000 shp, twin screws
Speed:	40 knots
Armament:	2 x 20-mm Oerlikon AA gun (or 1 x 40-mm Bofors gun), 2 x 21-in torpedo tubes (as MTB); or 1 x 4.5-in gun and 2 x 20-mm Oerlikon guns (as MGB)
Complement:	13
Pennant No.:	P1041

Britannia

The last Royal Yacht

The last and best known Royal Yacht, which served for more than forty years; now open to the public as a static exhibit at Leith, Scotland

Launched in 1953 as a replacement for *Victoria and Albert*, *Britannia* gave nearly forty-four years' service as a Royal Yacht, all of it in the reign of Queen Elizabeth II. In this time she steamed more than one million nautical miles and carried members of the Royal Family on 968 official visits, calling at more than 600 ports in 135 countries. She finally paid off in December 1997, signalling the end of an unbroken succession of Royal Yachts dating back to the reign of Charles II, and is now on display at Leith in Scotland.

Design and Build

Victoria and Albert had been launched in 1899, and by 1936 was in need of replacement. In that year, during the brief reign of King Edward VIII, initial discussions about a new ship took place but were interrupted by the abdication crisis. The issue was revived in 1938 when King George VI told the Admiralty that, to avoid criticism of the spending on a new Royal Yacht, the new ship should be capable of rapid conversion to a hospital ship in the event of war. The new proposals received Cabinet backing in June 1938 and the design process was set in motion. In August 1939 *Victoria and Albert* undertook what was to be her last royal duty when the King reviewed the Reserve Fleet at Portland. In the same month invitations to tender for the final design and construction of a new Royal Yacht were issued to eleven shipbuilders, with responses required by 12 September 1939.

However, war was declared with Germany before that date arose, and the plans were shelved. *Victoria and Albert* spent the war at moorings in Portsmouth Harbour, and for part of the time was an accommodation ship for the gunnery school at Whale Island. In October 1945, shortly after the end of the war, she was declared unseaworthy, but it was not until June 1951 that a decision to build a replacement was made. For reasons of economy and speed it was decided to adapt an existing design, that of the North Sea ferries *Amsterdam* and *Arnhem* – which had recently been built by John Brown & Co. Ltd at Clydebank, who were also to build the new Royal Yacht. The new ship was to have worldwide ocean-going capability (unlike *Victoria and Albert* which was only used in Home, European and Mediterranean waters) and was – in line with the pre-war decision – to be convertible to a hospital ship.

The instruction to proceed with the detailed design and construction was passed to John Brown's on 4 February 1952, though this event was quickly overshadowed by the death of the King the following day. Queen Elizabeth II and, especially, Prince Philip (a recently serving naval officer) were involved in further discussions on the design, and the keel was laid on 11 June 1952. Further work on the design of the Royal Apartments took place, and was heavily influenced by the architect and painter, Sir Hugh Casson. The idea was to produce elegant

ABOVE *Britannia* leaves the
Pool of London on 6 May
1960 with Princess Margaret
and Anthony Armstrong-Jones
aboard, after their wedding at
Westminster Abbey.

modern spaces without ostentatious and over-elaborate decoration. Whereas *Victoria and Albert*'s
hull was black, a decision was taken to adopt the livery of Prince Philip's *Dragon*-class yacht
Bluebottle for the hull: dark blue with scarlet red boot topping, and a 5½-inch-wide gold leaf
band around the top of the hull. This was complemented by white topsides and a buff funnel,
as on *Victoria and Albert*.

On 16 April 1953 she was launched by the new Queen and named *Britannia*. The name,
a closely guarded secret, was chosen by the royal couple from a shortlist of five names prepared
by the Admiralty Ships' Names Committee (the others being *Commonwealth*, *Prince Royal*, *Royal
Charles* and *Princess Anne*). This meant that HMS *Britannia*, the Royal Naval College at
Dartmouth, had to be renamed Britannia Royal Naval College, releasing the ship name for HM
Yacht *Britannia*. As the fitting out proceeded, the opportunity was taken to include items from
Victoria and Albert, including most of the pictures, the dining room chairs, the silver, linen and
glasses, a silver lantern, and one of two binnacles that had originally been fitted in *Royal George*,
an earlier Royal Yacht that had been broken up in 1905. The wheel from King Edward VII's
racing yacht *Britannia* was fitted in the wheelhouse.

In appearance the ship was intended to be dignified and modern, but not futuristic. The
clipper bow and modified cruiser stern gave a graceful profile without the excessive overhangs
of the *Victoria and Albert* and the 1939 design. Three masts were a requirement for a Royal Yacht,
and the single funnel gave a well-balanced look. The Royal Apartments were positioned aft on
the shelter deck between the main and mizzen masts with a verandah at the after end leading

ABOVE The engine room (left) and the bridge (right) on *Britannia*.

on to a sun deck. Below these, on the upper deck, were the State Apartments including the dining room, drawing room and anteroom, all of which were extended to the full width of the superstructure without obstruction from pillars. The State apartments were connected to the Royal Apartments by a broad main staircase. All these functional requirements meant that the aft superstructure was larger than might normally have been desired from an aesthetic point of view, but did not detract unduly from the overall appearance. The weather decks were sheathed with 2-inch teak and the upper deck was protected all round by bulwarks 3 feet 6 inches deep amidships rising to 6 feet at the bow. The sundeck was stiffened at the after end so that it could be used, if required, as a helicopter landing deck. The complement of boats was large and included a 40-foot Royal Barge, two 35-foot medium-speed motor boats, a 32-foot motor cutter, two 27-foot jolly boats, two 16-foot fast motor dinghies and two 14-foot sailing dinghies. The Royal Barge had originally been built by Vosper in 1938 for use with *Victoria and Albert*.

In the event of the ship being employed as a hospital ship the Royal and State Apartments, and spaces below them occupied by the Royal Household and staff on the main and lower decks were to be converted into wards, accommodating 200 patients. The operating theatre and other specialist facilities would be on the lower deck. The ship would then be manned by a merchant navy crew plus a medical party of eight doctors and dentists, five nursing sisters and forty-seven male orderlies.

Early Service

On 3 November 1953 *Britannia* began her contractor's sea trials. Powered by two geared steam turbines (which burned heavy fuel oil) she achieved a full speed of 22.85 knots, with the ship at 4,320 tons displacement, during the measured mile speed trials off the Isle of Arran. *Britannia* was accepted by the Admiralty on 11 January 1954, hoisting the White Ensign for the first time. For the next three weeks she worked up in the Firth of Clyde area, and then sailed around the north of Scotland to Invergordon and Rosyth for further trials and exercises. At Rosyth she carried out a trial embarkation of a Rolls Royce car, which was carried aboard in a garage on the Boat Deck inboard of the Barge, for use ashore on official visits. *Britannia* left Rosyth on 15 February for further working up at Portland and thence to Portsmouth, her home port, where she arrived for the first time on 26 February 1954.

At this time the Queen and Prince Philip were away on their Commonwealth Tour aboard the liner *Gothic* which had been adopted as a temporary substitute for the Royal Yacht. On 14 April the first royal party embarked – comprising the young Prince Charles and Princess Anne, with the Queen Mother and Princess Margaret – and the ship sailed for Tobruk where the Queen and Prince Philip joined them on 30 April for visits to Malta and Gibraltar. On 2 May, in a highly impressive spectacle, the Mediterranean Fleet, with Lord Louis Mountbatten as Commander-in-Chief, steamed past *Britannia* at 25 knots in two columns, with one column going down each side. This was followed by diving displays by submarines, flying displays by aircraft from HMS *Eagle*, and a flypast of aircraft from RAF Luqa. On the following day *Britannia* entered Grand Harbour, Malta, passing between two lines of warships of the Mediterranean Fleet outside the breakwater.

After her visit to Gibraltar *Britannia* sailed up the English Channel on 14 May and was joined by eighteen ships of the Home Fleet, including the battleship *Vanguard*. Off Yarmouth, Isle of Wight, the Prime Minister, Sir Winston Churchill, was embarked for the remainder of the voyage to London where the royal family were to disembark. In the spirit of the time the banks of the Thames were lined with huge crowds of cheering people as *Britannia*, escorted by Royal Navy fast patrol boats, sailed upriver, and onboard the Royal Marines of the Royal Yacht Band played 'Rule Britannia' as the ship passed under Tower Bridge to enter the Pool of London. On 19 May she sailed from the Thames and undertook an overnight passage to Portsmouth, thus completing her first spell of royal duty.

In 1954 her itinerary included the first crossing of the Atlantic by a Royal Yacht, for a Canadian tour, and in that year *Britannia* steamed 17,646 miles, a figure that subsequently

LEFT *Britannia* alongside at Leith.

peaked at 44,499 miles in 1964 but was rarely lower than 10,000 miles in any one year. In total she steamed 1,087,623 miles in the course of her forty-four years' service. In August 1955 after her first visit to Cowes, Isle of Wight, for Cowes Week, the Yacht took the royal family on the first Western Isles cruise as part of their move from Buckingham Palace to Balmoral for the summer break, and – like Cowes Week – this cruise became a regular fixture. On 28 August 1956 *Britannia* left Portsmouth for her first world cruise – the World Tour of Prince Philip – which included the Olympic Games in Melbourne. She circumnavigated the globe, taking in ports in the Indian Ocean, the South Pacific, Antarctica and the South Atlantic, and after six months the deployment concluded with the Queen's state visit to Portugal.

In January 1959 the Yacht commenced a second round-the-world voyage and once again Prince Philip was the Royal passenger. After her first passage of the Suez Canal she visited Vizagapatam (India), Rangoon (where Prince Philip embarked), Singapore, Sarawak and Hong Kong. This was followed by a passage across the Pacific to the British Solomon Islands and the Gilbert and Ellis Islands. The Yacht then headed for her first transit of the Panama Canal en route to the Bahamas and Bermuda. *Britannia* crossed the Atlantic and arrived at Portsmouth on 7 May, exactly four months after she had left. In the following month she re-crossed the Atlantic for the opening by the Queen of the St Lawrence Seaway. The visit included a review of the Royal Canadian Navy's Atlantic Fleet in Gaspe Bay, the opening of the Seaway at Montreal, visits to Toronto (on Lake Ontario), Windsor (on Lake Erie), Chicago (on Lake Michigan) and Port Arthur and Fort William (on Lake Superior, 600 feet above sea level), and then back to Halifax, Nova Scotia. The distance sailed from the lake port of Fort William to the sea port of Halifax was 2,800 miles.

ABOVE The drawing room (top) and the sun lounge (bottom) in the Royal Apartments.

Service in the Sixties

October and November 1961 saw the Queen's tour of West Africa with official visits to Ghana, Liberia, Sierra Leone, Gambia and Senegal. In December 1962 the Yacht left Portsmouth for her third circumnavigation, this time sailing west-about via Jamaica, the Panama Canal and Tahiti for Fiji, where the Queen and Prince Philip embarked and carried out the first engagements of their tour, which also took in New Zealand and Australia. A year later the Yacht retraced her path to the Pacific for the start of another planned tour of Australia and New Zealand, this time by the Queen Mother. However, on reaching Fiji it was heard that the tour was to be cancelled due to the Queen Mother's appendicitis. The Yacht set off for the United Kingdom via the Panama Canal but later received instructions to make for Kingston, Jamaica, where the Queen Mother would join the Yacht for a three-week convalescence cruise around the West Indies during which fourteen islands were visited.

In July 1964 a new 41-foot Royal Barge built by Camper and Nicholsons was accepted to replace the pre-war original. In October and November 1964 the Yacht visited Canada, Mexico, the Galapagos Islands, Panama and the West Indies for visits that variously involved

Princess Mary, the Queen and Prince Philip. She then entered Portsmouth Dockyard for her quadrennial refit, during which air-conditioning was installed in the forward half of the Yacht for the crew (it had been fitted in the Royal Apartments at the time of building). In January 1966 *Britannia* left for another circumnavigation, starting with a tour of the Caribbean by the Queen and Prince Philip. The Yacht then crossed the Panama Canal to the Pacific for a tour of Fiji and New Zealand by the Queen Mother, returning via the Suez Canal. In June and July 1967 there was another tour of Canada, while Brazil was the highlight of the 1968 itinerary. While in Brazil the Yacht was used for the first time to promote British trade to business people and other VIPs during two Sea Days, and similar events occurred intermittently in her later career. In May 1969 the Queen in *Britannia* reviewed a fleet of NATO warships from twelve nations, at Spithead to mark the twentieth anniversary of the formation of NATO. This was followed in July by a review of the Royal Navy's Western Fleet in Torbay, where thirty-eight ships had gathered.

Service in the Seventies

The year 1970 marked the bicentenary of Cook's landing in Australia at Botany Bay and the Queen was to be present at a re-enactment there in April. *Britannia*'s deployment lasted six months, and also included the by now familiar destinations of the Galapagos, Fiji and New Zealand. The following year the attraction of the royal family to the Pacific led to yet another six-month deployment to the Pacific, including visits to many South Sea islands and Australasia, and concluding with a tour of the Canadian west coast. The early part of 1972 was spent on the Queen's tour of South East Asia – visiting Thailand, Singapore, Malaysia and Brunei. The ability of the Yacht to allow the Queen to visit remote island communities was then evidenced by visits to Penang, the Maldives and Gan en route across the Indian Ocean to the Seychelles and Mauritius.

In October 1972 a long process of refit and modernisation began at Portsmouth, which included the fitting of full bunk sleeping accommodation for the crew, the Yacht having been the last ship in the Royal Navy in which sailors still slept in hammocks. The next major deployment started on 30 October 1973 and was another six-month global programme. It included the West Indies honeymoon cruise of Princess Anne and Captain Mark Phillips, the Commonwealth Games in New Zealand and a tour of Australia, Indonesia and several Pacific islands. The early part of 1975 saw engagements in Mexico and Bermuda, and the Yacht returned to the latter in July of the following year to embark the Queen and Prince Philip for a tour of the east coast of America and Canada.

On 28 December 1976 *Britannia* sailed from Portsmouth for her sixth circumnavigation of the globe, the principal part of which was the Silver Jubilee Tour of Australasia by the monarch and her consort. This theme continued on the ship's return to the United Kingdom, with the Silver Jubilee Fleet Review at Spithead on 28 June 1977. As *Britannia* sailed through the lines she passed 101 British warships, among them the aircraft carriers *Ark Royal* and *Hermes*, and seventy-nine ships from seventeen other nations, including the Australian aircraft carrier *Melbourne*. The year ended with the Queen's Silver Jubilee Tour of the West Indies.

Service in the Eighties

The next global deployment began in July 1981 with the Mediterranean honeymoon cruise of The Prince and Princess of Wales, before continuing via the Suez Canal to support the tour of Australia and New Zealand by the Queen and Prince Philip. On 2 April 1982 Argentina invaded the Falklands, and it seemed that the Yacht might be sent there to join the Royal Navy task force and act as a hospital ship for the first time. However, it was decided against this because *Britannia*'s need for heavy fuel oil (shared only by the flagship HMS *Hermes*) would create logistical problems, and also the Yacht might offer a prime target for the Argentinians, thus diverting disproportionate resources to protect her from attack. While these reasons might seem plausible, the decision gave ammunition to *Britannia*'s critics since part of the case for maintaining a Royal Yacht had been negated. So it was business as usual in August 1982 when the Yacht sailed for yet another Pacific tour by the Queen and Prince Philip, taking in the Commonwealth Games in Brisbane and visits to several Pacific islands. This was closely followed between January and March 1983 by visits to Mexico and the west coast of America. On 29 September 1983 *Britannia* entered dry dock for an extended refit, lasting six months, during which she was converted to burn diesel fuel – a decision stimulated by the dilemma of her absence from the Falklands campaign.

In June 1984 she crossed the Atlantic to Canada, only for the Queen's tour to be cancelled because of Canadian elections, so the ship returned to Portsmouth before setting out again in September for the rescheduled tour. In February 1985 she supported Prince Philip's visit to the west coast of Africa, and then moved to Lisbon for the Queen's visit and Italy for the tour of the Prince and Princess of Wales. In the autumn of that year the Yacht supported the Queen's Caribbean tour, and on New Year's Eve left Portsmouth for New Zealand and Australia via the Suez Canal. As *Britannia* passed down the Red Sea she was diverted to Aden to evacuate British nationals trapped in South Yemen by a civil war. Being a non-combatant ship the Yacht was able to enter South Yemeni territorial waters while warships, including HMSs *Newcastle* and *Jupiter* and RFA *Brambleleaf*, could not enter. The Royal Apartments were converted to accommodate the evacuees who were taken off beaches by the Yacht's boats, against a backdrop of a tank battle between the rival forces. Evacuees were either taken to Djibouti on the east African coast or transferred to other ships in international waters. The operation lasted seven days during which time *Britannia* rescued 1,082 of the 1,379 people of fifty-five nationalities saved by British ships. This demonstrated that the Yacht could have a secondary role during wartime as a casualty evacuation ship with medical facilities on board, even though the limited extent of the latter meant that she could not be considered a fully-fledged hospital ship.

Britannia resumed her passage to Auckland for the Queen's tour. In July 1986 she undertook her fourth and final honeymoon cruise, this time to the Azores for Prince Andrew and Sarah Ferguson. October of that year found the Yacht in Shanghai for the historic state visit of the Queen and Prince Philip to China and Hong Kong. In January 1987 *Britannia* entered Devonport Dockyard for a major ten-month refit, during which her worn teak decks were replaced with new teak planking – all fourteen miles of it. The 1988 programme included a six-month global tour taking in the Caribbean, the Galapagos Islands, Los Angeles, Australia and Italy. In 1989 there was a major tour of the Far East, including Singapore, Malaysia, Brunei, Indonesia and Hong Kong.

Final Service

In 1990 the programme began with royal visits to west Africa, followed by Iceland and then the Caribbean and Brazil. The next year she returned to Brazil for Sea Days before proceeding to support royal visits in Miami and Portugal. In the autumn of 1991 *Britannia* sailed for Toronto and Montreal, where the Prince and Princess of Wales undertook official engagements. In 1992 there were state visits to Malta and Bordeaux, and 1993 began with Mexico, the Caribbean and Palm Beach, followed by a deployment to Turkey, Cyprus, the Arabian Gulf and India. In 1994 the programme directed *Britannia* to New York and the Caribbean, including the Yacht's last visit to HMS *Malabar*, the Royal Navy's dockyard in Bermuda, which was due to close the following year.

In June 1994 the Yacht undertook an important role in the events marking the fiftieth Anniversary of the D-Day Landings when she led a review of ships at Spithead with the

Technical details

Displacement:	3,990 tons (4,715 tons full load)
Length:	412ft 3in (125.65m)
Beam:	55ft (16.76m)
Draught:	(normal load) 15ft 9in (16.76m)
Propulsion:	Single reduction geared steam turbines, 12,000 shp; two oil-fired boilers; two shafts
Speed:	21 knots in continuous seagoing
Range:	2,000 miles at 20 knots
Complement:	271 as Royal Yacht
Capacity for receptions:	250 guests; capacity for state banquets, 56 guests. Nominal patient capacity as hospital ship, 200, plus naval medical complement of 60
Armament:	2 x 3-pounder saluting guns (removed in October 1954)
Pennant No.:	A00 (not displayed on hull side)

Queen and President Clinton on board, and then proceeded to the Normandy coast for wreath laying and other ceremonies. In October *Britannia* was at St Petersburg for the Queen's state visit to Russia, including a state banquet on board for President Yeltsin. The highlight of the 1995 programme was the Queen's state visit to South Africa, for which she and Prince Philip embarked at Simonstown before rounding the Cape of Good Hope for Cape Town, where they were greeted by President Mandela. Early in 1996 there were visits to the east coast of America and Canada. In July *Britannia* was at Marchwood on Southampton Water for the Queen Mother's re-launching of the restored RAF rescue launch *HSL 102*.

The next year, 1997, was to be the last in service for *Britannia*. In January it was confirmed that she would decommission at the end of the year, but the Conservative government, which had prevaricated on the issue, announced that a replacement was to be built – and design studies were well underway. However, 1997 was also a general election year, and the Labour party campaigned on a pledge that the Yacht would not be replaced. Meanwhile *Britannia* embarked on her last major deployment, to the Middle East, Pakistan, India, Thailand, Malaysia and Japan. She then made a high-profile visit to Hong Kong where the Prince of Wales joined to represent the Queen for the formal return of the colony to China. *Britannia*'s departure from Hong Kong, escorted by HMSs *Chatham*, *Peacock*, *Plover* and *Starling*, and the RFA *Sir Percivale*, was for many a moving occasion symbolising both the end of an imperial era and the beginning of the end for the Royal Yacht.

On 10 October the new Labour government announced that no new Royal Yacht would be built and *Britannia* would not be refitted. The cost of a replacement was estimated at £80 million (which can be compared with the original construction costs of £2.1 million for *Britannia*). The annual operating costs of *Britannia* in the 1990s varied between £7.5 million and £12.5 million, while the annual cost in the financial year 1987/88 – when she had had her last major refit – was £22.4 million. Thus a major refit might have been expected to cost more than £10 million and, at a time when the stock of the Royal Family with the public had been damaged, these sums were considered unacceptable. On 20 October 1997 the Yacht began her final duty, a clockwise circumnavigation of the United Kingdom, visiting eight major ports – at most of which members of the royal family joined for various events. The last of these visits was to the Pool of London after which *Britannia* sailed for Portsmouth. She arrived on 22 November, streaming her paying off pennant and accompanied by HMS *Southampton* and a large number of private boats. On 11 December in the presence of the Queen and thirteen other members of the royal family, she was formally decommissioned.

Preservation

Seven ports had submitted bids to display *Britannia* as a tourist attraction, and it was finally announced that Forth Ports' bid to berth her in Leith had won. On 1 May 1998 she was handed over at Portsmouth Dockyard to the trust that had been set up by Forth Ports to preserve her, and left undertow for Leith where she arrived on 5 May. She entered dry dock three days later to begin a £2.5 million conversion into a static museum ship. Much of the original furniture, which had been removed after decommissioning, was retrieved, although some items had to be reproduced. Access and display arrangements had to be made on board and in October, by which time she had left the dry dock and was at a temporary berth, she was opened to the public.

In her first year 436,619 members of the public paid to visit her. This was an exceptional figure; latterly the figures have been between 250,000 and 300,000 each year. In September 2001 she was moved to her new permanent berth at Leith's Ocean Terminal, and additional areas of the Yacht, including the crew's accommodation, became open to visitors. The most popular areas remain the Royal Apartments, which include the Queen's and the Duke of Edinburgh's separate cabins and dayrooms and the honeymoon suite, though the immaculate engine room amazes many with its gleaming chrome and brass dials and fittings. The bridge and chart room, State Rooms, galleys, wardroom, laundry, petty officers' mess, chief petty officers' mess, Marines' mess, admiral's cabin and admiral's day room can also be seen.

Appendix

Other Vessels of 60 feet or more, in the Core and Designated Lists of the National Historic Ships Register

Name	Type	Year Built	Builder	Gross tonnage	Location
Amy Howson	Humber sloop	1914	Joseph Scar & Sons, Beverley	69	South Ferriby, Lincs.
Barcadale	Drifter	1938	Herd & MacKenzie, Buckie	31	Oban
Basuto	Clyde puffer	1902	W. Jacks & Co., Port Dundas	64	Ellesmere Port
Bronington	Coastal minesweeper	1953	Cook, Welton & Gemmell, Beverley	360	Birkenhead
Carola	Excursion vessel	1898	Scott & Co., Bowling	40	Irvine
City of Adelaide	Clipper ship	1864	William Pile and Hay & Co., Sunderland	860	Irvine
Comrade	Humber keel	1923	Warren Shipyard, New Holland	69	South Ferriby, Lincs.
Coronia	Excursion vessel	1935	Fellows & Co., Great Yarmouth	75	Scarborough
Esperance	Steam yacht	1869	T. B. Sneath & Co., Rutherglen	15	Windermere
Esther	Grimsby smack	1888	Collinson, Grimsby	85	Grimsby
Excelsior	Sailing trawler	1921	John Chambers & Co., Lowestoft	55	Lowestoft
Feasible	Steam drifter	1912	John Duthie, Aberdeen	150	Penzance
Grab No. 1	Grab dredger	1927	Blyth Shipbuilding Co., Blyth	101	Blyth
Gypsy Race	Grab dredger	1940	Lobnitz & Co. Ltd, Renfrew	145	Bridlington
Harriet	Fishing ketch	1893	Singleton, Wyre Dock, Fleetwood	25	Fleetwood
Hurlingham	Excursion vessel	1915	Salter Bros, Oxford	114	Lambeth
H.Y. Tyne III	Wooden lightship	1879	Unknown	205	Blyth
John Adams	Tender	1934	Thorne	94	Bideford
Kenya Jacaranda	Brixham trawler	1923	R. Jackman & Sons, Brixham	31	Tilbury
Lady of the Lake	Excursion vessel	1877	T. B. Sneath & Co., Rutherglen	43	Ullswater
Landfall	Landing craft	1944	Hawthorn Leslie, Hebburn-on-Tyne	350	Birkenhead
Largo Law	Pilot cutter	1924	J. N. Miller & Son Ltd, St Monans	45	Charlestown, Fife
Leader	Brixham trawler	1892	A. W. Gibb, Galmpton	110	Brixham
LV 12	Light vessel	1927	Goole Shipbuilding and Repair Co. Ltd, Goole	200	Hull
LV 16	Light vessel	1840	William Pitcher, Northfleet	158	Borstal, Kent
LV 91	Light vessel	1937	Philip & Son, Dartmouth	225	Swansea
Manxman	Short-sea ferry	1955	Cammell Laird Ltd, Birkenhead	2495	Sunderland
Massey Shaw	Fire float	1935	J. Samuel White & Co., Cowes	51	Woolwich
Maud	Norfolk wherry	1899	D. S. Hall, Reedham	20	Upton Dyke, Norfolk
Medway Queen	Paddle steamer	1924	Ailsa Troon Shipbuilding, Glasgow	316	Kingsnorth, Kent
MTB 331	Motor torpedo boat	1941	John I. Thornycroft, Hampton	17	Upper Heyford
Navigator	Admiralty MFV	1943	Richards Ironworks Co. Ltd, Lowestoft	116	Dartmouth
North Carr	Light vessel	1932	A. & J. Inglis, Pointhouse	250	Dundee
Perseverance	Grab dredger	1934	J. Pollock, Son & Co. Ltd, Faversham	70	Ellesmere Port
Pilgrim	Brixham trawler	1895	Uphams, Brixham	74	Cremyll, Cornwall
Provident	Brixham trawler	1924	Sanders & Co., Galmpton	85	Brixham
Pyronaut	Fire float	1934	C. Hill & Sons Ltd, Bristol	20	Bristol
Raven	Steam barge	1871	T. B. Sneath & Co., Rutherglen	41	Windermere
Raven	Excursion vessel	1889	T. B. Sneath & Co., Rutherglen	63	Ullswater
Reaper	Fifie	1901	J. & G. Forbes, Sandhaven	61	Anstruther, Fife
Regal Lady	Excursion vessel	1930	Fellows & Co., Great Yarmouth	72	Scarborough
Research	Sailing drifter	1903	W. & G. Stephen, Banff	Not known	Anstruther, Fife
Solace	Norfolk pleasure wherry	1903	D. S. Reed, Reepham	40	Wroxham, Norfolk
Spider T.	Humber sloop	1926	Warrens Shipyard, New Holland	70	Keadby Lock, Lincs.
Stalker	Tank landing ship	1944	Canadian Yarrow, Esquimalt	2,256	Portsmouth
Swan	Excursion vessel	1938	Vickers-Armstrong, Barrow	251	Windermere
Swan	Fifie	1900	Hay & Co., Lerwick	57	Lerwick, Shetland Isles
Teal	Excursion vessel	1936	Vickers-Armstrong, Barrow	251	Windermere
Tern	Excursion vessel	1891	Forrest & Sons Ltd, Wyvenhoe	120	Windermere
The King	Excursion vessel	1902	H. Tagg, East Moseley	41	Borstal, Kent
Vigilance	Brixham trawler	1926	J. W. Upham, Brixham	39	Brixham
Vigilant	Customs cutter	1901	Cox & Co., Falmouth	140	Faversham
Violette	Coastal schooner	1919	J. Pollock & Co. Ltd, Faversham	300	Hoo, Kent
Western Lady III	Excursion vessel, ex ML	1941	Southampton Steam Joinery Ltd	108	Swanage
Wincham	Weaver packet	1948	W. J. Yarwood & Sons Ltd, Northwich	210	Canning Half Tide Dock, Liverpool

For further details of these vessels see www.nationalhistoricships.org.uk

Glossary

Acronyms and abbreviations

AA – anti-aircraft (guns or missiles)

bhp – brake horse power

CMB – coastal motor boat

CMS – coastal minesweeper

HA – high angle (gun, suitable for anti-aircraft fire)

HDML – harbour defence motor launch

HSL – high speed launch

ihp – indicated horse power

LCT – landing craft (tank)

LST – landing ship (tank)

MGB – motor gunboat

MTB – motor torpedo boat

NSC(L) – naval stores craft (lighter)

SDML – seaward defence motor launch

shp – shaft horse power

TID – a small utility tug (there are various explanations of the acronym, including Tug Invasion Duty)

VIC – a class of standard steam victualling lighters built in the Second World War

aftercastle – a castle (or platform) built up over the stern of an old fighting ship, where archers could be stationed and guns mounted

articles (ship's articles) – legally binding documents signed by a ship's crew when they enlisted (on a merchant vessel)

ASDIC – an echo-sounding system (later known as sonar) for detecting submarines

athwartships – from one side of the ship to the other

ballast tanks – tanks on the sides of a submarine into which water is flooded when submerging, and blown out (with compressed air) when surfacing

barque – a three- or four-masted sailing ship, *square-rigged* except for the after (mizzen) *mast* which is *fore-and-aft rig*ged

beam – (1) the transverse measurement of a ship at her widest part; (2) a transverse member of a ship's frames on which the decks are laid

binnacle – the wooden housing of a ship's compass

boatswain – officer or warrant officer responsible for sails, rigging, anchors, cables, etc

Bofors gun – 40-mm anti-aircraft gun of Swedish design

Bonaventure – an additional mizzen sail, *lateen* in shape, which was carried on a fourth mast, known as a Bonaventure mizzen in the sixteenth and seventeenth centuries

boot-topping – painted part of the hull in the waterline area

bowsprit – large spar projecting over the bow of a sailing vessel

brail – line used to gather a sail up towards the mast

breech-loading gun – one in which the shot or shell is loaded at the back end of the barrel, behind the bore

broadside (as in firing) – the full weight of metal that can be fired simultaneously from the guns that bear on one side of a warship

bulkhead – a vertical partition, either fore and aft or athwartships, dividing the hull into separate compartments

bulwarks – the planking or plating along the sides of a ship above her upper deck

cannon – in the sailing navy, a large-calibre gun with medium length and range

capstan – a cylindrical barrel used for heavy-lifting work, for example, of anchors and cables

caravel – the smaller type of trading vessel in southern Europe of the fourteenth to seventeenth centuries, three-masted with *square-rig* on the foremast and *lateen*-rig on the other two; later the mainmast also became square-rigged

carrack – the larger type of European trading vessel of the fourteenth to seventeenth centuries, with three *mast*s, square-rigged except for the mizzen-mast, which was *lateen*-rigged

carronade – a short, light carriage gun firing relatively heavy shot for a limited range

carvel construction (or carvel-built) – a wooden hull form in which the side planks are all flush, with edges butting up to one another

caulk – driving rope fibres into the seams between wooden planks to prevent water ingress

chainshot – two cannon balls, connected together by either a chain or iron bar (the latter also called bar shot), which, when fired from a gun rotated at great speed through the air

clinker construction (or clinker-built) – a wooden hull form in which the side planks overlap at their edges, the upper over the lower

clipper – generic name for various types of fast sailing ships

compound engine – a steam engine with two cylinders, the steam exhausted from the first cylinder being used at a lower pressure by the second cylinder, for increased efficiency

conning tower – raised platform above the deck of a submarine, used to direct operations when on the surface, and to house periscopes, etc (this structure is now often called a sail); also a similar directing tower on a surface ship

corvette – (1) a flush-decked warship of the seventeenth to eighteenth centuries, with a single gun deck but smaller than a *frigate*; (2) small anti-submarine escort of the Second World War

counter – overhanging part of stern above the waterline

coxswain – senior petty officer on a small warship; also senior crewmember and helmsman of ship's boat

crack ship – one of the fastest in a fleet of sailing ships

culverin – a sixteenth-century gun with a relatively small calibre in proportion to its length, and of greater range than a cannon

cutter – (1) in the sailing navy, a clinker-built ship's boat of 24–32 feet length, with eight to fourteen oars plus sails; (2) later used for a pilot or coastguard vessel

davit – small crane aboard a ship, e.g. used to raise and lower the ship's boats

displacement – the actual weight of a ship, equalling the weight of water displaced by the hull when floating with full (or light) load; used for warships

draught (or draft) – the depth of water that a ship draws

Fifth Rate – sailing warship, which in the eighteenth century had between twenty-eight and forty-four guns; also known as a *frigate*

First Rate – the largest sailing warship, with 100 guns or more after about 1700

flagship – ship carrying an admiral's flag in the Royal Navy (or the flag of the commodore or senior captain in a merchant shipping line)

flying bridge – platform above the normal bridge (which is itself a platform from which the ship is navigated and controlled)

fore-and-aft rig – the arrangement of sails that abut the *masts*, or are attached to vertical stays (wires or ropes), so that the sails are parallel with the *fore-and-aft* line of the vessel (unless they are filled by wind)

forecastle – (pronounced fo'c'sle and sometimes written thus) – the accommodation space beneath the short raised deck forward; originally a castle (or platform) built up over the bows of an old fighting ship, in which archers could be stationed

frigate – (1) in the sailing navy, a three-masted ship with 24–38 guns carried on a single *gundeck*; (2) twentieth–twenty-first-century warship, similar in size to a destroyer, for escort work

gaff – a spar to which the head of a four-sided *fore-and-aft* sail is laced and hoisted on the after side of the mast

galleon – a development of the *carrack*, without the high *forecastle*, used for both warships and merchant ships

galley – (1) oared fighting ship with long length in relation to beam; (2) the ship's kitchen

gingerbread work – gilded scroll work and carving used as decoration on a sailing ship

gross tonnage – a registered measurement of a merchant ship's size, calculated from the capacity of the ship's hull below the upper deck (100 cubic feet equalling 1 ton)

gundeck – deck on a sailing warship that contains a large number of guns; a *First Rate* had three gundecks, a *frigate* normally had only one

gunports – square openings in the side of a fighting ship from which guns may be fired; normally covered by a port-lid that is raised before action

hard-chine – hull shape with a sharp angle in the cross-section, rather than rounded

Hedgehog mortar – ahead-throwing anti-submarine mortar which fired a pattern of twenty-four bombs

hogged – describes a hull shape in which the bow and stern slope downwards from the centre of the ship

hold – large compartment in a ship, either for the stowage of cargo, or – in sailing warships – to stow provisions and other stores

Hotchkiss gun – late nineteenth-century gun, variants such as the 6-pounder were still in use in the First World War

hydroplane – (1) a fin-like attachment which enables a submarine to alter the angle of the hull when diving or surfacing; (2) light fast motor boat designed to skim over the surface of the water

in ordinary – (for a ship) in reserve

jib – a triangular *fore-and-aft* sail attached to the stays of the foremast

keel – the lowest and principal timber of a wooden ship, or the lowest line of plates on an iron or steel ship, which extends the whole length of the vessel

ketch – sailing vessel with two *masts*, the after one (the mizzen) being lower than the main-mast and positioned forward of the rudder-head

knee – right-angled timber or iron bracket, supporting a beam on a ship

lateen – a narrow triangular sail set on a very long *yard* which is positioned obliquely on the mast

lateen rigged – with triangular *fore-and-aft* sails that helped the ship sail to windward

leeboard – a pivoting board on the side of the hull which, when lowered, reduces the *leeway* made when sailing into the wind

leeway – the distance a ship is moved away from her course by the wind or tide

limbo – three-barrelled ahead-throwing anti-submarine mortar, of later design than *Squid*

master – (1) captain of a merchant ship; (2) officer on a sailing warship responsible for the navigation.

masts (mizzen, etc) – a three-masted ship has fore, main and mizzen masts in order from bow to stern

mate – the rank in the merchant service next below the master

messdeck – lower deck where the crew ate and socialised and, often, slept

midshipman – a non-commissioned rank in the Navy, next below a sub-lieutenant

Mulberry harbour – an artificial harbour made of prefabricated sections, used off the coast of Normandy in the Second World War

muzzle-loading gun – gun in which the shot or shell is loaded at the forward end of the barrel

Oerlikon gun – 20-mm rapid-firing light anti-aircraft gun of Swiss design

orlop deck – the lowest deck in a ship, being the platform laid on beams low down in the hull

paravane – towed, underwater device used to cut mooring wires on mines when minesweeping

pennon – long, coloured streamer flown from fighting ships in the fifteenth and sixteenth centuries

planing – fast, forward movement of a vessel during which the front part of the hull is lifted above the water, thus reducing resistance

poopdeck (or poop) – short, raised deck near the stern of a ship

post-captain – Royal Navy rank in a sailing warship, given to an experienced captain of a large ship

pressure hull – the main hull structure of a submarine, it is circular in cross-section and built to withstand the pressure of water at the deepest diving depth; outside of the pressure hull are the casing (on top of the pressure hull) and the *ballast tanks*

privateer – privately owned vessel armed with guns, which operated in time of war against the trade of an enemy

prize – vessel captured at sea by a ship of war

puffer – small steam cargo ship, mainly built on the Clyde for use around the lochs and islands of west Scotland

purser – paymaster and officer responsible for provisions and clothing on a ship

quarterdeck – part of the upper deck of a ship which, on a sailing ship, is abaft the mainmast

quartermaster – a petty officer who assists the *master* of a ship and his *mates*; also the senior helmsman who maintains the navigational equipment

reciprocating engine – steam engine in which the piston moves back and forth inside a cylinder, transmitting its motion by connecting rod and crank to a driving shaft

'Roaring Forties' – the area in the south Indian Ocean between latitudes 40° and 50° south, where the prevailing winds blow very strongly from the west

roller-reefing – system for reducing the area of a sail by rolling it around a stay

Royal Fleet Auxiliaries (RFAs) – civilian-manned naval support vessels, e.g. tankers and stores ships

Royal Naval Reserve (RNR) – supplementary force of the Royal Navy, originally comprised of merchant sailors and retired Royal Navy personnel, who normally had other full-time jobs, but since 1958 included other volunteers; deployed as required during hostilities or emergencies

Royal Naval Volunteer Reserve (RNVR) – supplementary Royal Navy force of volunteers who were trained on a part-time basis for use during hostilities; in 1958 became part of the Royal Naval Reserve

running rigging – that part of the rigging which moves, e.g. to raise and adjust sails

schooner – *fore-and-aft* rigged vessel with two or more *masts*; the foremast is lower than the mainmast

screw – propeller

sheer – the upward curve of the deck of a ship towards the bows and stern

ship (rig) - sailing vessel, normally with three *masts*, all *square-rigged*

ship-of-the-line – a major warship, usually with at least two *gundecks* and a least sixty guns (from 1750s) or seventy-four guns (from about 1800)

'show the flag' – a visit by a naval vessel to a port (usually foreign) for diplomatic and public-relations purposes

Sixth Rate – sailing warship typically with twelve to twenty-eight guns, the smallest warship commanded by a full captain in the Royal Navy

sloop – (1) originally a single-masted sailing vessel; (2) later used for intermediate-sized warships for patrol, minesweeping or anti-submarine work, from Victorian times onward

snort mast – air tube that can be raised by a submarine to enable running of a diesel engine when submerged (usually to recharge batteries); based on the German schnorkel

sonar – see ASDIC

spanker – additional sail hoisted on the mizzen-*mast*

of a *square-rigged* sailing ship, later also referred to the largest sail on the mizzen-mast of a *fore-and-aft* rigged vessel

Special Air Service (SAS) – army unit trained to work behind enemy lines on special operations

Special Boat Squadron (SBS) – army or Royal Marine unit for special amphibious operations

square-rig – the arrangement of sails that are laced to *yards* (spars) which lie square to the sides of the ship

Squid – three-barrelled ahead-throwing anti-submarine mortar

standing rigging – that part of the rigging which is fixed and permanent, particularly to support the masts

staysail – a triangular *fore-and-aft* sail attached to a stay (the part of the rigging which supports the *mast*)

stem – the foremost timber or steel member forming the bow of a vessel

stepped (as in a stepped mast) – *mast* erected by fitting the bottom of it into a step (or square framework) on the keelson (an internal member attached to the keel)

superstructure – structures above the level of the upper deck, including deckhouses and the bridge

sweep – a patrol intended to clear an area of water of enemy ships

taking a sounding – measuring the depth of water, e.g. using a lead weight attached to a line

topgallant – the sail that is third above the deck on a *square-rigged* ship

topsail – a *square-rig* sail on the topsail yard (and above the mainsail on a *fore-and-aft* rigged vessel)

transom – the timbers of a flat stern

triple-expansion engine – steam engine with three cylinders, which uses the steam three times at successively lower pressures

tween deck – between decks, the deck below the main deck, which was often used for cargo but temporarily partitioned to provide basic accommodation, e.g. for emigrants

vanguard (or van) – the leading part of a fleet in battle

waist – the part of the upper deck between the *forecastle* and the *quarterdeck*; on a sailing ship, the part of the upper deck between the fore- and main- masts

warrant officer – rank between commissioned officer and petty (non-commissioned) officer

White Ensign – the Royal Navy flag flown by its ships and shore stations: comprises a St George's flag on a white field with the Union flag in the upper canton

working up – period of training and exercises during which the new crew of a warship is brought up to full efficiency

'with despatch' – with speed

yard – a large wooden or metal spar crossing the *masts* of a ship horizontally or diagonally, from which a sail is set

Select Bibliography

Adams, R., *Red Funnel and Before*, (Kingfisher, Southampton, 1986)

Allison, R., *HMS Caroline*, (Blackstaff, Belfast, 1974)

Benham, H., *Down Tops'l*, (Harrap, London, 1971)

Bennett, G., *Naval Battles of the First World War*, (Penguin, London, 2001)

Best, N., *Trafalgar*, (Wiedenfeld & Nicolson, London, 2005)

Boniface, P., *HMS Cavalier - Past and Present*, (Periscope, Penzance, 2004).

Bradford, E., *The Story of the Mary Rose*, (Hamilton, London, 1982).

Brouwer, N., *International Register of Historic Ships*, (Anthony Nelson, Oswestry, 1993)

Brown, D., *The Royal Navy and the Falklands War*, (Cooper, London, 1987).

Brown, D.K., *The Design and Construction of British Warships*, (Conway Maritime Press, London, 1996)

—, *Warrior to Dreadnought*, (Chatham, London, 1997)

—, *The Grand Fleet*, (Chatham, London, 1999)

—, *Nelson to Vanguard*, (Chatham, London, 2000).

—, *Rebuilding the Royal Navy*, (Chatham, London, 2003)

Brown, P. J., *Maritime Portsmouth*, (Tempus, Stroud, 2005)

Burton, A., *The Past Afloat*, (BBC/Deutsch, London, 1982)

Buxton, I., *His Majesty's Monitor M33*, (Hampshire County Council, 2001)

Castle, C., and I. MacDonald, *Glenlee – The Life and Times of a Clyde-Built Cape-Horner*, (Brown, Son & Ferguson, Glasgow, 2005)

Colledge, J., *Ships of the Royal Navy*, vol. 2, (Greenhill Books, London 1989)

Colledge, J., and B. Warlow, *Ships of the Royal Navy*, (Chatham, London, 2006)

Corlett, E., *SS Great Britain – The Iron Ship*, (Conway Maritime Press, London 1990)

Costello, J., and T. Hughes, *Jutland 1916*, (Futura, 1976)

Davies, D., *The Thames Sailing Barge, Her Gear and Rigging*, (David & Charles, Newton Abbot, 1970)

Dixon, C., *Ships of the Victorian Navy*, (Ashford, Shedfield, 1987)

Eglinton, E., *The Last of the Sailing Coasters*, (HMSO, London, 1982)

Elliott, C., *Maritime Heritage*, (Tops'l Books, Sulhamstead, 1981)

Finch, R., *Sailing Craft of the British Isles*, (Collins, London, 1976)

Firstbrook, P., *The Voyage of the Matthew*, (BBC, London, 1997)

Goodwin, P., *Nelson's Victory: 101 Questions and Answers about HMS Victory*, (Conway Maritime Press, London, 2000)

Fogg, N., *SS Great Britain – Brunel's Flagship of the Steam Revolution*, (Bristol, SS Great Britain Project, Bristol, 1996)

Friedman, N., *British Destroyers and Frigates*, (Chatham, London, 2006)

Gardiner, R., (ed.), *The Line of Battle – The Sailing Warship 1650-1840*, (Conway Maritime Press, London, 1992)

Greenhill, B., *The Ship – The Life and Death of the Merchant Sailing Ship*, (HMSO, London, 1980)

Haines, R., *Life and Death in the Age of Sail*, (National Maritime Museum, London, 2003)

Hannan, B., *Fifty Years of Naval Tugs*, (Maritime, Liskeard)

Humphries, S., *The Call of the Sea*, (BBC, London, 1997)

Hutchinson, R., *Submarines – War Beneath the Waves*, (HarperCollins, London, 2001)

Ireland, B., *Naval Warfare in the Age of Sail 1756–1815*, (HarperCollins, London, 2000)

Jefferson, D., *Coastal Forces at War*, (Patrick Stephens, Yeovil, 1996)

Johnstone-Bryden, R., *Britannia – the Official History*, (Conway Maritime Press, London, 2003)

Jones, J., *Historic Warships*, (McFarland, London, 1993)

Kemp, P., ed., *The Oxford Companion to Ships and the Sea*, (Oxford University Press, Oxford, 1988)

Lambert, A., *Warrior: Restoring the World's First Ironclad*, (Conway Maritim Press, London, 1987)

—, *Trincomalee, The Last of Nelson's Frigates*, (Chatham Publishing, Rochester, 2002)

Lambert, J., *Allied Coastal Forces of World War II* vol. 2, (Conway Maritime Press, London, 1993)

Leather, J., *Barges*, (Adlard Coles, London, 1984)

Lenton, H., *British and Empire Warships of the Second World War*, (Greenhill Books, London, 1998)

Lubbock, B., *The China Clippers*, (Brown, Son & Ferguson, Glasgow, 1914)

—, *The Log of the Cutty Sark*, (Brown, Son & Ferguson, Glasgow, 1924)

Marsden, P., *Sealed by Time – the Loss and Recovery of the Mary Rose*, (The Mary Rose Trust, Portsmouth, 2003)

McGowan, A., *The Ship – The Century before Steam*, (HMSO, London, 1980)

—, 1999, *HMS Victory – Her Construction, Career and Restoration*, (Chatham Publishing, London, 1999)

Munro, A., *HMS/HQS Wellington*, (The Wellington Trust, London, 2006)

Preston, J., and J. Major, *Send a Gunboat*, (Conway Maritime Press, London, 2007)

Robertson, T., *Walker, RN*, (Evans, London, 1956)

Rodger, N. A. M., *The Safeguard of the Sea*, (HarperCollins, London, 1997)

—, *The Command of the Ocean*, (Allen Lane, London, 2004)

Savours, A., *The Voyages of the Discovery*, (Virgin Books, London, 1994)

Smith, K., *Turbinia – The Story of Charles Parsons and his Ocean Greyhound*, (Newcastle Libraries and Information Service and Tyne and Wear Museums Newcastle, 1996)

Smith, P., *Heritage of the Sea*, (Balfour, Huntingdon, 1974)

Taylor, G., *London's Navy*, (Quiller, London, 1983)

Thomas, D., *Battles and Honours of the Royal Navy*, (Leo Cooper, Barnsley, 1998)

Thornton, E., *South Coast Pleasure Steamers*, (Stephenson, Prescott, 1962)

Villiers, A., *The Cutty Sark*, (Hodder & Stoughton, London, 1953)

Warlow, B., *Shore Establishments of the Royal Navy*, (Maritime Press, Liskeard, 2000)

Warren, C., and J. Benson, *Above Us The Waves*, (Harrap, London, 1953)

Warwick, P., *Voices from the Battle of Trafalgar*, (David and Charles, Newton Abbott)

Watton, R., *The Cruiser HMS Belfast*, (Conway Maritime Press, London, 2003)

Waverley Excursions, *Waverley – the Golden Jubilee*, (Condie, Nuneaton, 1997)

Wells, J., *The Immortal Warrior*, (Kenneth Mason, Emsworth, 1997)

Williams, G., *HMS Wellington –One Ship's War*, (Self Publishing Association, Hanley Swan, 1992)

Winfield, R., *British Warships in the Age of Sail 1793–1817*, (Chatham Publishing, 2005)

Wingate, J., *In Trust for the Nation: HMS Belfast 1939–72*, (Imperial War Museum, London, 2004)

Winton, J., *Hurrah for the Life of a Sailor*, (Joseph, London, 1977)

Woodman, R., *Arctic Convoys*, (Murray, London, 1994)

Periodicals

Classic Boat
Mariners Mirror
Navy News (various editions)
Sea Breezes
Ships Monthly
Traditional Boats and Tallships
Warship World

Visitor guidebooks and websites associated with various ships

ADM/various (Admiralty records), The National Archives, Kew, London

Twentieth Century Warships – Service Histories, National Maritime Museum, Greenwich

Service Histories of Coastal Forces, British Military Powerboat Trust

Submarine Service Histories, Royal Navy Submarine Museum, Gosport

Useful Websites

Further information about the ships featured in this book including, where relevant, directions, opening times and entry prices, are available on the following websites:

Balmoral – www.waverleyexcursions.co.uk
British Military Powerboat Trust – www.bmpt.org.uk
Britannia – www.royalyachtbritannia.co.uk
Bronington – www.tca2000.co.uk/ton
Calshot – www.tugtendercalshot.co.uk
Cambria – www.cambriatrust.org.uk
Challenge – www.stchallenge.org
Chatham Historic Dockyard – www.chdt.org.uk
City of Adelaide – www.scottishmaritimemuseum.org/carrick
www.sunderlandmaritimeheritage.org.uk/adelaide
Courageous – www.royalnavy.mod.uk/server/show/ConMediaFile.20734
Cutty Sark – www.cuttysark.org.uk
Daniel Adamson – www.danieladamson.co.uk
Discovery – www.rrsdiscovery.com
Edmund Gardner – www.liverpoolmuseums.org.uk/maritime/collections/edmundgardner
Freshspring – www.rmasfreshspring.mysite.orange.co.uk
Garlandstone – www.morwellham-quay.co.uk
Glenlee – www.glenlee.co.uk
Golden Hind (Brixham) – www.goldenhind.co.uk
Golden Hinde (London) – www.goldenhinde.org
Grand Turk – www.turks.co.uk
Great Britain – www.ssgreatbritain.org
Imperial War Museum, Duxford – www.iwm.org.uk/duxford
John H. Amos – www.mqwebmaster.pwp.blueyonder.co.uk/jha
Kerne – www.tugkerne.co.uk
Kingswear Castle – www.pskingswearcastle.wanadoo.co.uk
Kyles – www.scottishmaritimemuseum/renfrew
Lydia Eva – www.lydiaeva.org.uk
M33 – www.hants.org/m33
Maid of the Loch – www.maidoftheloch.com
Mary Rose – www.flagship.org.uk/mary_rose
Matthew – www.matthew.co.uk
Medusa – www.trinitystar.co.uk/medusa
Mirosa – www.ironwharf.co.uk/charters
MTB 102 – www.mtb102.com
National Historic Ships Register – www.nationalhistoricships.org.uk
Otus – www.hms-otus.com
Portwey – www.stportwey.co.uk
Robin – www.ssrobin.com
Royal Navy Submarine Museum – www.rnsubmus.co.uk
Shieldhall – www.ss-shieldhall.co.uk
Thames Barges – www.thamesbarge.org.uk
www.thamesbarges.co.uk
www.bargetrust.org
www.thamesbargeracing.co.uk
TID 164 – www.tid164.co.uk
Trincomalee – www.hms-trincomalee.co.uk
Turbinia – www.twmuseums.org.uk/discovery
Unicorn – www.frigateunicorn.org
VIC 56 – www.vic56.co.uk
Victory – www.hms-victory.com
Warrior – www.hmswarrior.org
Waverley – www.waverleyexcursions.co.uk
Wellington – www.thewellingtontrust.com
Wingfield Castle – www.hartlepoolsmaritimeexperience.com

Picture Credits